ACTION
RESEARCH

3
EDITION

ACTION RESEARCH

Improving Schools and Empowering Educators

3

EDITION

Craig A. Mertler

University of West Georgia

Los Angeles | London | New Delhi
Singapore | Washington DC

For information:

SAGE Publications, Inc.
2455 Teller Road
Thousand Oaks, California 91320
E-mail: order@sagepub.com

SAGE Publications Ltd.
1 Oliver's Yard
55 City Road
London EC1Y 1SP
United Kingdom

SAGE Publications India Pvt. Ltd.
B 1/I 1 Mohan Cooperative Industrial Area
Mathura Road, New Delhi 110 044
India

SAGE Publications Asia-Pacific Pte. Ltd.
33 Pekin Street #02-01
Far East Square
Singapore 048763

Printed in the United States of America

Library of Congress Cataloging-in-Publication Data

Mertler, Craig A.
Action research: improving schools and empowering educators / Craig A. Mertler.—3rd ed.
    p. cm.
Includes bibliographical references and index.
ISBN 978-1-4129-8889-6 (pbk.: acid-free paper)
    1. Action research in education. I. Title.

LB1028.24.M47 2012
370.72—dc22   2010032333

This book is printed on acid-free paper.

11   12   13   14   15   10   9   8   7   6   5   4   3   2   1

Executive Editor:	Diane McDaniel
Associate Editor:	Leah Mori
Assistant Editor:	Aja Baker
Editorial Assistant:	Ashley Conlon
Production Editor:	Brittany Bauhaus
Copy Editor:	Jovey Stewart
Typesetter:	C&M Digitals (P) Ltd.
Proofreader:	Jennifer Gritt
Indexer:	Diggs Publication Services, Inc.
Cover Designer:	Gail Buschman
Marketing Manager:	Erica DeLuca
Permissions Editor:	Adele Hutchinson

Brief Contents

Detailed Contents

PART II. "HOW DO I BEGIN MY ACTION RESEARCH STUDY?"   51

3 Planning for Action Research   53

8 Sharing and Reflecting 217

9 Writing Up Action Research 241

Preface

Purpose of the Text

Most, if not all, graduate students in education—and, in particular, in-service teachers seeking graduate degrees—are required to complete a course in educational research methods. The majority of these methods courses provide a broad overview of educational research methods, designs, and techniques. However, I would argue that graduate-level research methods courses taught to in-service teachers could be more suitable provided the appropriate instructional materials were available to instructors and students, such that they focus on a classroom-based approach to research. Most research methods courses—and, therefore, their appropriate textbooks—follow the description that I offer above, in that they are "survey" courses (i.e., those that provide an overview of a variety of research methods). There are numerous texts on the market that meet this description.

In contrast, there are relatively few books that focus specifically on action research as a methodology, and there are even fewer that do so with the target audience of practicing educators in mind. The purpose of this book is to introduce educators to the process of conducting their own classroom-based or school-based action research. Detailed, but practical, information describing each step of the cyclical, iterative process is presented in a sequential manner. Educators are provided with an overview of traditional educational research prior to examining action research as a mechanism for designing and conducting their own applied research projects. The focus is not on the theoretical aspects of educational research but rather on the practical facets of conducting applied classroom and/or school research. As presented in this textbook, action research is not simply a means of conducting applied research. It is also a mechanism for engaging educators in reflective practice and customizing professional development opportunities in order to capitalize on the unique interests of individual educators or teams of educators.

The reason behind my desire to write a textbook on this topic is fairly straightforward. I have taught educational research methods for more than 15 years. The vast majority of the students enrolled in this course are in-service teachers seeking master's degrees in various fields, including curriculum, teaching, administration, and counseling. This course is intended to serve as an overview of research methods used to conduct research in the broad field of education, focusing primarily on quantitative methods. The focus is on very formal methodological approaches, such as descriptive, correlational, causal-comparative, experimental, and quasiexperimental research methods. The educators enrolled in a research methods course—especially those who intend on remaining in the K–12 setting—typically experience substantial difficulty in being able to see the application of these formal methodological approaches in their educational settings. The bottom line is that they do not really need to understand the application of these approaches to conducting research, since the majority will likely never design or conduct such formal methodological procedures. It is my belief that this is the case for many graduate programs in education across the country.

On the other hand, when we reach the topic of *action research,* the discussion typically piques student interest. The students can actually see how *this* methodological approach could be used in their schools, in their classrooms, with their students, and so on. Since action research is conducted by practitioners—yet still incorporates a good degree of rigor—students begin to see themselves designing and carrying out action research studies. By focusing our attention on a broad overview of research methods, I feel that we are doing an injustice to these practicing educators. We are not providing them with the tools necessary to design and conduct research studies that provide meaningful and immediate solutions to local-level problems. In other words, we are not adequately preparing them to investigate problems and seek solutions in their local settings and in a professional manner.

The *practical* nature of the book stems from the fact that it focuses on research methods and procedures that teachers, administrators, counselors, intervention specialists, etc. can use in conjunction with their everyday instructional practices and activities in schools and classrooms. Educators are shown how to design and conduct school-based research in order to make their instructional practices more effective. The numerous examples—many of which are supplied by me, while others come from published action research studies—of the principles, procedures, and techniques discussed in the narrative make it easy for students to understand the material in this book. Theoretical aspects of research, as well as highly technical concepts and procedures, which are unlikely to be used by practicing educators, are deemphasized—producing a textbook that provides comprehensive coverage of action research methods for practicing educational professionals without being unnecessarily technical; that is, it is a practical book for educators. This book provides them with the knowledge and skills necessary to design research studies that seek solutions to local-level problems, conduct those studies, and communicate the results to local stakeholders and other interested parties. Although it is based on the research literature, the book takes a very practical approach, never losing sight of its intended audience—the practicing educator.

Text Targets Graduate Students, Educators

This book was written with graduate students as the primary target audience. Specifically, this audience includes, but of course is not limited to, K–12 classroom teachers, administrators, counselors, special educators, and intervention specialists. In all likelihood, this text would be used as the primary book for a graduate course in action research, although it could also serve as a supplemental text for other graduate-level courses not focusing on research methods (e.g., courses in curriculum, supervision). The book is appropriate for educators in all areas of education (e.g., elementary and secondary mathematics, science, social studies, languages, music, art, physical education, special education, administration, counseling, and special education); examples, as well as sample articles, throughout the book come from a variety of settings and situations.

Text Organized Sequentially, Like an Action Research Study

The main topics covered in the book pertain most closely to designing and conducting classroom-based applied research. These general topic areas—and the chapters where they are addressed in the book—include the following:

- An overview of educational research (Chapter 1)

- An overview of action research (Chapter 1)

- The characteristics of action research (Chapter 1)

- The action research process (Chapter 2)

- Identifying an area of focus for action research (Chapter 3)

- Reviewing related literature (Chapter 3)

- Designing an action research study (Chapter 4)

- Collecting and analyzing data (Chapters 5 and 6)

- Developing an action plan (Chapter 7)

- Sharing the results of an action research study (Chapter 8)

- Reflecting on the process of action research (Chapter 8)

- Writing up action research (Chapter 9)

The book was arranged in this manner because it presents, in sequential order, the process of designing and conducting an action research study—beginning with the development of the topic to be investigated, reviewing related research, designing the study, actually carrying out the procedures, developing an action plan, and ultimately sharing the results and reflecting on the process. It is, however, important to note that action research proceeds through this process in a cyclical manner.

Pedagogical Features and Benefits to Students (as Well as Instructors)

When compared to other action research books currently on the market, this book provides similar coverage of content. There are, however, several aspects that distinguish it from similar works. These aspects include the following:

- Since the book takes an extremely applied approach, it includes numerous examples—not simple discussions or descriptions—of such things as data collection instruments (e.g., checklists, attitude surveys, interview protocols, and journal prompts) and presentation of research results (e.g., tables and graphs resulting from the analysis of quantitative data; summary tables resulting from the analysis of qualitative data, actual reports of action research).

- In addition to the various narrative examples that appear throughout the book, two detailed case studies of action research, called "Action Research Portraits," are developed in Chapter 3 and are extended in each subsequent chapter through Chapter 8. In each chapter, the case study discussions continue from the previous chapter, highlighting the application of content from the particular chapter as integrated into three practically based action research studies, one of which is conducted by an individual teacher and the other, by a group of teachers. In addition, a third "Action Research Portrait" appears on the book's accompanying website (http://www.sagepub.com/mertler3study).

- Numerous online resources are available for teachers to use in order to learn more about action research, address questions that they may have about the process, or promote dissemination of their action research results. A section titled "Related Websites" is included near the end of each of the nine chapters.

- Special sections, titled "Writing Up Action Research," are also included in Chapters 3 through 8. These sections provide annotated excerpts from published or otherwise disseminated action research reports, highlighting specific concepts presented in each particular chapter.

- On the first page of each chapter is a visual organizer for the main contents of that chapter.

- Two new appendices follow Chapter 9. Each includes a complete written report of a teacher-conducted action research project. We have also included the four complete written reports of teacher-conducted action research projects (i.e., two from the first edition and two from the second edition) on the website (http://www.sagepub.com/mertler2study).

- Each chapter includes a bulleted "Summary" of the main points included in the chapter.

- Each chapter also includes a final section titled "Questions and Activities" that can be used to extend student knowledge, understanding, and application.

- The text also includes a complete glossary of terms related to action research, a list of references used to compile the book, and a comprehensive subject and author index.

New Features in the Third Edition

There are several new features in the third edition of *Action Research: Improving Schools and Empowering Educators*:

- First and foremost, a new subtitle for the book has been developed in order to stress that the target audience for the book is not limited to classroom teachers, but includes professional educators at all levels and types of responsibilities in educational settings.

- An additional section titled "Connection of (action research) to School Improvement" has been added to Chapter 1.

- Information about additional searchable electronic databases (e.g., Google Scholar, ProQuest) has been added to the discussion in Chapter 3 as sources for locating related research.

- The discussion in Chapter 3 about developing and writing a literature review has been supplemented to add clarity to the explanation of the "funneling effect" of a review; a figure showing this process has also been added.

- In Chapter 4, discussions of research ethics have been enhanced by adding information on institutional review boards, parental consent forms, and minor assent forms. Examples of a parental consent form and a minor assent form have also been added.

- Sections on "Reflective Teaching," "Formative and Summative Classroom Assessments," and "Standardized Test Scores" have been added to Chapter 5 as additional sources of data for action research studies.

- Additional clarification of the differences between the two types of t tests and ANOVA has been added to Chapter 6, along with an explanatory figure.

- A new section titled "A Note About 'Analyzing' Standardized Test Scores" has been added to Chapter 6. References to several web-based statistics calculators have also been added to the "Related Websites" section of this chapter.

- The discussion in Chapter 8 of "Action Research Communities" has been substantially updated and enhanced to include more information on professional learning communities.

- A section titled "District-Level Action Research Conferences" has also been added to Chapter 8.

- Finally, two new examples of complete action research reports have been added as Appendix A and Appendix B. The two complete written reports of teacher-conducted action research projects from the second edition (along with the two originally published in the first edition) are available on the website that accompanies this book (http://www.sagepub.com/mertler3study).

Ancillary Material on the Web

Open-Access Student Study Site: www.sagepub.com/mertler3study

This web-based student study site provides a variety of additional resources to enhance students' understanding of the book content and take their learning one step further. The site includes:

 Video vignettes of the author and several educator-researchers discussing various aspects of conducting action research. These vignettes are integrated with specific chapter content throughout the book.

- **Self-quizzes** allow students to independently assess their progress in learning course material.

- **E-flashcards** are study tools to reinforce student understanding and learning of key terms and concepts that are outlined in the chapters.

- Chapter-specific **PowerPoint presentations** offer assistance by highlighting essential content, features, and artwork from the book.

- A *Learning From SAGE Journal Articles* feature provides access to recent, relevant full-text articles from SAGE's leading research journals. Each article supports and expands on the concepts presented in the chapter.

- Carefully selected, web-based **video resources** feature relevant content for use in independent and classroom-based exploration of key topics.

- Links to relevant **web resources** direct students to additional tools for further research on important chapter topics.

- *Sample Action Research Reports* and a link to an author created and supported **online professional learning community** are also included.

A Note About Action Research Projects

One concern that both instructors and students face is how to fit into one semester both the content coverage of the book and the completion of a student-conducted action research project. My advice is first to reinforce with students, who are just learning about action research, that the important aspect of an action research project as a course assignment is to become familiar with the process of designing and conducting action research and that they should worry less about the final product of their study. If they can become familiar and comfortable with the process as a whole, they will later be able to design and conduct larger-scale research projects that may require more time.

For a typical 15-week academic term, I might suggest the following week-by-week activities, for both content coverage of the book and the associated action research project:

Week	Content	Project Activity
1	Introduction to the course and to action research	
2	Chapter 1: Overview of research	Brainstorm list of possible research topics
3	Chapter 1: Continued Chapter 2: Overview of action research	Continue brainstorming, discussing possible topics with instructor
4	Chapter 3: Topic refinement	Begin process of narrowing topic
5	Chapter 3: Reviewing related literature	Begin search for related literature
6	Chapter 4: Developing a research plan	Continue reviewing related literature; develop preliminary research design
7	Chapter 5: Data collection	Draft instrumentation, interview guides, etc.
8	Chapter 5: Continued	Revise instrumentation, interview guides with instructor
9	Chapter 6: Data analysis	Begin data collection
10	Chapter 6: Continued	Data collection continues
11	Chapter 7: Developing action plans	Data collection continues; begin data analysis
12	Chapter 8: Sharing and reflecting	Data analysis continues; draft action plan
13	Chapter 9: Writing up results of action research	Finalize action plan; begin writing final paper
14	Informal presentations of projects and results	Complete written report
15	Submit final written report	

For a typical 10-week academic term, I might suggest the following week-by-week activities:

Week	Content	Project Activity
1	Introduction to the course and to action research	
2	Chapter 1: Overview of research	Brainstorm list of possible research topics
3	Chapter 2: Overview of action research	Continue brainstorming, discussing possible topics with instructor
4	Chapter 3: Topic refinement and reviewing related literature Chapter 4: Developing a research plan	Begin process of narrowing topic; search for related literature; develop preliminary research design
5	Chapter 5: Data collection	Continue reviewing related literature; draft and revise instrumentation, interview guides, etc.
6	Chapter 6: Data analysis Chapter 7; Developing action plans	Data collection; begin data analysis
7	Chapter 8: Sharing and reflecting	Draft action plan
8	Chapter 9: Writing up results of action research	Finalize action plan; begin writing final paper
9	Informal presentations of projects and results	Complete written report
10	Submit final written report	

A Final Note for Students of Action Research

I enjoy and value classroom-based/school-based action research because it has the potential to empower educators and to engage them directly in the process of educational improvement. I will not mislead you into thinking that this is necessarily an easy road to travel. Learning how to conduct action research studies that will enhance your professional practice does, in fact, take time and practice. However, by gaining familiarity and experience with designing and conducting action research projects, you will, I trust, realize the substantial and positive professional, reflective outcomes of action research discussed repeatedly throughout this book. I sincerely wish you the best of luck in your action research endeavors!

Acknowledgments

I would like to acknowledge the contributions of several individuals to this project. I would like to recognize and sincerely thank my editorial team at Sage Publications—namely, Diane McDaniel (acquisitions editor). Her support and understanding (as well as her general positive outlook!), especially during the early stages of the development of the first edition, made the process of writing this book an extremely smooth one. Her fabulous encouragement continued throughout the work on this revision. I would also like to recognize Leah Mori (associate editor) and Ashley Conlon (assistant editor) for their support and timely responses to all of my questions. I would like to thank Brittany Bauhaus (production editor) and Jovey Stewart (copy editor) for their assistance in working with me on the drafts and on the final appearance of the book. I offer my sincere thanks to those individuals who served as reviewers for this revised edition—their comments and feedback were greatly appreciated and extremely helpful:

Maryann Byrnes, *University of Massachusetts-Boston*

John Huss, *Northern Kentucky University*

Gabrielle Kowalski, *Cardinal Stritch University*

Terrence Stange, *Marshall University Graduate School*

Tamara Walser, *University of North Carolina-Wilmington*

I would also like to thank those individuals who served as reviewers for the second edition of this book:

Eugene Bartoo, *University of Tennessee at Chattanooga*

Kevin Carr, *George Fox University*

Dana Fredebaugh, *Nova Southeastern University*

Terrance Jakubowski, *California State University at Northridge*

Maja Miskovic, *National-Louis University*

Phillip Mutisya, *North Carolina Central University*

Cynthia Williams Resor, *Eastern Kentucky University*

Gail Ritchie, *George Mason University*

Margaret Waterman, *Southeast Missouri State University*

Finally, I would also like to thank those individuals who served as reviewers of both the original prospectus and the first edition of this book:

Lois McFadyen Christensen, *University of Alabama at Birmingham*

Christopher J. Della Pietra, *Southeastern Louisiana University*

Michael P. Grady, *Saint Louis University*

K. Fritz Leifeste, *Angelo State University*

Marilyn Lichtman, *Virginia Tech*

Jeanne M. McGlinn, *University of North Carolina at Asheville*

Jill C. Miels, *Ball State University*

Cathy Mogharreban, *Southern Illinois University at Carbondale*

Ted J. Singletary, *Boise State University*

Shelley H. Xu, *California State University at Long Beach*

As always, I would like to thank my wife, Kate, for her continued support of my extensive writing projects and for her feedback on various aspects of the book, from a classroom teacher's perspective, and our son, Addy, for providing the student's perspective.

"What Is Action Research?"

Part I of this book provides an introduction to and overview of action research. In Chapter 1, you will learn what action research is (and is not), how it compares to traditional forms of educational research, why it is important for teachers to become involved in action research, and some examples of its applications. You will also see several models of the process of conducting action research. In Chapter 2, you will learn more about the various steps in the action research cycle and see how it can be conducted within a contextualized example.

CHAPTER 1

Introduction to Action Research

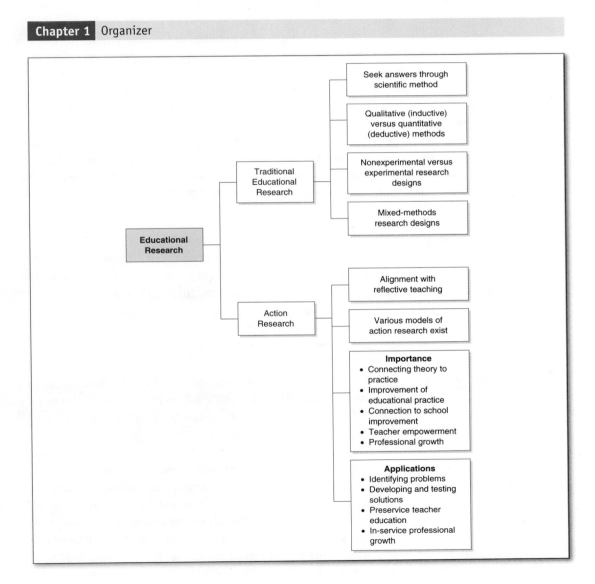

Research: Think about it for a few moments. What types of images come to mind? For many people, the term *research* tends to evoke images of scientists in white laboratory coats coaxing mice through a maze, observing their every move, action, and reaction. They closely monitor stopwatches, recording the amount of time that passes as the mice reach each stage of the maze. Further images called to mind might include chemists (yes, also wearing white lab coats!) with beakers, flasks, and Bunsen burners conducting experiments that involve mixing chemicals in order to make new solutions or to further study the properties of those solutions. Another visualization could involve medical researchers who work with animals or directly with human "subjects" to investigate possible cures for devastating diseases. Still others may envision research as something done by college or university professors as a regular aspect of their work. For quite some time, research has been conducted primarily by professionals whose principal education included training in the conduct of research studies. Admittedly, much research continues to be conducted by professionals, such as those described in the four examples above. However, more and more research is being conducted by *practitioners*—people whose primary education and training is *not* in research methodology. The specific procedures for conducting this type of research are somewhat different from those that serve as the foundation for more formal types of research, but the guiding principles are the same. It is this type of practitioner-based research—known as *action research*—upon which we will focus our attention in this book.

What Is Action Research?

Over the last decade, action research has begun to capture the attention of teachers, administrators, and policymakers around the country (Mills, 2011). Educators at a variety of levels have embraced it as something that makes conducting research a more "manageable" task and that brings about results that are more informative and have immediate and direct application. But just what is action research? What does it look like? What does it purport to accomplish?

Action research is defined as any systematic inquiry conducted by teachers, administrators, counselors, or others with a vested interest in the teaching and learning process or environment for the purpose of gathering information about how their particular schools operate, how they teach, and how their students learn (Mills, 2011). More important, action research is characterized as research that is done by teachers for themselves. It is truly a systematic inquiry into one's own practice (Johnson, 2008). Action research allows teachers to study their own classrooms—for example, their own instructional methods, their own students, and their own assessments—in order to better understand them and to be able to improve their quality or effectiveness. It focuses specifically on the unique characteristics of the population with whom a practice is employed or with whom some action must be taken. This, in turn, results in increased utility and effectiveness for the practitioner (Parsons & Brown, 2002). The basic process of conducting action research consists of four steps:

1. Identifying an area of focus

2. Collecting data

3. Analyzing and interpreting the data

4. Developing a plan of action (Mills, 2011)

You will learn much more about the process of action research later in this chapter and in Chapter 2.

Introduction to Educational Research

As classroom teachers—who are the ultimate, or at least the most likely, consumers of educational research—it is essential to have a basic understanding of several key terms and essential concepts related to the notion of research. Research is simply one of many means by which human beings seek answers to questions. Questions arise constantly throughout a day, whether they be personal or professional in nature. As an example of a personal question in need of an answer, imagine a coworker who asks if you would like to go to lunch this afternoon. You will need to give that person a yes or no answer, but you must factor in some information first—for example, do you already have plans for lunch? Can you afford to give up the time to go to lunch today? Do you have enough money for lunch?

Answers to questions of a professional nature often require much more information; however, human nature prompts us to try to find answers to those questions as quickly as possible. Consider the following scenario: You have a student, Arthur, whom you informally classify as an "unmotivated reader." You approach a colleague and ask about ideas for intervention strategies for motivating Arthur. She provides several strategies that she says have worked for other students, but you are not sure if they will work for Arthur. In addition, you know that there are undoubtedly many more strategies out there, but you need an answer now—the school year is off and running, and you do not want to lose any more valuable time by not encouraging Arthur to read more. But where do you go to find the answers you are looking for?

Mertler and Charles (2011) suggest that we usually consult sources for answers that are most convenient to us and with which we are most comfortable; however, these sources have the potential to be fraught with problems. These sources of information include tradition, authority, and common sense. **Tradition** refers to ways in which we have behaved in the past. Interventions that have worked in the past may in fact still work today, but there is no guarantee. In addition, there may now be newer interventions that will work better than our old standby. **Authority** refers to the use of the opinions of experts, whom we assume will know what will work best. However, simply finding someone who has a strong opinion about a given intervention or instructional strategy does not necessarily support the use of that strategy. In fact, it is typically safe to assume that as soon as you find an expert who supports any given technique, you will quickly find another who is willing to denounce it as being inferior. Finally, **common sense** refers to the use of human reasoning as a basis for answering questions. While human reasoning has gotten our global culture far throughout history, it is most reliant on dependable information. If information that we collect in order to help us make common-sense decisions is of substandard quality or accuracy, our common-sense decisions will reflect those various deficiencies.

The main problem with these familiar sources of information is that they have a tendency to provide unreliable information. This is largely due to the fact that answers based on tradition, authority, and common sense use information that is biased to some degree. This bias occurs primarily because the information was collected in an unsystematic and subjective manner. In order for the answers we seek to be accurate and of high quality, we must obtain information that is both valid and reliable. This is best accomplished by using the scientific method. The **scientific method** is a specific strategy used to answer questions and resolve problems. You may recall the scientific method from a junior or senior high school science course when you may have been required to complete some sort of science fair project. What makes the scientific method such a useful strategy is that it is a very systematic, step-by-step set of procedures. In 1938, American philosopher John Dewey described the scientific method as a procedure for thinking more objectively (Mertler & Charles, 2011). He presented the procedure as a series of the following steps:

1. Clarify the main question inherent in the problem.

2. State a hypothesis (a possible answer to the question).

3. Collect, analyze, and interpret information related to the question, such that it will permit you to answer the question.

4. Form conclusions derived from your analyses.

5. Use the conclusions to verify or reject the hypothesis.

It would be misleading to assume that all researchers—and therefore all research studies—follow these steps exactly. For example, it may not be necessary to formally state a hypothesis in some studies. Although not all research studies conduct the procedure exactly as described above, they do have one important thing in common. Collecting, analyzing, and interpreting information (Step 3 above) is always done in research. It is the result of this step that provides the necessary impetus that allows us to answer our initial questions.

How, then, is the scientific method related to research in the broad field of education? There is a great deal of similarity between the two. Simply put, **educational research** involves the application of the scientific method to educational topics, phenomena, or questions in search of answers. Educational research is typically carried out in the following manner:

1. Specify the topic about which a concern exists.

2. Clarify the specific problem on which the research will focus.

3. Formulate research questions and/or hypotheses concerning the main problem.

4. Carry out procedures by which data (a more appropriate term for "information") are collected, analyzed, and interpreted.

5. State the findings determined as a result of the data analysis.

6. Draw conclusions related to the original research questions and/or hypotheses. (Mertler & Charles, 2011)

Note the similarities between Dewey's list of steps in the scientific method and those used to conduct educational research. The major components are common to both lists. In either case, it is important to remember that in practice these steps do not always occur as neatly as presented here, nor do they always follow the sequence listed.

Johnson (2008) also reminds us that, as consumers of research as well as potential researchers, we must be aware of the differences between science and pseudoscience. Science—that is, the use of the scientific method for inquiry—uses perceived reality (typically in the form of collected data) to determine beliefs. In other words, data are collected and analyzed in order to determine what is believed:

| perceptions (data) | ⟶ | determine | ⟶ | beliefs |

An example of scientific inquiry is the Trends in International Mathematics and Science Study (or TIMSS). TIMSS resulted from the American education community's need for reliable and timely data on the mathematics and science achievement of our students compared to that of students in other countries. Since 1995, TIMSS has provided trend data on students' mathematics and science achievement from an international perspective. TIMSS uses standardized achievement tests, administered and scored in identical fashion, as the means of collecting student data. The tests are similar in content, form, and length in order to allow for comparisons. What makes this study "science" is the standardization and objectivity incorporated into the research design.

In contrast, pseudoscience uses beliefs to determine perceived reality. One begins with a strong belief and then looks for data to support that belief (Johnson, 2008):

| beliefs | ⟶ | determine | ⟶ | perceptions |

Pseudoscience is often used as a marketing tool by companies to sell products or by groups or individuals in an attempt to demonstrate that their ideas, methods, or products are the best or most effective. Clearly, this approach is not systematic, nor is it objective; it does not utilize the scientific method. Therefore, it is not science, and it is not research.

deductive — general to specific

Overview of Educational Research

Traditional research in education is typically conducted by researchers who are somewhat removed from the environment they are studying. This is not to say that they are not committed to the research study and truly interested in the ultimate results but rather to say that they are studying people, settings, or programs with which they are seldom personally involved (Schmuck, 1997). They may in fact be removed from the actual research site, in many instances. Furthermore, traditional researchers often seek explanations for existing phenomena and try to do so in an objective manner. The primary goal of traditional educational research is "to explain or help understand educational issues, questions, and processes" (Gay & Airasian, 2000, p. 24). In traditional research, different research methods—the specific procedures used to collect and analyze data—provide different views of a given reality. These various research methods tend to be put into two broad categories—quantitative approaches and qualitative approaches—based on different assumptions about how to best understand what is true or what constitutes reality (McMillan, 2004). Generally speaking, quantitative research methodologies require the collection and analysis of numerical data (e.g., test scores, opinion ratings, attitude scales); qualitative research methodologies necessitate the collection and analysis of narrative data (e.g., observation notes, interview transcripts, journal entries).

Quantitative research methodologies utilize a deductive approach to reasoning when attempting to find answers to research questions. **Deductive reasoning** works from the more general to the more specific, in a "top-down" manner (Trochim, 2002a). As depicted in Figure 1.1, the quantitative researcher might begin by thinking up a theory about a given topic of interest.

Figure 1.1   Process of Deductive Reasoning as Applied to Research

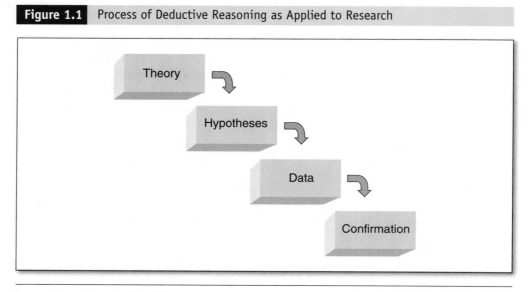

Source: Adapted from Trochim, 2002a.

That topic would then be narrowed down to more specific hypotheses that could be tested. This process of narrowing down goes even further when data are collected in order to address the hypotheses. Finally, the data are analyzed, and conclusions about the hypotheses are drawn—this allows for a confirmation (or not) of the original theory.

On the other hand, qualitative research methods typically use an inductive approach to reasoning. **Inductive reasoning** works in the exact opposite direction when compared to deductive reasoning. Using a "bottom-up" approach (see Figure 1.2), inductive reasoning begins with specific observations and concludes with broader generalizations and theories (Trochim, 2002a). One begins with specific observations (data), notes any patterns in those data, formulates one or more tentative hypotheses, and finally develops general conclusions and theories. It is important to note that, in some cases, the purpose of qualitative research is not to analyze data in order to form hypotheses or theories. Rather, in these cases, the purpose may simply be to provide a "thick description" of what is going on in the particular setting being studied. You will read more about deductive and inductive reasoning, as they relate to data analysis, in Chapter 6.

It is important to note that both quantitative and qualitative approaches to conducting educational research are guided by several sets of philosophical assumptions. These philosophical assumptions are composed primarily of several basic underlying beliefs about the world itself and how best to discover or uncover its true reality. The underlying beliefs held

| Figure 1.2 | Process of Inductive Reasoning as Applied to Research |

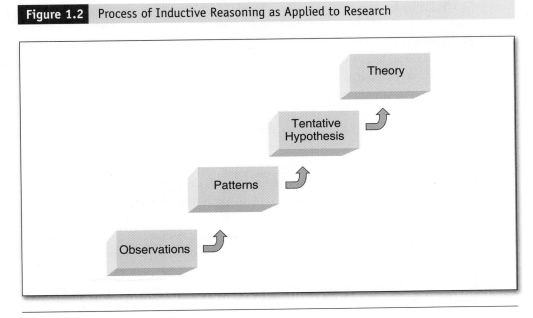

Source: Adapted from Trochim, 2002a.

by quantitative researchers differ substantially from those held by qualitative researchers. It is my conviction that an understanding of these beliefs is not requisite to understanding or being able to successfully conduct an action research study. This is largely due to the fact that action research, as we will view it throughout this text, typifies a grassroots effort to find answers to important questions or to foster change. It is entirely practical—and not necessarily philosophical—in its application. Mills (2011) refers to this as "practical action research" (p. 7), which he contrasts with the more philosophically based critical action research. The focus of this particular textbook is on the former; in-depth discussions of more philosophically based forms of action research are beyond the scope of this book. If the reader is interested in learning more about these various underlying philosophical assumptions and their connection to action research, several excellent resources include Johnson (2008), McMillan (2004), and Mills (2011).

Recall that the goal of quantitative research is to describe or otherwise understand educational phenomena. To accomplish this, researchers collect data by measuring **variables** (factors that may affect the outcome of a study or characteristics that are central to the topic about which the researcher wishes to draw conclusions) and then analyze those data in order to test **hypotheses** (predicted outcomes of the study) or to answer **research questions**. For example, a quantitative research study might involve collecting data on elementary school discipline referrals and absenteeism (numerical variables) in order to answer the question: Are there differences in the rates of disciplinary problems and absenteeism in schools with a K–8 grade span versus those with other grade span configurations (e.g., K–5, K–6)?

The type of **research design** employed by the researcher refers to the plan that will be used to carry out the study. Research designs may be either nonexperimental or experimental. In **nonexperimental research**, the researcher has no direct control over any variable in the study, either because it has already occurred or because it is not possible for it to be influenced. In other words, in nonexperimental research, variables cannot be controlled or manipulated by the researcher. The previous illustration of a study of school discipline and absenteeism problems is an example of a nonexperimental study, as the type of grade configuration, the number of discipline referrals, and the number of absences cannot be controlled or influenced by the researcher. The fact that variables cannot be controlled in nonexperimental studies is an important distinction between nonexperimental research and experimental research, especially when it comes to drawing conclusions at the end of a study. This usually means that conclusions to nonexperimental studies can describe only variables or relationships between variables. Some examples of nonexperimental research designs include *descriptive*, *comparative*, *correlational*, and *causal-comparative* research (McMillan, 2004). *Descriptive* studies simply report information about the frequency or amount of something (e.g., What percentage of the time do teachers use performance-based assessments in their classrooms?). *Comparative* studies characteristically build on descriptive studies by comparing two or more groups to that which is measured (e.g., Is there a significant difference between elementary and secondary teachers' use of performance-based assessments?).

Correlational studies measure the degree to which a relationship exists between two or more variables (e.g., What is the relationship between years of teaching experience and use of performance-based assessments?). Finally, *causal-comparative* studies (also sometimes referred to as ex post facto studies) compare groups—where group membership is determined by something that occurred in the past—on subsequent data on another variable in such a way that it makes possible drawing potential causal relationships between the two variables (e.g., Do teachers who completed a stand-alone preservice course in classroom assessment use performance-based assessment more than teachers who did not complete such a course?). Notice that based on the sample research questions provided it is quite possible to use any of the various types of nonexperimental research designs to study a given topic—in this case, classroom teachers' use of performance-based assessments.

In **experimental research**, the researcher has control over one or more of the variables included in the study that may somehow influence (or cause) the participants' behavior. The variables over which the researcher has control are known as the **independent variables**; these are the variables that are manipulated by the researcher, meaning that the researcher determines which subjects will receive which condition. For example, if the effectiveness of a new math program was being investigated, those students exposed to the new program would constitute the **experimental** or **treatment group**; their performance would be compared to a **control group** that receives the standard math instruction. The ultimate variable of interest (i.e., the "behavior" variable mentioned above, perhaps "math achievement" in our example) is referred to as the **dependent variable** (since its value depends on the value, or group membership, of the independent variable).

There are a wide variety of experimental research designs, the discussion of which is beyond the scope of this book. However, an illustration of experimental research is likely in order. Suppose a history teacher wanted to determine whether students performed better when taught American history using the more traditional forward (i.e., past to present) approach versus a backward (i.e., present to past) approach. She randomly assigns half of her classes to be taught using the forward approach and the other half to be taught using the backward approach. The independent variable for her study is the type of instruction. There are two levels to this variable that "define" the two groups—the experimental group receives the innovative backward approach to instruction; the control group receives the more traditional forward approach. Finally, the academic performance (dependent variable) of all students is measured using the same instrument (e.g., a final exam) for both groups. The aspect that makes this study experimental in nature is that the teacher herself determines which group will receive which version of the treatment (i.e., instruction); in other words, she is manipulating or controlling the independent variable.

Data collected as part of quantitative research studies are numerical and therefore naturally analyzed statistically. Analyses may include descriptive statistics, inferential statistics, or both. **Descriptive statistics** allow researchers to summarize, organize, and simplify data. Specific techniques include such statistics as the mean, median, mode, range, standard

mean / median / mode

deviation, correlations, and standardized scores. **Inferential statistics** are more complex and permit researchers to test the statistical significance of the difference between two or more groups or to test the degree of correlation between two variables. **Statistical significance** refers to a decision made from the results of statistical procedures that enable researchers to conclude that the findings of a given study (e.g., the size of the difference between two groups or the strength of the relationship between two variables) are large enough in the sample studied in order to represent a meaningful difference or relationship in the **population** from which the sample was drawn.

Whereas quantitative research studies focus on a relatively small number of variables, qualitative research studies utilize a much broader, more holistic approach to data collection. Qualitative research designs use systematic observation in order to gain knowledge, reach understanding, and answer research questions. There is no attempt to control or manipulate any variable in a qualitative study; researchers simply take the world as it exists and as they find it (Johnson, 2008). Qualitative research tends to emphasize the importance of multiple measures and observations (Trochim, 2002b). Therefore, guiding research questions tend to be more broad and open-ended. This allows the researcher to collect a wide variety of data for the purpose of getting a more holistic picture of the phenomenon under investigation. This also permits the researcher to engage in triangulation. **Triangulation** is a process of relating multiple sources of data in order to establish their trustworthiness or verification of the consistency of the facts while trying to account for their inherent biases (Bogdan & Biklen, 2007; Glesne, 2006). It is important to note that "triangulation" does not necessarily mean that the researcher is using three (as in "tri-") sources of data; it simply means that there is more than one source of data—perhaps, a more appropriate term would be "*polyangulation*" (since the prefix "*poly-*" is defined as "more than one or many"). Ultimately, this enables the researcher to try to get a better handle on what is happening in reality and to have greater confidence in research findings (Glesne, 2006). For example, in a qualitative study, one might collect data through firsthand observations, videotaped observations, and interviews. Triangulating these sources of data would involve examination in order to determine, for example, if the behaviors exhibited and comments made by participants are consistent regardless of the type of data representing them. In other words, did a specific person act the same way he said he acted, or did he verbally portray his behavior differently from his actual behavior?

Similar to quantitative research, there are a variety of qualitative research designs. These include phenomenology, ethnography, grounded theory, and case studies (McMillan, 2004). **Phenomenological studies** engage the researcher in a long process of individual interviews in an attempt to fully understand a phenomenon (e.g., What characteristics of teachers are needed in order for them to be viewed as compassionate by their students?). **Ethnographic research** attempts to describe social interactions between people in group settings (e.g., What meaning does the teachers' lounge have for the staff at Main Street Elementary School?). **Grounded theory** research studies attempt to discover a theory that relates to a particular environment (e.g., What types of personal and school characteristics serve to motivate teachers?). Finally, **case studies** are in-depth studies of individual programs, activities, people, or groups (e.g., What is the nature of the school culture at Washington Middle School?).

Data collected during a qualitative research study may be quite diverse. Recall that qualitative data are typically narrative and consist primarily of observations, interviews, and existing documents and reports (McMillan, 2004). Resulting qualitative data are analyzed by means of a process known as **logico-inductive analysis**, a thought process that uses logic to make sense of patterns and trends in the data (Mertler & Charles, 2011).

Although quantitative and qualitative approaches to conducting research are quite different on a variety of levels, they need not be considered mutually exclusive. It is not uncommon to see research studies that employ both types of research data. These types of studies are often referred to as **mixed-methods research designs**. The combination of both types of data tends to provide a better understanding of a research problem than one type of data in isolation. In other words, these types of studies capitalize on the relative strengths of both quantitative and qualitative data. Creswell (2005) considers action research studies to be most similar to mixed-methods designs, since they often utilize both quantitative and qualitative data. The only real difference between the two is the underlying purpose for the research. The main goal of mixed-methods studies is more traditional (i.e., to better understand and explain a research problem); the main goal of action research is to address local-level problems with the anticipation of finding immediate solutions.

Overview of Action Research

For decades, there has been pressure from both public and governmental sources for improvement in our schools. The public, fueled by the mass media, has criticized schools for low levels of achievement in math, science, reading, writing, and history (Schmuck, 1997). Business leaders fault schools for not preparing students for the workforce. Although teachers are on the receiving end of the brunt of this criticism, it is my firm belief that teachers in the United States have been doing—and continue to do—an outstanding job in the classroom. However, that being said, I also believe that true school improvement must begin from within the proverbial "four walls of the classroom." Teachers must be able and willing to critically examine their own practice as well as how students (both collectively and individually) learn best.

Often, school improvement leaders look toward the enormous body of educational research literature as a means of guiding their improvement efforts. However, many practitioners do not find that either formal or applied academic research is very helpful (Anderson, 2002). This is largely due to the fact that traditional educational researchers have a tendency to impose abstract research findings on schools and teachers with little or no attention paid to local variation (i.e., not all schools are the same) and required adaptations (i.e., the extent to which research findings generalize across entire populations; Metz & Page, 2002). I believe that, due to this continued imposition of more traditional research findings, there is a real need for the increased practice of teacher-initiated, classroom-based action research.

Schmuck (1997) defines action research as an attempt to "study a real school situation with a view to improve the quality of actions and results within it" (p. 28). Its purpose is also to improve one's own professional judgment and to give insight into better, more effective means of achieving desirable educational outcomes. McMillan (2004) describes action research as being focused on solving a specific classroom or school problem, improving practice, or helping make a decision at a single local site. Action research offers a process by which current practice can be changed toward better practice. The overarching goal of action research is to improve practice immediately within one or a few classrooms or schools (McMillan, 2004).

Due to the fact that action research is largely about examining one's own practice (McLean, 1995), reflection is an integral part of the action research process. **Reflection** can be defined as the act of critically exploring what you are doing, why you decided to do it, and what its effects have been. In order for teachers to be effective, they must become active participants in their classrooms as well as active observers of the learning process; they must analyze and interpret classroom information—that has been collected in a systematic manner—and then use that information as a basis for future planning and decision making (Parsons & Brown, 2002). **Reflective teaching** is a process of developing lessons or assessing student learning with thoughtful consideration of educational theory, existing research, and practical experience, along with the analysis of the lesson's effect on student learning (Parsons & Brown, 2002). This process of systematic collection of information followed by active reflection—all with the anticipation of improving the teaching process—is at the core of action research.

Accordingly, action research is also largely about developing the professional disposition of teachers and the teaching profession (Mills, 2011). Through action research, teachers are encouraged to become continuous, lifelong learners in their classrooms and with respect to their practice. This notion is central to the very nature of education—action research encourages teachers to examine the dynamics of their classrooms, critically think about the actions and interactions of students, confirm and/or challenge existing ideas or practices, and take risks in the process (Mills, 2011). A goal of every classroom teacher should be to improve her or his professional practice, as well as student outcomes. Action research is an effective means by which this can be accomplished.

Models of Action Research

Numerous authors and researchers have proposed models for the action research process. Because this process is somewhat dynamic, various models look a bit different from one another but possess numerous common elements. Action research models begin with a central problem or topic. They involve some observation or monitoring of current practice, followed by the collection and synthesis of information and data. Finally, some sort of action is taken, which then serves as the basis for the next stage of action research (Mills, 2011). In addition, some models are simple in their design, while others appear relatively complex. This range of complexity—from simpler to more complex—can be seen in the following examples:

- Stringer (2007), in his action research interacting spiral, describes action research as a "simple, yet powerful framework" consisting of a "look, think, and act" routine (p. 8). During each stage, participants observe, reflect, and then take some sort of action. This action leads them into the next stage (see Figure 1.3).

Figure 1.3   Stringer's Action Research Interacting Spiral

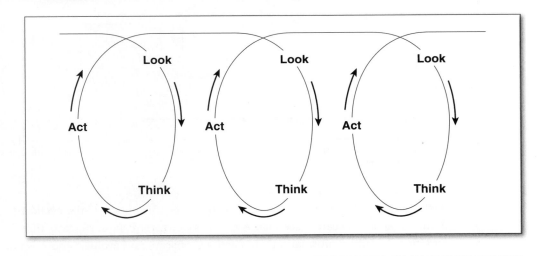

Source: Adapted from *Action Research* (p. 9), by Ernest T. Stringer, 2007, Thousand Oaks, CA: Sage. Copyright 2007 by Sage. Reprinted with permission of the publisher. All rights reserved.

- Kurt Lewin (Smith, 2007)—who, by the way, is credited with coining the term "action research"—also depicts an action research spiral, which includes fact finding, planning, taking action, evaluating, and amending the plan, before moving into a second action step (see Figure 1.4).

- Calhoun's (1994) action research cycle, while not appearing as a "spiral," still represents a process that is built around a cyclical notion. As she describes, the solid lines indicate the primary direction of the action research cycle through the phases, in numerical order. The dotted lines indicate backward and forward movement within the cycle as refinement or clarification of information is warranted (see Figure 1.5).

Figure 1.4	Lewin's Action Research Spiral

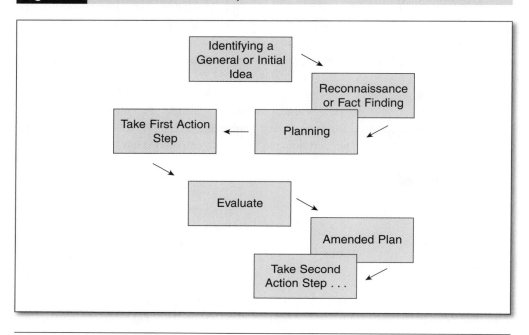

- Bachman's (2001) action research spiral continues this notion of the cyclical nature of action research (see Figure 1.6). His downward spiral suggests that participants gather information, plan actions, observe and evaluate those actions, and then reflect and plan for a new cycle of the spiral, based on the insights that were gained in the previous cycle.

- Riel's (2007) progressive problem solving through action research model takes the participant through four steps in each cycle: planning, taking action, collecting evidence, and reflecting (see Figure 1.7).

- Piggot-Irvine's (2006) action research model continues to depict this spiraling nature of the action research process. In her upward spiral, she shows these similar steps—planning, acting, and reflecting—through three subsequent action research cycles (see Figure 1.8).

- *Hendricks's* (2009) action research model is shown in Figure 1.9. In her model, which she has placed in a school-based context, she focuses on acting, evaluating, and reflecting.

4 Best 4-stage

| **Figure 1.5** | Calhoun's Action Research Cycle |

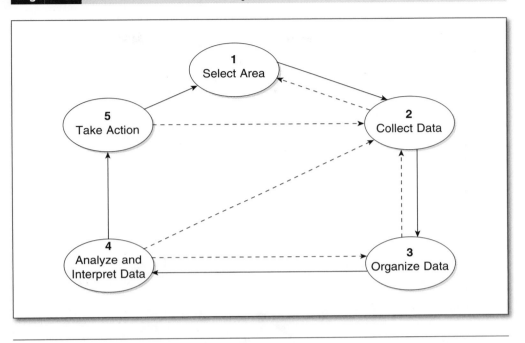

Which model should you follow? Personally, I do not think it really matters, as I see them essentially as variations on the same theme (as evidenced by their shared elements). Generally speaking, my version of the action research process is composed of a four-stage procedure (Mertler & Charles, 2011), which will be expanded in more detail in the next chapter. For the time being, these four stages are as follows:

1. The planning stage

2. The acting stage

3. The developing stage

4. The reflecting stage

Within this framework—and as you saw earlier in the various models presented—action research is a recursive, cyclical process that typically does not proceed in a linear fashion (Johnson, 2008). Teacher-researchers engaged in action research often find themselves repeating some of the steps several times or perhaps doing them in a different order.

Figure 1.6   Bachman's Action Research Spiral

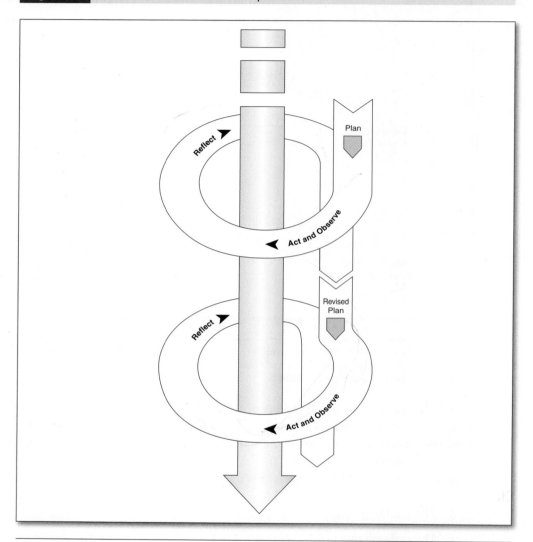

Source: Adapted from "Review of the Agricultural Knowledge System in Fiji: Opportunities and Limitations of Participatory Methods and Platforms to Promote Innovation Development" (unpublished dissertation), by Lorenz Bachman, 2001, Berlin, Germany: Humboldt University to Berlin. Copyright 2001. Retrieved January 17, 2008, from http://edoc.hu-berlin.de/dissertationen/bachmann-lorenz-b-r-2000–12–21/HTML/bachmann-ch3.html. Reprinted with permission of the author.

Depending on the nature of a given action research project, there may never be a clear end to the study—teachers may continue to go through subsequent cycles of planning, acting and observing, developing a new plan, and reflecting, which seemingly spiral from 1 year

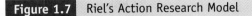

| **Figure 1.7** | Riel's Action Research Model |

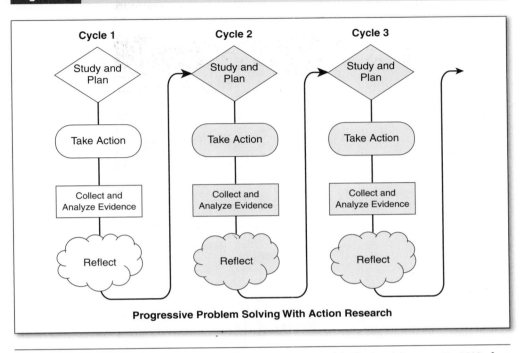

Source: Adapted from *Understanding Action Research*, by Margaret Riel. Retrieved January 17, 2008, from http://cadres.pepperdine.edu/ccar/define.html. Copyright 2007 by the Center for Collaborative Action Research, Pepperdine University. Reprinted with permission of the author.

into the next (Mertler & Charles, 2011). You will learn more about the specific steps in conducting action research in Chapter 2.

Characteristics of Action Research: What It Is and What It Is Not

Although action research can be a fairly straightforward process, it is sometimes misunderstood by educational practitioners (Mertler & Charles, 2011). There are many aspects of this methodology that characterize its uniqueness as an approach to conducting educational research. It is imperative for educators to have a sound, foundational understanding of just what action research is and is not. The following list, compiled from several sources (Johnson, 2008; Mertler & Charles, 2011; Mills, 2011; Schmuck, 1997), is an attempt to describe what action research is:

- Action research is a process that improves education, in general, by incorporating change.

Figure 1.8   Piggot-Irvine's Action Research Model

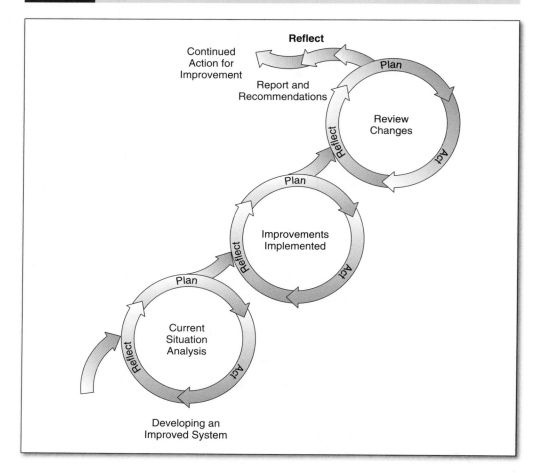

Source: Adapted from "Sustaining Excellence in Experienced Principals? Critique of a Professional Learning Community Approach," by Eileen Piggot-Irvine, 2006, *International Electronic Journal for Leadership in Learning*, *10*(16). Retrieved January 17, 2008, from http://www.ucalgary.ca/iejll/vol10/irvine. Copyright 2006 by the University of Calgary Press. Reprinted with permission of the publisher.

- Action research is a process involving educators working together to improve their own practices.

- Action research is persuasive and authoritative, since it is done by teachers for teachers.

- Action research is collaborative; that is, it is composed of educators talking and working with other educators in empowering relationships.

Figure 1.9	Hendricks's Action Research Process

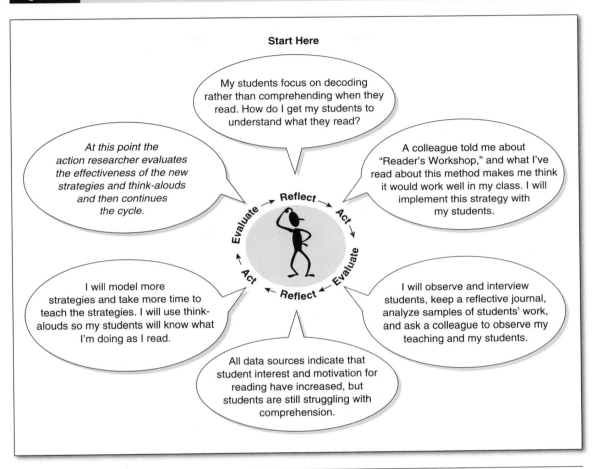

Source: Adapted from *Improving Schools Through Action Research: A Comprehensive Guide for Educators* (p. 9), by Cher Hendricks, 2009, Boston: Allyn & Bacon.

- Action research is participative, since educators are integral members—not disinterested outsiders—of the research process.

- Action research is practical and relevant to classroom teachers, since it allows them direct access to research findings.

- Action research is developing critical reflection about one's teaching.

- Action research is a planned, systematic approach to understanding the learning process.

- Action research is a process that requires us to "test" our ideas about education.

- Action research is open-minded.

- Action research is a critical analysis of educational places of work.

- Action research is a cyclical process of planning, acting, developing, and reflecting.

- Action research is a justification of one's teaching practices.

Of equal importance is that educators understand what action research is not (Johnson, 2008; Mertler & Charles, 2011; Mills, 2011; Schmuck, 1997):

- Action research is not the usual thing that teachers do when thinking about teaching; it is more systematic and more collaborative.

- Action research is not simply problem solving; it involves the specification of a problem, the development of something new (in most cases), and critical reflection on its effectiveness.

- Action research is not done "to" or "by" other people; it is research done by particular educators, on their own work, with students and colleagues.

- Action research is not the simple implementation of predetermined answers to educational questions; it explores, discovers, and works to find creative solutions to educational problems.

- Action research is not conclusive; the results of action research are neither right nor wrong but rather tentative solutions that are based on observations and other data collection and that require monitoring and evaluation in order to identify strengths and limitations.

- Action research is not a fad; good teaching has always involved the systematic examination of the instructional process and its effects on student learning. Teachers are always looking for ways to improve instructional practice, and although teachers seldom have referred to this process of observation, revision, and reflection as research, that is exactly what it is.

The Importance of Action Research

At this point, you may find yourself asking a basic—albeit legitimate—question: Why should I become involved in an action research project, especially with all the demands and responsibilities placed on me as an educator today? Mertler and Charles (2011) have provided at least some partial answers to this question:

Video Clip 1.1
View a clip of
Dr. Mertler
discussing the
importance of
action research.

[First,] action research deals with your problems, not someone else's. Second, action research is very timely; it can start now—or whenever you are ready—and provides immediate results. Third, action research provides educators with opportunities to better understand, and therefore improve, their educational practices. Fourth, as a process, action research can also promote the building of stronger relationships among colleagues with whom we work. Finally, and possibly most importantly, action research provides educators with alternative ways of viewing and approaching educational questions and problems and with new ways of examining our own educational practices. (Mertler & Charles, 2011, p. 339–340)

Unfortunately, the answers to the initial question may have prompted another query in your mind: If the benefits are so substantial, why doesn't everyone do action research? Again, Mertler and Charles (2011) suggest answers to this question:

First, although its popularity has increased over the past decade, action research is still relatively unknown when compared to more traditional forms of conducting research. Second, although it may not seem the case, action research is more difficult to conduct than traditional approaches to research. Educators themselves are responsible for implementing the resultant changes, but also for conducting the research. Third, action research does not conform with many of the requirements of conventional research with which you may be familiar— it is therefore less structured and more difficult to conduct. Finally, because of the lack of fit between standard research requirements and the process of conducting action research, you may find it more difficult to write up your results. (Mertler & Charles, 2011, p. 340)

These sets of responses to our hypothetical (or perhaps very realistic) questions provide compelling reasons for both conducting and not conducting action research projects. The following is a discussion of four broad but vitally important ways in which action research can be used successfully in educational settings: to effectively connect theory to practice, to improve educational practice, to empower teachers, and as a means for promoting professional growth.

Connecting Theory to Practice

Research is often used to develop theories that eventually help determine best practices in education (Johnson, 2008). These best practices are then used to help teachers develop effective learning experiences for their students. Johnson (2008) describes how this unidirectional flow of information, in the specific form of research findings, from researchers to practitioners, often breaks down. Frequently, a gap exists between what is learned by researchers, who conduct and report their research on educational topics, and practicing classroom teachers. This apparent gap may be described this way: Research occurs in the ivory towers, whereas practice takes place in the trenches (Parsons & Brown, 2002). What goes on in public school classrooms often does not reflect research findings related to instructional practices and student learning (Johnson, 2008).

Johnson (2008) further offers two possible explanations for this noticeable breakdown. First, he cites the fact that research (i.e., that conducted by university and college professors and other researchers) is characteristically written and therefore published in such a way that does not consider a teacher's typical day-to-day schedule. Research articles often are overly descriptive, contain an overabundance of jargonistic terms, and use research methods that do not "fit" with the daily needs of and resources available to teachers. Many teachers who have taken my educational research methods course over the years have shared with me the fact that they believe most, if not all, education research is impractical and irrelevant to their needs. Second, Johnson suggests that this one-way flow of information from researcher to teacher creates an environment in which the researcher expects the practicing teacher to be a passive receiver of this information. Often, these research findings do not appreciate or even take into account teachers' points of view, the complexities of the teaching-learning process, or the practical challenges teachers must address in their classrooms on a daily basis.

Video Clips 1.2 & 1.3 View clips of educator-researchers discussing the importance of action research.

Action research provides one possible solution to bridging this gap by creating a two-way flow of information. Research findings offered from researchers can still be used to inform best practices and to better understand what is happening in classrooms. Simultaneously, data collected and analyzed by practicing teachers in their own classrooms can be used to inform theories and research related to best practices (Johnson, 2008). Parsons and Brown (2002) effectively explain this two-way flow of information by stating that "teaching decisions are not only shaped by theory and research, but in turn help give shape and new directions to educational theory and research" (p. 7).

Improvement of Educational Practice

As was discussed previously, a main focus of action research is the improvement of classroom practice. When teachers are reflective and critical of their own practice, they use the information they collect and phenomena they observe as a means of facilitating informed, practical decision making (Parsons & Brown, 2002). The clear strength of action research is that it is reflective and collaborative and that it can ultimately lead to improvements in educational practice (Parsons & Brown, 2002).

This sometimes requires a bit of a shift in the way we think about and approach our own classroom practice. Many teachers believe that they have mastered their profession and that they will be successful if they simply keep doing what they have been doing. Ironically, however, the truly successful teachers (i.e., those whom we call experts or "master teachers") are those who constantly and systematically reflect on their actions and the consequences of those actions. This constant reflection results in the acquisition of new knowledge as it pertains to the teaching and learning process. It is important to remember that, as teachers, we work all day long with other human beings; each one is exceptional in her or his own special way. Each human being has different needs, desires, motivations, interests, learning styles, strengths, and weaknesses. Each student or group of students constantly provides us with unique challenges and opportunities, many of which require unique approaches (Parsons & Brown, 2002). Systematic reflection in the form of action research can provide the stimulus for changing and improving practice in order to make it appropriate for these unique individuals with whom we work.

Connection to School Improvement

The discussion in the previous section focused on the use of action research as a reflective means of improving individual classroom practice. Action research can also be organized and facilitated in such a way as to promote more systemic types of improvements. One way to accomplish this is to approach action research as a collaborative venture. One of the benefits of sharing the responsibilities of such a process is that it brings together different perspectives, ideas, experiences, and resources (Mertler, 2009). Collaboratively designed and implemented action research—a concept known as **collaborative action research** (or CAR), as opposed to "individual action research" (Clauset, Lick, & Murphy, 2008, p. 2)—is an ideal mechanism for engaging teachers, administrators, and support personnel in systemic, self-initiated school improvement. This concept can even spread so far as to include *every* educator in a school; this concept is known as "schoolwide action research" (Clauset, Lick, & Murphy, 2008, p. 2). As a means of improving schools and empowering educators (as you will read in the next section), I firmly believe that this process will lead to better instruction, better learning, and more productive students coming out of our classrooms.

Teacher Empowerment—Teacher as Decision Maker

Another important aspect of action research is that it advances the notion of teacher empowerment. When teachers collect their own data in order to assist in making decisions about their own students and classrooms—a concept known as "teacher as decision maker"—they become empowered. Teacher empowerment allows teachers to bring into their classrooms their own unique expertise, talents, and creativity so that they can implement instructional programs to best meet the needs of their students (Johnson, 2008). Teachers are allowed—even encouraged—to take risks and make changes to their instructional practice whenever and wherever they believe it to be appropriate. This approach to school leadership and improvement is in complete opposition to the standard top-down, administrator-driven leadership. This is not meant to imply that the skills and abilities of building- and district-level administrators are not needed; the leadership skills of these individuals are quite necessary. They simply take on different roles (e.g., the roles of facilitator, supporter, and mentor). The locus of control is in essence returned to the classroom level, thereby enhancing the effectiveness of schools and promoting school improvement (Johnson, 2008).

Gives teachers a voice

Professional Growth

Johnson (2008) characterizes traditional teacher in-services as a gathering of teachers, usually after a long day of teaching or on a jam-packed workshop day, who sit and listen to an expert describe a new methodology, a new approach, or new instructional material that they typically do not believe relates directly to their classroom situations or teaching styles. Teachers are not provided with enough time, content, or activities in order to effectively increase their knowledge or positively affect their practice. Action research has been shown to serve as a means of improving teachers' problem-solving skills and their attitudes toward professional development and school change, as well as of increasing their confidence and professional self-esteem (Parsons & Brown, 2002). Furthermore, action research affirms the professionalism of teaching by giving teachers a real voice in their own professional development, as opposed to being told by someone else that a specific goal or topic is what is needed by every teacher in the building or district (Schmuck, 1997).

Applications of Action Research

There are several ways in which the basic principles of action research can be applied. Four of the most essential—the identification of educational problems, the development and testing of possible solutions, preservice teacher education, and in-service teacher professional growth—are outlined here.

Identifying Problems

Action research can be used effectively as a means of identifying problems in school settings. In fact, as you will see in the next chapter, the identification of a particular problem is the first major step in the process of conducting an action research study. If a goal of action research is to promote improvement and change, obviously the specific target of that improvement or change must first be identified (Johnson, 2008). The basic process of problem identification occurs when a situation is observed and there is recognition that something within that situation could probably be done better (Johnson, 2008). Identifying, defining, and limiting the problem involves its specification, followed by actively pursuing further understanding of the situation and then uncovering its possible causal factors. You are, in essence, trying to answer the question: Why are things as they are (Johnson, 2008)? Examples might include the following:

- Why are my students not retaining what they have been taught?
- Why do Adam, Betty, and Carlos seem to lack the motivation to read?
- What are the specific reasons behind Devin's behavior problems?
- How can I use my instructional time more effectively?

Developing and Testing Solutions

Action research can also be used to find solutions to problems you have identified and ultimately test their effectiveness. Once you have specified a problem (i.e., posed a question in need of an answer, as we did above), problem-solving strategies can be used to arrive at possible solutions (Johnson, 2008). For example, creative problem solving (Johnson, 2008) is a process that follows the identification of a problem with the generation of as many potential solutions as possible; the selection of one solution that seems best; the refinement and implementation of the solution; and finally the evaluation and revision of the solution, focusing on its limitations, for future use.

Action research—recall its systematic nature—allows teachers to be more flexible in their thinking, more receptive to new ideas, and more organized in their approach to problem solving (Johnson, 2008). All of these facets enable teachers to become better able to solve problems.

Once possible solutions have been developed, they must be tested or tried out in order to determine their effectiveness (Johnson, 2008). Every new idea must be tested in order to see if, or how well, it works. Often, during the initial implementation of a solution, procedures must be revised and adjusted. This requires some level of continuous monitoring. Action research allows for the integration of both formative and summative evaluation, a sort of "data-driven decision making." **Formative evaluation** occurs during the implementation phase; **summative evaluation** occurs following the completion of the implementation phase. Both types of evaluative decisions are essential in determining the extent to which a solution has worked.

Preservice Teacher Education

As we all know, teaching is an extremely complex professional undertaking. If we can say that, as experienced classroom teachers, imagine what those who are making the transition from student to beginning teacher must feel. The preservice teacher's knowledge base and understanding of the complexities of the "typical" classroom environment is quite limited. Without this knowledge base and understanding, the everyday decision-making process takes substantially more time for the preservice teacher when compared to the in-service teacher (Johnson, 2008). Action research can add to this limited knowledge base by helping preservice teachers see things in the classroom that they would not normally notice (Johnson, 2008). This can help speed up the process of assimilating to a new classroom environment, thus allowing them to make better and quicker decisions.

As in-service teachers, most of you will not have the occasion to change the nature of preservice teacher education. However, I offer this small piece of advice: If you are ever afforded the opportunity to take a preservice teacher under your tutelage, consider providing that person with a unique preprofessional development opportunity—his or her own mini action research project, done collaboratively with you. Preservice teacher action research projects can focus on observations of students, observations of other classroom teachers (including you), or observations of their own practice. In all likelihood, they will be required to do some of this anyway but probably not using a systematic, action research approach. Action research can serve as a vehicle through which preservice teachers, in-service teachers, and university faculty can work together. Schools and teachers within those schools provide real-world experiences for university students and faculty; university students and faculty provide schools and teachers with access to current best practices. Through action research, preservice teachers, in-service teachers, and university faculty can work together toward a common goal—the improvement of student learning. One cautionary note, however: Be sure to consider small-scale topics or problems—perhaps through the integration of performance-based assessments—so as not to overwhelm the preservice teacher, whose mind may already be spinning (Johnson, 2008).

In-Service Professional Growth

As has been previously discussed, action research is an effective means for teachers to develop and grow professionally. In fact, Johnson (2008) believes action research to be perhaps "the most efficient and effective way to address the professional development of teachers" (p. 44). Action research affords teachers opportunities to connect theory with practice, to become more reflective in their practice, and to become empowered risk takers. All of these opportunities enable the in-service classroom teacher to grow professionally and ultimately to realize growth in student learning.

"Rigor" in Action Research

Research, of any kind, is a scientific endeavor. Quality research must meet standards of sound practice. The basis for establishing the quality of traditional (i.e., experimental) research lies in concepts of validity and reliability. Action research, because of its participatory nature, relies on a different set of criteria (Stringer, 2007). Historically, however, one of the "weaknesses" of action research has been its perceived lower level of quality. People falsely believe that, since action research is conducted by teachers, and not academicians or researchers, it must be of lesser quality. Stringer (2007) tells of his experience of submitting a proposal, which was ultimately rejected for presentation, to present an action research paper at a national educational research conference. Accompanying the rejection notification was the feedback from one reviewer, who referred to the topic of the paper as "nonsense" (p. 191).

This idea that action research is of lesser quality is, of course, not true. However, it is critical for the action researcher to ensure that the research is sound. The extent to which it reaches a standard of quality is directly related to the usefulness of the research findings for its intended audience. This level of quality in action research can be referred to as its "rigor."

rigor

In general, **rigor** refers to the quality, validity, accuracy, and credibility of action research and its findings. Rigor is typically associated with the terms validity and reliability in quantitative studies, referring to the accuracy of instruments, data, and research findings, and with accuracy, credibility, and dependability in qualitative studies (Melrose, 2001). (These terms will be discussed further in Chapter 5.) Many action researchers use the term rigor in a much broader sense, making reference instead to the entire research process, not just to its aspects of data collection, data analysis, and findings (Melrose, 2001). Rigor in action research is typically based on procedures of checking to ensure that the results are not biased or that they reflect only the particular perspective of the researcher (Stringer, 2007).

As mentioned, the determination of rigor is often contingent on the intended audience for the sharing of action research results. Classroom-based action research can be disseminated to a wide variety of audiences (e.g., teachers, administrators, counselors, parents, school boards, professional organizations), and the usefulness of the results of action research often depends on their particular perceptions about rigor, since it can have different connotations depending on the particular audience (Melrose, 2001). For example, if the research is intended for limited dissemination (e.g., sharing with members of the action research group or building staff), the necessary level of rigor is much different than if the dissemination is intended for scholarly academic output (e.g., formally presenting the results at a national research conference or publishing the study in a journal). It is necessary for the broader dissemination to be concerned more with generalizability, meaning that the results of the study will extend beyond its scope to other settings and people.

However, action research intended for more local-level dissemination—and, as an aside, I believe that the majority of classroom-based action research falls into this category—has an altogether different focus. It is important to remember that participants in action research studies make mistakes and learn from them (Melrose, 2001); this is inherent in the action research process. The research questions and design are often emergent, changeable, and therefore unpredictable. Therefore, there may be no generalizable conclusions at all, as the findings are context specific and unique to the particular participants and their setting and situation. What matters is typically the improvement of practice, as evidenced by the resulting, visible change, not the study's rigor (as defined by its ability to be generalized).

There are numerous ways in which to provide rigor within the scope of teacher-led action research studies. The following list has been adapted from Melrose (2001), Mills (2011), and Stringer (2007):

- *Repetition of the cycle*—Action research is, by its very nature, cyclical. Most action researchers firmly believe that once through an action research cycle is simply not enough. In order to develop adequate rigor, it is critical to proceed through a number of cycles, where the earlier cycles are used to help inform how to conduct the later cycles (Melrose, 2001). In theory, with each subsequent cycle, more is learned, and greater credibility is added to the findings.

- *Prolonged engagement and persistent observation*—In order to gather enough information to help participants fully understand the outcomes of an action research process, they must be provided "extended opportunities to explore and express their experience" (Stringer, 2007, p. 58) as it relates to the problem being investigated. However, simply spending more time in the setting is not enough. For example, observations and interviews must be deliberately and carefully conducted (Mills, 2011; Stringer, 2007). These should not be indiscriminate research activities.

- *Experience with the process*—In many cases rigor and credibility will depend on the experience of the action researcher(s). If a teacher has (or other school personnel have) conducted previous studies, or even previous cycles within the same study, this individual can perform confidently and will have greater credibility with respective audiences (Melrose, 2001). However, if the teacher-researcher is a novice, the entire process may benefit from the use of an experienced facilitator.

- *Polyangulation of data*—Rigor can be enhanced during the action research process when multiple sources of data and other information are included (Mills, 2011; Stringer, 2007). This permits the action researcher to cross-check the accuracy of data (Mills, 2011) and to clarify meanings or misconceptions held by participants (Stringer, 2007). Accuracy of data and credibility of the study findings go hand-in-hand.

- *Member checking*—Participants should be provided with opportunities to review the raw data, analyses, and final reports resulting from the action research process (Mills, 2011; Stringer, 2007). The rigor of the research is enhanced with this activity by allowing participants to verify that various aspects of the research process adequately and accurately represent their beliefs, perspectives, and experiences. It also gives them the opportunity to further explain and/or extend the information that they have already provided.

- *Participant debriefing*—Similar to member checking, debriefing is another opportunity for participants to provide insight. However, in this case, the focus is on their emotions and feelings, instead of the factual information they have offered (Mills, 2011; Stringer, 2007). They may address emotions that might have clouded their interpretations of events or inhibited their memories.

Needless to say, rigor in action research is very important, albeit for reasons that are different from those of more traditional forms of educational research.

Related Websites: What Is Action Research?

This annotated list of related websites represents merely a partial offering of information on the Internet that can help you understand more about conducting action research.

- Action Research Resources **http://www.scu.edu.au/schools/gcm/ar/arhome.html**

  Bob Dick, of Southern Cross University in Lismore, New South Wales, Australia, maintains this extensive site. The main page includes links to action research journals, discussion lists, papers, theses, dissertations, and much more. Included on the page titled "Action Research Theses and Dissertations" (http://www.scu.edu.au/schools/gcm/ar/art/arthome.html) are links to full-text action research theses and dissertations, as well as a wonderful paper offering an overview of the action research process, titled "You Want to Do an Action Research Thesis?" (http://www.scu.edu.au/schools/gcm/ar/art/arthesis.html). Everyone should definitely take a look at this paper!

- Classroom Action Research **http://oldweb.madison.k12.wi.us/sod/car/carhome page.html**

  This site is maintained by the Madison Metropolitan School District in Madison, Wisconsin. It is an extensive action research resource site for teachers. (I will be referencing this site numerous times in the Related websites sections of later chapters.) The first link is titled, "What is Action Research?" (http://oldweb .madison.k12.wi.us/sod/car/carisandisnot.html) and provides a nice summary of what classroom-based action research is and is not.

- Action Research Introduction **http://www.accessexcellence.org/LC/TL/AR/**

  Sharon Parsons, of San Jose State University, provides a brief overview and introduction to action research. Included in her discussion are suggestions for getting started on an action research project, concentrating on the following steps: deciding on a focus for the project, developing a research plan, analyzing the data, and reporting on what has been learned. Several examples of classroom-based action research projects are also provided.

- Action Research by Teachers for Teachers **http://rubble.heppell.net/TforT/default .html**

  This interesting website showcases action research projects undertaken by teachers that focus on the integration of technology in the classroom. Teachers can learn about projects, ideas, and solutions offered by other teachers. There is even a link providing information about how you can contribute to the collection.

- Dissecting My Classroom: A Teacher Experiments With Action Research **http:// www.alliance.brown.edu/pubs/voices/3qrt1999/actref.shtml**

  If you find yourself wondering if you can really do action research in your classroom, read this brief reflection piece offered by Julie Nora, an ESL (English as a Second Language) teacher in Providence, Rhode Island. She explains how her attitude toward educational research changed after attending an action research conference. She continues by explaining how she decided to integrate action research into her daily teaching, how it eventually caused her to change her teaching, and how it ultimately resulted in substantial improvements in student achievement.

- Comparing Formal Research and Action Research **http://mypage.iusb.edu/ ~gmetteta/Research_about_Teaching_and.htm#Comparison**

  Gwynn Mettetal, of Indiana University South Bend, offers a brief comparison of traditional and action research methodologies. This web page may help solidify many of the things discussed in this first chapter.

- Action Research Links **http://www.emtech.net/actionresearch.htm**

  This final site is a compilation of links to websites related to action research. There are over 160 links contained on this site.

SUMMARY

★ Educational research involves the application of the scientific method to educational problems.

- Answers to questions typically come from common sources, such as tradition, authority, and common sense.

- The scientific method is a more systematic, objective procedure for finding answers to questions.

- Traditional research is often conducted by individuals who are somewhat removed from the environment they are studying.

★ Two broad types of research methods are quantitative and qualitative.

- Quantitative research methodologies require the collection of numerical data and utilize a deductive approach to reasoning; they include both nonexperimental (e.g., descriptive, correlational, causal-comparative research) and experimental designs.

- Qualitative research methodologies require the collection of narrative data and utilize an inductive approach to reasoning; they include phenomenology, ethnography, grounded theory, and case studies.

- Mixed-methods research designs combine both quantitative and qualitative types of data.

★ Action research is any systematic inquiry conducted by educators for the purpose of gathering information about how their particular schools operate, how they teach, and how their students learn.

- Action research is done *by* teachers *for* teachers, working with students and colleagues.

- Teacher reflection is an integral part of action research.
- The basic process of action research consists of the following four stages: planning, acting, developing, and reflecting.
- Most action research studies are cyclical and iterative.
- Action research can be used effectively to bridge the gap between theory and practice, to improve educational practice, to empower teachers, to provide professional growth opportunities for teachers, to identify educational problems, to develop and test solutions, and to expand the knowledge base of preservice teachers.

QUESTIONS AND ACTIVITIES

1. List or describe at least five things (e.g., problems, things you would like to improve) within your classroom or school that interest you and that you might want to pursue further. Do you think any of the things on your list might be appropriate for an action research study?

2. Describe a situation where someone other than you made a decision that affected your classroom practice. If it had been up to you, would you have made the same decision? If not, what would your decision have been, and why do you suppose there was a difference?

3. Think about your own views of research and what you have learned in this chapter. In a chart (see the example below), develop a list of advantages and limitations for both traditional research and action research.

4. Do you think that traditional research can benefit you and your students? If so, how can it benefit you? If not, why do you believe that it cannot?

5. Do you think that action research can benefit you and your students? If so, how? If not, why not?

	Advantages	Limitations
Traditional Research		
Action Research		

STUDENT STUDY SITE

Visit the Student Study Site at **www.sagepub.com/mertler3study** for these additional learning tools:

- Video clips
- Web resources
- Self quizzes
- E-flashcards

- PowerPoint slides
- Sample action research reports
- Full-text SAGE journal articles
- Chapter summaries

CHAPTER 2

Overview of the Action Research Process

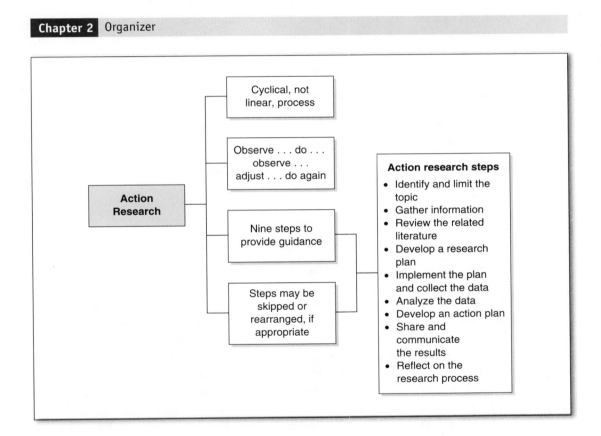

Action Research

- Cyclical, not linear, process
- Observe . . . do . . . observe . . . adjust . . . do again
- Nine steps to provide guidance
- Steps may be skipped or rearranged, if appropriate

Action research steps

- Identify and limit the topic
- Gather information
- Review the related literature
- Develop a research plan
- Implement the plan and collect the data
- Analyze the data
- Develop an action plan
- Share and communicate the results
- Reflect on the research process

In Chapter 1, the general process of conducting action research was briefly introduced as a four-stage procedure. To reiterate, these four stages are:

1. The *planning* stage

2. The *acting* stage

3. The *developing* stage

4. The *reflecting* stage

However, it is critical at this time that we begin to examine the *specific* steps of conducting an action research study. The focus of this chapter is to introduce the nine specific steps that comprise the process of action research. These steps will then be detailed across Chapters 3 through 8. The nine steps in the process (followed parenthetically by the chapters where they are addressed in this book) are as follows:

1. Identifying and limiting the topic (Chapter 3)

2. Gathering information (Chapter 3)

3. Reviewing the related literature (Chapter 3)

4. Developing a research plan (Chapter 4)

5. Implementing the plan and collecting data (Chapter 5)

6. Analyzing the data (Chapter 6)

7. Developing an action plan (Chapter 7)

8. Sharing and communicating the results (Chapter 8)

9. Reflecting on the process (Chapter 8)

Upon comparing the general four-stage procedure with the nine specific steps, you probably will not find it too difficult to see how the two fit together (see Figure 2.1). Stage 1 (the *planning* stage) is composed of Steps 1, 2, 3, and 4 since these are planning activities done prior to the implementation of the project. Stage 2 (the *acting* stage) is composed of Steps 5 and 6, where the action researcher implements the plan and then collects and analyzes the data. Step 7 is, in essence, its own stage, namely Stage 3 (the *developing* stage). This is the step where the revisions, changes, or improvements arise and future actions (known as an "action plan") are developed. Finally, Stage 4 (the *reflecting* stage) is composed of Steps 8 and 9; the action researcher summarizes the results of the study, creates a strategy for sharing the results, and reflects on the entire process. It is important to mention that you will see variations of Figure 2.1 near the beginning of each of Chapters 3 through 8, with the specific step or steps being addressed in that particular chapter highlighted in the figure.

not a linear process

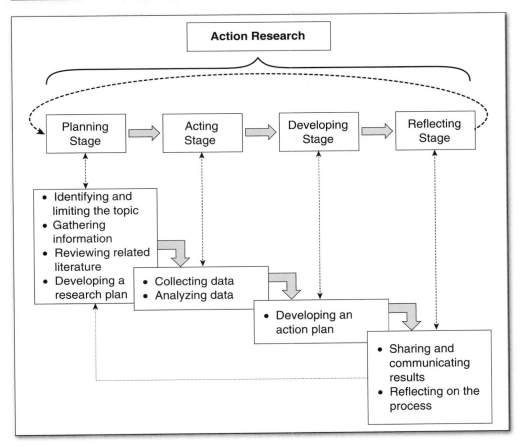

Figure 2.1 Integration of Two Organizational Schemes for the Step-by-Step Process of Action Research

It is critical at this point to reiterate the fact that action research, contrary to the way it is depicted in Figure 2.1, is not a linear process (the purpose of Figure 2.1 is merely to show the relationship between the two schemes for summarizing the action research process). Action research has historically been viewed as cyclical in nature (Mertler & Charles, 2011). That is to say, whereas action research has a clear beginning, it does not have a clearly defined endpoint. Ordinarily, teacher-researchers design and implement a project, collect and analyze data in order to monitor and evaluate the project's effectiveness, and then make revisions and improvements to the project for future implementation. In all likelihood, the project would then be implemented again—perhaps with next semester's or next year's students—when the effectiveness of the revisions would be monitored and evaluated, with new improvements developed for the next phase of implementation. One may be able to see that a given project may never have a clear end—the teacher may continue to go through subsequent cycles of implementation, evaluation, and revision, spiraling from one semester or year to the next (Mertler & Charles, 2011). Parsons and Brown (2002) describe the process as one of "observing-doing-observing-adjusting" and then doing it again (p. 8). The process of action research, with its cyclical and spiraling nature, is portrayed in Figure 2.2.

As we begin to examine the nine specific steps in greater detail, Johnson (2008) reminds us that these steps are meant to serve as guidelines in conducting action research projects. They must be adapted to a particular research problem or topic. Furthermore, the steps themselves should not necessarily be seen as cast in stone. If and where appropriate, teacher-researchers may find themselves skipping steps, rearranging their order, or repeating some steps more than once (Johnson, 2008). Action research can take on many forms,

Figure 2.2   The Process of Action Research

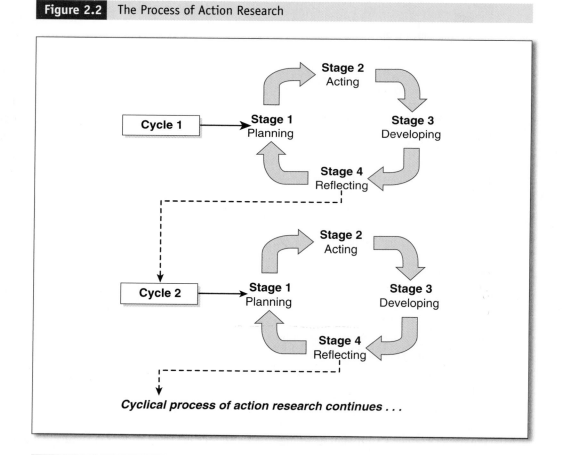

Source: Adapted from Mertler and Charles, 2011.

thus employing a wide range of methodologies. The key to worthwhile teacher-conducted action research rests in the questions addressed by the project and the extent to which the results are meaningful and important to *that* teacher (Parsons & Brown, 2002) and not necessarily in the means by which those results were realized.

Step 1: Identifying and Limiting the Topic

What first step

The first step in any research study is deciding exactly *what* to study. Since personal and professional experiences are so central to teacher-initiated action research, possible topics for investigation might be anything about which you are curious, that piques your interest, or that intrigues you in any way. Essentially, you are looking to identify some topic that you would genuinely like to examine in depth (Johnson, 2008). It is important to remember that the goal of any action research project is a desire to make things better, improve some specific practice, or correct something that is not working as well as it should (Fraenkel & Wallen, 2003). These goals must be kept in mind when initially identifying, and later narrowing the focus of, the topic.

Video Clip 2.1
View a clip of Dr. Mertler discussing the process of conducting action research

In addition, in order to investigate a topic for action research, it must be manageable (Fraenkel & Wallen, 2003). With all due respect, large-scale complex issues and research projects are probably better left to professional researchers. Action research studies designed and conducted by classroom teachers should take into consideration such things as the time requirements (or restrictions), the data collection and analysis skill levels of the individual(s) conducting the research, and any budgetary limitations. For these reasons, action research topics are generally narrow in focus (Fraenkel & Wallen, 2003).

Suggestions for identifying and narrowing the focus of action research topics are discussed more extensively in Chapter 3.

reconnaissance

Step 2: Gathering Information

After identifying and limiting the topic, the next step is preliminary information gathering, a process that Mills (2011) refers to as **reconnaissance**. Information gathering can be as simple as talking with other teachers, counselors, or administrators in your school or district in order to gauge their perceptions of your proposed research problem and perhaps to query them for ideas. You may skim teacher's manuals or other types of curricular guides, again looking for ideas, suggestions, and the like that may inform your topic.

More formally, doing reconnaissance involves taking time to reflect on your own beliefs and to gain a better understanding of the nature and context of your research problem (Mills, 2011). Doing reconnaissance takes three forms: self-reflection, description, and explanation. These will be discussed in detail in Chapter 3.

Step 3: Reviewing the Related Literature

"Related literature" can be loosely defined as any existing source of information that can shed light on the topic selected for investigation. These sources of information might include professional books, research journals, complete websites or individual web pages, teacher resource manuals, school or district documents, and even discussions with colleagues (Creswell, 2005; Johnson, 2008). There really is no limit to what can be used as related literature because the purpose of reviewing this information is to help the teacher-researcher make informed decisions about the research focus and plan. This related information can provide guidance for defining or limiting the problem, for developing an appropriate research design, or for selecting legitimate instruments or techniques for collecting data (Parsons & Brown, 2002). Again, this activity provides an opportunity for the action research to connect existing theory and research to actual classroom practice (Johnson, 2008).

Much more information, including specific recommendations and techniques, for reviewing related literature is also presented in Chapter 3.

Step 4: Developing a Research Plan

In a traditional educational research study, the development of a research design and plan for collecting data is known as the **research methodology**. Inherent in designing an action research study are several specific decisions that must be made during this step in the action research process. Once the research problem or topic has been identified and focused, it is then appropriate to state one or more research questions and possibly to develop from those questions specific hypotheses (Parsons & Brown, 2002). As you will see in Chapter 4, a *research question* is the fundamental question inherent in the research problem; it is *the* question the action researcher seeks to answer through conducting the study. The research question provides the guiding structure to the study itself. Every part of the action research study should be done so as to facilitate finding an answer to the research question. This is largely the reason behind why it is important to specify the research question prior to making any other decisions about the methodology.

It is typically best to try to keep the study as simple as possible by stating only *one* research question. However, in some instances, it may be appropriate to state an additional question that may be subordinate to (i.e., important but not as important as) the main question. These questions are sometimes referred to as *subquestions* (Mertler & Charles, 2011). If the teacher-researcher has enough previous experience with the topic at hand, it may be possible to also state the research question, as well as any subquestions, as research hypotheses. A *research hypothesis* is simply a specification of the expected answer—or a prediction, of sorts—to the research question. While a convention in more traditional forms of research—especially, quantitative research—hypotheses are seldom used in action research.

Integrated into the specification of research questions and hypotheses is the identi-fication of the variables that are central to the action research investigation. Recall from Chapter 1 that a *variable* is any characteristic that is central to the research topic and, therefore, the research question, about which the researcher wishes to draw conclusions. Therefore, a variable is in essence the actual characteristic or behavior upon which data will be collected. For this reason, it is critical that variables be observable and measur-able. For example, it is not possible to observe or measure *"understanding* of addition and subtraction facts" because actual understanding of these facts and skills occurs only in a student's brain. And since we cannot see into someone's brain, we cannot actually measure or observe how much the student understands. A more appropriate variable might be the *"accuracy* of applying addition and subtraction facts." Students could be given a set of addition and subtraction problems to complete. Their accuracy could then be measured by simply counting the number of problems each student answers correctly.

procedure

Closely related to decisions about which specific characteristics will be measured or observed are the procedures to be used to collect the data on those characteristics; these are the particular decisions related to the design of the research study. The action researcher needs to decide who can provide the data that are needed, how many participants are needed for the study, and how to gain access to those individuals (Creswell, 2005). Any of the methodologies briefly described in Chapter 1—whether they be quantitative, qualitative, or mixed methods in nature—can be used (although usually in somewhat simplified and less sophisticated form; Fraenkel & Wallen, 2003). Surveys, comparative studies, correla-tional studies, experiments, observations, interviews, analysis of existing records, and ethnographies are just some of the methodological designs that can be considered and effectively utilized. Also, remember that action research is systematic; therefore, data col-lection must be focused, and decisions about the various elements of research design and data collection must be determined *before* implementing the actual study (Johnson, 2008). Remember also that the data to be collected relate directly to the research questions that are guiding the action research study.

Also important during the planning stage of action research studies is paying close atten-tion to the issue of **research ethics**. Research ethics deals with the moral aspects of con-ducting research, especially research involving human beings. Consideration must be paid to how participants who are involved in a study are treated, the level of honesty and open-ness that participants are afforded, and the manner in which results are reported. As Mills (2011) states, it basically involves "doing the right thing" from a research perspective (p. 29). At a minimum level, research ethics addresses such values as honesty, caring, and fairness, among others. Details regarding research questions and hypotheses, research designs, ethics, and other decisions related to the development of a research plan are discussed more thoroughly in Chapter 4.

Step 5: Implementing the Plan and Collecting Data

Video Clips 2.2 & 2.3 View clips of educator-researchers discussing the process of conducting action research

The next step in the process of conducting action research is the determination of the specific data to be collected and how to *actually* collect them. In other words, decisions must be made about the instruments or other data collection techniques that will be used in the study. Fraenkel and Wallen (2003) suggest three main categories of data collection techniques. First, teachers can *observe* participants involved in the educational process. These participants might include students, other teachers, parents, and administrators. Whenever observations are made by teachers, it is a good idea to record as much as possible of what is observed. **Field notes** or journals are typically used to describe in detail what is seen and heard.

Second, **interviews** may also be used to collect data from students or other individuals. When we think of interviews, we typically think of an oral question-and-answer exchange between two or more individuals. However, interviews can also be conducted in written form through the use of a pencil-and-paper medium. This type of written question-and-answer data collection is known as a **questionnaire** or **survey**. Often, data collected from observations can lead quite nicely to additional follow-up data collected through the use of interviews or surveys (Fraenkel & Wallen, 2003).

Finally, a third category of data collection techniques involves the examination and analysis of **existing documents** or **records**. Analysis of existing records is often the least time consuming, since the data have already been collected; it is the job of the action researcher to make some sense of what is already there. A few examples of this type of data include attendance records, minutes of faculty meetings, school newspapers, lesson plans, policy manuals, seating charts, and student portfolios—the list is potentially endless.

I would like to add a fourth category to the list provided by Fraenkel and Wallen (2003) above. This fourth category is composed of quantitative measures, such as **checklists**, **rating scales**, **tests**, and other formal assessments that are routinely used in schools. Checklists and rating scales are often used in classrooms by teachers, usually in the form of scoring rubrics. In that sense, they may be considered existing records. However, they may also be specifically designed to collect data as part of an action research study. Tests, whether standardized or teacher developed, as well as other types of formal assessment techniques, are also existing forms of data that can be used quite efficiently for action research purposes.

Action research allows for the use of all types of data collected through the use of a wide variety of techniques. As both Frankel and Wallen (2003) and Johnson (2008) point out, it is important to collect multiple measures on the variables of interest in a given study. This allows—and, in fact, *encourages*—the teacher-researcher to *polyangulate* the collected data. Recall from Chapter 1 that **polyangulation** is the process of relating or integrating two or more sources of data in order to establish their quality and accuracy. For example, by comparing one form of data to the other, student comments about group dynamics made during interviews could be used to substantiate behaviors observed when those same students were videotaped during a small-group exercise.

Much more information, including examples of various data collection instruments and techniques, is provided in Chapter 5. Both qualitative (e.g., observations, interviews, journals) and quantitative (e.g., surveys, checklists, rating scales, tests) techniques are presented.

Step 6: Analyzing the Data

Analysis of data occurs primarily at two points during the process of a research study. In *traditional quantitative* research studies, data analysis typically occurs following the completion of all data collection. In *traditional qualitative* research studies, data analysis typically begins during data collection, continues throughout the remainder of the process of collecting data, and is completed following data collection. Action research combines these two approaches. Johnson (2008) suggests that "as you collect your data, analyze them by looking for themes, categories, or patterns that emerge. This analysis will influence further data collection [and analysis] by helping you to know what to look for" (p. 63). He continues by stating that there should also be a final stage of data analysis once everything has been collected.

Decisions about which type of data analysis to use are based initially on whether the data are qualitative or quantitative. Moreover, it is imperative to remember that the analysis of data must "match" the research question(s) being addressed, and hopefully answered, by the study. Most qualitative data are appropriately analyzed by means of an inductive process, where the action researcher examines all data for patterns and similarities. Quantitative data may be analyzed through the use of either descriptive statistics or inferential statistics. In most cases, descriptive statistics will suffice for the analysis of action research data; however, inferential statistics may be required if it is necessary to compare groups or measure relationships between variables (Creswell, 2005).

At this point, you might want to consider this advice: Try not to become overwhelmed at the anticipation of analyzing your data, especially if you have experienced stress, frustration, and confusion whenever you read published articles resulting from traditional research studies. The analysis of action research data is typically much less complex and detailed than in other, more formal research studies (Fraenkel & Wallen, 2003). In addition, do not feel that it is a requirement for *you* to analyze the data; you are certainly free to enlist the help of other teachers, administrators, or data analysts (Creswell, 2005). Information about analytical techniques—both qualitative and quantitative—is presented in Chapter 6.

Step 7: Developing an Action Plan

Once the data have been analyzed and the results of the analysis interpreted, the next step in the action research process is the development of an action plan. This is really the ultimate goal of any action research study—it is the "action" part of action research. The important outcome from the development of an action plan is the existence of a specific and tangible approach to trying out some new ideas as a means to solve the original problem (Creswell, 2005). The action plan is essentially a proposed strategy for implementing the results of your action research project. As the action plan is implemented, its effectiveness must continually be monitored, evaluated, and revised, thus perpetuating the cyclical nature of action research.

The action plan may be proposed for an individual teacher or classroom, collaboratively among a group of teachers, or on a schoolwide or even a districtwide basis. In some situations, it may be necessary to prepare a formal document outlining the action plan; often, clearly delineated guidelines for implementing possible solutions may suffice. There must be enough documented information about the plan for implementation; action researchers should never rely on their collective memories for future implementation of solutions.

Further information about the nature of an action plan and the various types of plans appears in Chapter 7.

Step 8: Sharing and Communicating the Results

An important part of any research study is the reporting or sharing of results with others in the educational community at large. Action research should be no different. Simply because you have undertaken this project in order to help you solve a problem that is more local and perhaps more personal in nature does not mean that no one else will be interested in the results that you have obtained. The vast majority of educators are constantly looking for ways to improve their practice—as we have discussed previously, it is the nature of their profession.

The presentation of results can take a variety of forms. For example, Johnson (2008) explains that the most appreciative audience for presentations of action research results is often your own colleagues. Results can be shared with this type of audience in an informal manner, perhaps taking the form of a brief presentation at a regularly scheduled faculty meeting or teacher in-service session (Johnson, 2008). Even an individual dialogue with a colleague may be an appropriate setting to share results. Presentations—which can sometimes include written summaries of results—can also be made to school boards, principals, other administrators, students, and parents.

On a more professional level, results of action research studies can also be disseminated to larger educational audiences, typically in more formal settings. Results can be formally presented at professional conferences or other types of teachers' conventions, usually conducted at the regional, state, or national levels (Johnson, 2008). Academic or professional journals are wonderful mechanisms for disseminating your results to a geographically broader audience. Journals that focus on a specific level of education—that is, elementary, middle, or high school—or on particular subject areas—for example, mathematics, science, social studies, language arts—are often quite appropriate for articles that report the results of action research. This, however, would require you to prepare a much more formal written paper of your study and its results.

Detailed suggestions for methods of sharing and communicating the results of your action research, both orally and more formally as a written document, are provided in Chapters 8 and 9.

Step 9: Reflecting on the Process

Action research is primarily about critical examination of one's own practice. In order for someone to critically examine her or his practice, that person must engage in systematic reflection of that practice. Reflection, as it pertains to action research, is something that must be done at the end of a particular action cycle. It is a crucial step in the process, since this is where the teacher-researcher reviews what has been done, determines its effectiveness, and makes decisions about possible revisions for future implementations of the project (which, in all likelihood, will comprise future action research cycles).

However, it is not only important to reflect at the end of a given cycle; effective teachers reflect on and critically examine their practice continuously *during* the process of teaching. When a teacher plans an innovative lesson, he might reflect on his planning of that lesson immediately after developing, but prior to delivering, the lesson; again after teaching the lesson; and perhaps once again after assessing his students on the content of the lesson. This allows him to be able to make revisions *during* instruction. Similarly, the teacher-researcher should engage in reflective practice *throughout* the entire action research project. Reflection following each step in the process permits the teacher-researcher to continuously monitor the progress of the action research project. This allows the teacher to make decisions and, more appropriately, *revisions* to the process throughout its implementation. By doing this, teacher-researchers are not confined to decisions made at the outset of a project; they can adapt their procedures if the situation warrants. In this manner, reflection is not really a final step but is integrated throughout the action research cycle.

Reflecting on the overall process of conducting action research is discussed in Chapter 8.

A Brief Example

Now that we have taken a concise look at each of the nine steps involved in conducting an action research study, let us consider the following example of an action research study, where each step has been briefly described. Our example begins with the department chair of a high school social studies department who, for some time, has been disappointed in the performance of students in the school's American history course. The course has always been taught in a traditional manner—with the content coverage beginning prior to the American Revolution and ending with events more recent. The department chair, who teaches multiple sections of the course along with another teacher, believes that there may be some merit in examining a "backward" approach to teaching history (i.e., beginning with current events and proceeding back through time in order to end at the American Revolution). The chair asks the other history teacher for assistance with this potential action research project, and she agrees.

Step 1: Identifying and Limiting the Topic

The two teachers meet on a couple of occasions over the summer in order to identify the specific topic they hope to address through the examination and trial of this alternative instructional approach. They determine that they believe that their students struggle most in making connections between seemingly unrelated historical events. The department chair argues that perhaps this backward approach (i.e., beginning with more recent historical events with which their students will be more familiar) will have a positive impact on how well they are able to make these types of connections. The teachers decide to focus their attention on any differences that the two instructional approaches have on students' abilities to make these connections.

Step 2: Gathering Information

The teachers decide to talk with the other social studies teachers, as well as teachers in other subject areas, in their building. They want to know what other teachers think about their assumption that students struggle with making connections between historical events, which occurred perhaps decades apart. They ask the others for their initial perceptions about the backward approach to teaching their content. Additionally, the two teachers spend time, independently, over the course of a few days to actually consider *why* they believe that this is the case for the struggles their students seem to experience. In other words, they carefully consider any "evidence" that may have led them to feel this way. They also strongly consider other possible solutions to this dilemma. At their next meeting together, they share what they had reflected on and decide that the backward approach continues to be worthy of investigating.

Step 3: Reviewing the Related Literature

The teachers then decide to collect more formal information—that based on research, in addition to what they had already obtained anecdotally from other teachers of history— about the effectiveness of backward approaches to teaching historical, chronological events; how other history teachers may have implemented this type of instruction; and any problems they may have encountered. They decide to split the tasks, with the department chair identifying and reviewing published research studies on the topic and the other teacher contacting history teachers through their professional organizations.

Step 4: Developing a Research Plan

Following the review of published literature and discussions with teachers from other schools and districts that have implemented this type of instruction, the teachers found enough evidence to support the focus of their proposed study (i.e., the backward approach to instruction is effective), although they also found some contradictory evidence (i.e., this approach is less or at least no more effective). The teachers decide on the following researchable question: *Is there a difference in instructional effectiveness between a backward approach and a forward approach to teaching American history?* Furthermore, based on their review of related literature and other information, the teachers state the following predicted hypothesis: *Students who are exposed to the backward approach will experience higher academic achievement, as evidenced by their abilities to make connections between historical events, than those exposed to the more traditional forward approach.*

Since their hypothesis implies a comparison study, the teachers decide to randomly split the eight sections of American history for the coming school year. Each teacher will teach four sections of American history—for each teacher, two sections will be taught using the forward approach and two sections will incorporate the backward approach. Achievement data, as well as other teacher-developed assessment data, will be collected from all students enrolled in the American history course for this academic year.

Step 5: Implementing the Plan and Collecting Data

Throughout the school year, the two history teachers design performance-based assessments, which examine the extent to which students were able to connect historical events. In addition, students will take an American history achievement test in the spring, a portion of which focuses on critical thinking skills as they apply to historical events.

Step 6: Analyzing the Data

Immediately following the end of the school year, data analysis is undertaken. Test scores resulting from the administration of the standardized achievement tests are statistically compared for the two groups (i.e., the backward group versus the forward group). It is determined that the test scores of the students who were taught using the backward instructional approach are significantly higher than those of the students taught in the more traditional manner. In other words, the original research hypothesis has been supported.

In addition, scores resulting from the various administrations of classroom-based performance assessments support the results of the standardized achievement tests. Again, the research hypothesis has been supported.

Step 7: Developing an Action Plan

With their findings in hand, the teachers decide to approach their principal and district curriculum coordinator about temporarily revising the American history curriculum in order to capitalize on the apparent effectiveness of the backward instructional approach. They agree that it will be imperative to continue to study the effectiveness of this approach in subsequent academic years. Similar findings in the coming years would provide a much stronger case for permanently changing the approach to teaching American history.

Step 8: Sharing and Communicating the Results

The principal and curriculum coordinator are quite impressed with the results of this action research study. They suggest to the department chair that the two teachers make

a presentation to the school board and to the entire school faculty at a regularly scheduled meeting at the beginning of the next school year. The two teachers develop and
make an effective presentation at the subsequent month's board meeting. A teacher
attending the board meeting later suggests that this study might make an interesting
contribution at an annual statewide conference on instructional innovations and best
practices held each fall.

Step 9: Reflecting on the Process

Over the summer, the two teachers meet in order to debrief and decide on any adjustments to the process that might be beneficial for next year. They consider several questions, including: How well did the process work? Are we sure that the data we collected
were the most appropriate in order to answer our research question? Were there additional types of data that could or should have been included in the data collection? Their
answers to these questions will help guide next year's implementation of the backward
approach to teaching American history.

Related Websites: The Action Research Process

This annotated list of related websites presents various interpretations of the action
research process.

- An Introduction to Action Research **http://physicsed.buffalostate.edu/danowner/
  actionrsch.html**

  In her 1995 presidential address to the National Association for Research in Science
  Teaching (NARST), Dorothy Gabel provides this thorough introduction to action
  research. Contained within are three different graphical depictions of the action
  research process. All are variations on the same theme but present different
  perspectives on the process.

- The Five Phases of Action Research **http://oldweb.madison.k12.wi.us/sod/car/
  carphases.html**

  The Classroom Action Research site of the Madison (Wisconsin) Metropolitan School
  District contains a specific page dedicated to reviewing the phases involved in
  conducting an action research study. Each of the five phases is described and
  summarized by posing to the reader a series of questions whose answers are central
  to completing that particular phase.

SUMMARY

★ The cyclical and iterative action research process comprises four stages: planning, acting, developing, and reflecting.

★ The *planning stage* consists of the following four steps:

- Identifying and limiting the topic

- Gathering information

- Reviewing the related literature

- Developing a research plan

★ The *acting stage* consists of the following two steps:

- Implementing the plan and collecting data

- Analyzing the data

★ The *developing stage* consists of the following step:

- Developing an action plan

★ The *reflecting stage* consists of the following steps:

- Sharing and communicating the results

- Reflecting on the process

QUESTIONS AND ACTIVITIES

1. Which of the nine steps in the action research process do you believe would be most difficult to carry out? Explain your answer.

2. Considering the process of action research as presented in the chapter, do you think it would be more feasible to conduct action research individually or in small groups? Develop a list of advantages and a list of disadvantages for doing it either way.

3. Discuss what you see as possible benefits of communicating the results of action research studies with various educational audiences.

4. Suppose that students in your school are not achieving at the desired level in the area of mathematics. Using the four-stage procedure for action research as presented in this chapter, briefly describe how you might *systematically* examine this problem.

5. Using the same scenario presented in Number 4 above, outline a specific action research study you might conduct conforming to the nine-step process as presented in the chapter.

STUDENT STUDY SITE

Visit the Student Study Site at **www.sagepub.com/mertler3study** for these additional learning tools:

- Video clips
- Web resources
- Self quizzes
- E-flashcards

- PowerPoint slides
- Sample action research reports
- Full-text SAGE journal articles
- Chapter summaries

"How Do I Begin My Action Research Study?"

Part II of this book introduces the initial steps in the action research process. In Chapter 3, you will learn about the process of identifying and narrowing your research topic, as well as the importance of gathering preliminary information related to your topic and conducting a review of the related literature. In Chapter 4, you will learn about research questions and hypotheses, basic qualitative and quantitative research designs, and ethical considerations for your action research. Finally, some practical planning guidelines are provided.

CHAPTER 3

Planning for Action Research

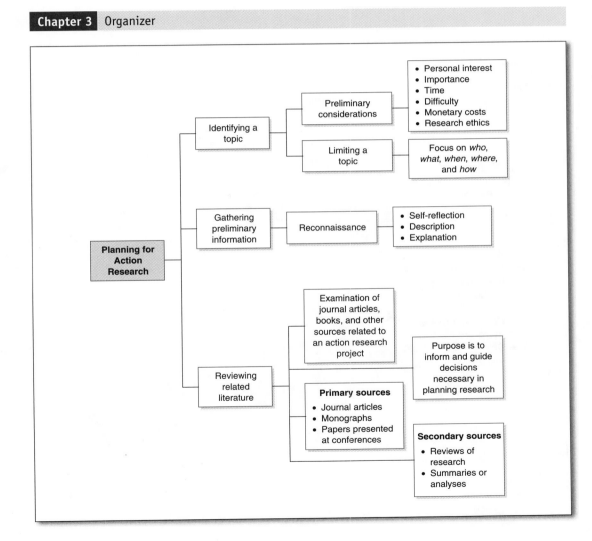

The first crucial steps in any research study are to clearly identify the topic under investigation and to examine the existing research, and any other related information, associated with the topic. In this chapter, we will explore various aspects of identifying a topic for research, including the whys and hows of gathering preliminary information and ways to narrow the focus of a topic. In addition, we will look at activities associated with reviewing related literature. These activities include identifying appropriate sources to consult for related literature, finding ways to search those sources, and writing a literature review. The steps of topic selection and reviewing related literature comprise two of the three initial steps when planning for action research.

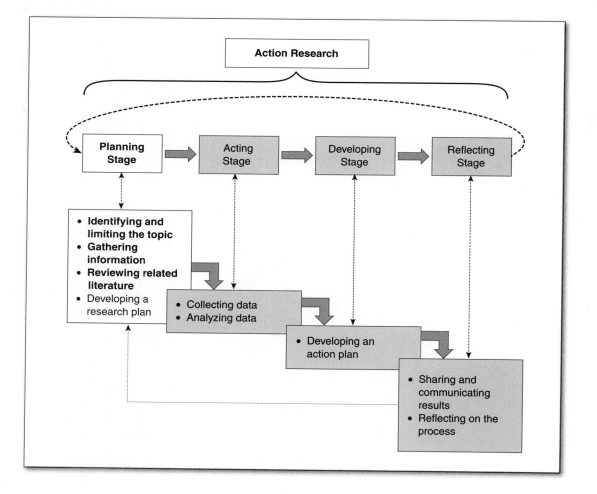

Identifying a Topic for Research

Identifying the topic to be investigated in an action research study is obviously the first step in the process of conducting the actual study. It is, however, also one of the most important steps in the process. Nothing shapes the remainder of a research study as much as the research topic or problem and the research questions that follow (Hubbard & Power, 2003). If the research topic is too broad or too vague, the researcher may become overwhelmed with too many possible variations in the data collection, too much data, and too little time. If the topic is too narrow, it may not be possible to collect appropriate data in order to be able to answer the question at hand. The matter of limiting the focus of a research topic will be discussed in more detail later in this chapter.

The research topic should address a realistic classroom problem, such as an academic problem or an issue of classroom management (Rousseau & Tam, 1996). Johnson (2008) provides an overview of three main topic areas within which many action research studies fall. These three possibilities are as follows:

1. *Trying a new teaching method.* Teachers often consider trying a new teaching method or technique; action research allows for the systematic investigation of the effectiveness of new teaching methods.

2. *Identifying a problem.* Frequently teachers will notice when there is a problem or when things are not going as well as they should, whether the problem occurs in an individual classroom or schoolwide; an organized and logical examination can help educators better understand the problem and its possible causes and can help them explore various solutions.

3. *Examining an area of interest.* Teachers are professionals, and, as such, their curiosity about particular topics in education is often aroused; action research can be used quite effectively to study such topics in an exploratory fashion.

Mertler and Charles (2011) have expanded this list by providing several categories of topics that could conceivably be considered for action research studies. They list the following categories, with only a few sample topics included here:

- Classroom environment—Topics in this category include the various aspects of the physical and psychosocial environments in classrooms and school buildings and their impact on student learning.

- Instructional materials—Topics might include the appropriateness of textbooks and other printed materials with respect to gender and ethnicity, the extent to which teachers find the materials useful and to which they support the curriculum, or the perceptions that students have of those materials.

- Classroom management—Possible research topics might include the level of satisfaction that both teachers and students have with the methods of managing student behavior, the degree to which the methods of managing behavior allow students to learn without unnecessary distraction, or how limiting those methods are with respect to the ability of teachers to teach as they would like.

- Instructional methods—Topics might include the effect of a given teaching method on student learning, the impact that different teacher personality styles can have on student learning or motivation to learn, or methods of providing effective feedback to students on their academic performance.

- The relation of human growth patterns to education—Possible topics might include ways to incorporate individual students' interests and learning preferences, teaching strategies that support self-regulated learning, or those that support individual rates of learning.

- Grading and evaluation—Teachers often have questions about the effects that grades and other forms of evaluative decisions have on student motivation, stress, achievement, and attitudes or on effective methods of incorporating authentic assessment and other nontraditional means of assessing students.

- Conferencing—Possible topics might involve (a) the ways in which parents and teachers value individual conferences or (b) strategies for improving the effectiveness of parent-teacher conferences.

Video Clip 3.1
View a clip of
Dr. Mertler
discussing how
to identify a
topic for study.

This list of categories represents merely a sampling of possible topic areas for action research investigations. There is a multitude of additional research topics that do not necessarily fall into these categories—curriculum, special education, counseling, psychological services, athletics, the arts, exceptionality services, student organizations, and gifted education. Bear in mind that in the broad field of education, you will not find a shortage of possible research topics for your action research projects.

Preliminary Considerations

Once you have decided on a general topic area that you are interested in examining further, it is a good idea to evaluate it against several important and practical considerations (Mertler & Charles, 2011). Schwalbach (2003) believes that such considerations as these help establish the parameters of your research project. First, you should have a *personal interest* in your potential topic. The level of personal interest should probably stem from the fact that the topic is associated with positive experiences or is associated with some unpleasant concern. In either case, the topic continues to suggest itself to you. If this is the case, the particular topic is likely one you should consider. In addition, you will be spending some amount of time investigating this topic—it might be as brief as a couple of months or it might last an entire school year. It is important to identify a topic with which you will enjoy working. Imagine spending an entire year engaged in an in-depth study of a topic that you really do not like.

Second, the topic you identify should be *important*; the results of your action research study should make some sort of difference—or should at least have the *potential* to make some sort of difference—in some aspect of education. If you believe that investigation of the topic will not result in such a difference, it should probably not be pursued. You may wish to discuss the potential benefit of your study with colleagues and administrators.

Third, it is important at this point in the process to reflect on (notice that we are already beginning to engage in the reflective process) and anticipate the *amount of time* that the study will require. You must compare the time requirements of the study to that which you have available. The last thing you want to happen is that your action research project begins to take time away from your regular teaching duties. All things being equal, it may be better to select a topic for investigation such that the study can be completed in a relatively short period.

Fourth, it is also critical to reflect on the anticipated *difficulty* of investigating the proposed topic. For a variety of reasons—many of them methodological in nature, as you will see in the next chapter—interesting topics are often difficult or simply impossible to research. To reiterate, the research topic must be practical. It is also important to design a research study within your personal research skill level. It is not wise to propose to undertake a study that will involve research skills beyond your individual capabilities. If you had absolutely no experience in conducting interviews, you probably would not want to select a topic that required that interviews be conducted and their transcriptions analyzed.

Fifth, consideration should also be given to the potential *monetary costs* associated with investigating the topic. If you select and develop a topic that will require you to spend money on supplies, materials, travel, and so on, you will likely want to find a different topic or, at a minimum, alter your ideas for the original topic. There are many good topics that will not involve monetary costs.

Finally, action researchers need to be cognizant of *research ethics*. Generally speaking, it is unethical and sometimes illegal to conduct research that exposes participants (i.e., students, teachers) to harm of any kind, including physical, emotional, and psychological harm. Any of these is considered mistreatment of human beings and is unacceptable in the field of educational research.

Limiting a Topic

Once a topic has been selected and evaluated against the considerations above, it usually must be refined or limited before it can be effectively researched. This is due to the fact that most topics are either: too broad, too vague, or too complex (Mertler & Charles, 2011). The process of evaluating your topic against the preliminary considerations as presented above will establish your research parameters and will typically help focus the size of your topic. Focusing the size of your topic usually requires that the topic be narrowed in scope. If you do not have a specific and clear focus to your action research study, the project can wander aimlessly, and you may waste valuable time (Schwalbach, 2003). In addition, the topic may need to be clarified—that is, reworded so that it is clear and unambiguous. Schwalbach (2003) suggests that when trying to narrow the topic, you should be mindful to choose a focus that will ultimately help your students learn. Provided in Table 3.1 are several examples of broad research topics and their revised, more focused counterparts.

Table 3.1   Examples of Broad and Narrow Topics for Action Research

Broad Topic		Narrowed Version of Topic
What teachers' lives are like outside of school	→	Leisure activities of elementary teachers and the amount of time spent on them
Factors that affect learning among culturally diverse students	→	Hispanic students' perceptions of factors that make academic success more difficult
Use of computers in the classroom program in helping students revise drafts of written stories	→	Effectiveness of a word processing program in helping students revise drafts of written stories
Importance of reading practice in developing reading skills	→	Effect of reading practice with fifth-grade "buddies" on the developing reading skills of first-grade students
Virtual dissection versus real dissection of lab specimens	→	Tenth-grade biology students' perceptions of virtual and real animal dissections

Once the topic is adequately narrowed and clarified, the process of specifically focusing it is continued by stating specific research questions or hypotheses directly related to the topic. Research questions and hypotheses will be discussed in more detail in the next chapter.

Gathering Preliminary Information

As mentioned in Chapter 2, after identifying and narrowing the scope of a research topic, the next step is to gather preliminary information. As a starting point, I often suggest simply talking with other teachers, administrators, or counselors in your school or district. The purpose of engaging them in this activity is to gauge their perceptions of your proposed research topic. Undoubtedly, they may have experiences that differ from yours, and that may give you further insight into your ideas for action research. They may also provide you with additional matters of importance about your topic—and perhaps its feasibility as a *researchable* topic—that you had not previously considered. You may want to ask them for ideas or for feedback on your ideas. During this step, you will also want to read quickly through recent editions of teacher's manuals or other types of curricular guides, teacher magazines or newsletters from professional educator organizations, and various other resource guides, all for suggestions that may inform your topic. Finally, do not forget that you have a wonderful and easily accessible resource in the Internet (please see the Related websites section later in this chapter).

While considering that the ideas and suggestions of others is important, it is critical to examine your *own* beliefs, knowledge, and context in which you are considering your potential action research topic. This process, which Mills (2011) calls *reconnaissance*, involves taking time to reflect on your own beliefs and to gain a better understanding of the nature and context of your research problem. The act of engaging in reconnaissance takes three forms: self-reflection, description, and explanation. When you try to gain insight into your area of action research, Mills (2011) suggests that you begin by reflecting on your own understanding of the following:

- The educational theories that impact your instructional practice

- The values that you hold about education

- Ways in which your work in schools, in general, contributes to the larger context of schooling

- The historical context of your school and teaching in that school and how they came to be that way

- The historical contexts about how and why you hold the beliefs that you do about teaching and learning

These activities do not produce the changes you might be seeking. However, they provide the necessary groundwork upon which to build your ideas about how to solve a problem or answer an educational question through action research.

The next step in doing reconnaissance is to describe as completely as possible the situation or problem that you want to change or improve. In order to accomplish this, you must focus your descriptive activities on the *who, what, where, when,* and *how* of your problem. Through careful description of these aspects, you ultimately clarify for yourself the true area of focus for your action research. Otherwise, there is sometimes a tendency to focus on too many things at once, making the action research endeavor appear too "chaotic" and disorganized. For example, you may want to collect information that would allow you to describe the following:

- What evidence exists that what you perceive as a problem really is a problem?

- Who are the students that (i.e., which groups) are affected by the problem?

- How is this material, concept, or skill currently taught?

- How often is the material, concept, or skill taught and/or reinforced?

- How is student mastery of the material, concept, or skill currently assessed?

- Where is the material taught in the scope and sequence of the course content?

- When during the school year is the material taught?

A final step in doing reconnaissance is to take this description of the current problem that you have developed and then try to explain *why* the problem occurs. In light of the description of your problem that you have developed above, are you able to offer possible explanations for the reasons behind the occurrence of the problem? Based on these possible explanations for the problem, a hypothesis to guide your action research study is typically developed at this point. Recall that a *hypothesis* is a tentative but informed guess about the findings of a study, made before the study begins. You are now at a point in the action research process where you can make an informed prediction. It is being informed by self-reflection about your beliefs about and the historical context of teaching and learning in your school. Furthermore, it is being guided by your close and careful scrutiny of the current state of affairs with respect to the condition you want to change or improve.

Reviewing the Related Literature

The next major step in the action research process that serves many purposes is reviewing the related literature. A **literature review** is "an examination of journal articles, ERIC documents, books, and other sources related to your action research project" (Johnson, 2008, p. 75). By reviewing related literature, you can identify a topic, narrow its focus, and gather information for developing a research design, as well as the overall project (Rousseau & Tam, 1996). You may also find examples of classroom applications, research questions, hypotheses, methods of data collection, and data analysis techniques (Johnson, 2008). A review of literature can reveal a study that could be systematically replicated in your classroom or provide you with potential solutions to the research problem you have identified.

The literature review can also help establish a connection between your action research project and what others have said, done, and discovered before you (Johnson, 2008). There is no reason to reinvent the wheel when it may not be necessary. A literature review allows you to use the insights and discoveries of others whose research came before yours in order to make your research more efficient and effective. In a manner of speaking, conducting a review of related literature can actually save you time in the development of your action research project (Mills, 2011). Instead of becoming bewildered in the research process because you are not sure of what to ask and how to pursue finding an answer, reflecting on your problem or situation through someone else's perspective can prove very informative. Finally, conducting a literature review can enable you to become more of an expert in the area you are proposing to study, not to mention a more knowledgeable professional educator. Not only does a literature review guide you in many phases of your action research project, but it also will likely enhance your ability to teach (Johnson, 2008). Figure 3.1 depicts the ways in which a review of related literature can inform various aspects of an action research study.

Before you actually begin searching for literature related to your topic, you should be aware of several things. First, there is an extremely wide range in the quality of books, articles, and conference papers that you will come across. Just because something has been published does not necessarily mean that it is of high quality. When you find an article, for example, it is important to consider whether it is simply someone's opinion or whether it has been well researched (Schwalbach, 2003). Well-researched articles and other types of manuscripts are based on the collection of original data; these types of studies are referred to as **empirical research**. Empirical studies are not inherently better, but they are based on data other than solely the author's individual opinions and perceptions.

A second key aspect of the research you locate is its objectivity. You will undoubtedly enter into your action research with some sort of expectation as to what you will discover at its end. Often, teacher-researchers will examine the related literature only for works that support what they anticipate finding. If you are to do a thorough job of gathering all—or, at least, a representative cross section—of the literature related to your topic, you should look for books, articles, and other published literature that both support and contradict your views (Schwalbach, 2003). For example, if you are proposing to study the effectiveness of whole-language instruction, you should also examine the literature related to the effectiveness of phonics instruction. Because things change in the field of education, there is often a historical context embedded within any body of literature. It is important to examine the entire body of literature in order to better understand how and why those things changed.

Third, be aware of the timeliness of the literature you find. Although it is important to examine the body of literature in its entirety, it is most applicable to your study to focus your review on the thinking and empirical research that is most current in that particular discipline (Schwalbach, 2003). If you did not consider the historical context and the fact that things change, and if you only examined literature from 20 years ago, you would very likely be missing out on newer, innovative, and more-timely research findings. Although it will vary from topic to topic, my recommendation is to initially look at literature produced or published within the last 5 years. Of course, there will be situations where you may need to look to older publications or other sources of related information. For example, if your topic is one that received much attention a decade or two ago and then experienced a lack of research attention but has now resurfaced as an area of interest in the field, it would likely be wise to examine those older sources of information.

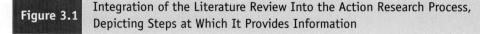

Figure 3.1 Integration of the Literature Review Into the Action Research Process, Depicting Steps at Which It Provides Information

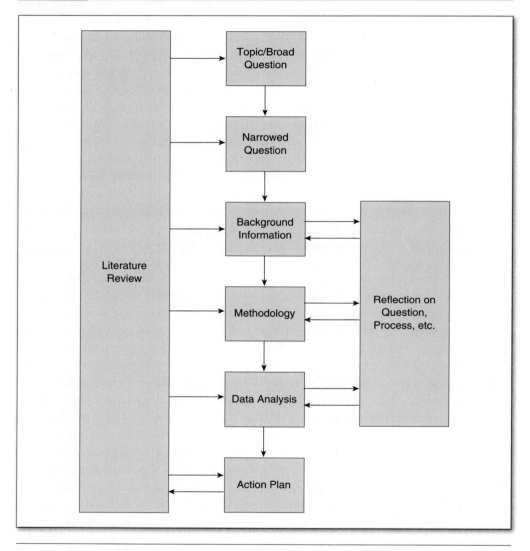

Source: Adapted from Schwalbach, 2003.

Finally, there are two questions related to literature reviews that I am probably asked most by my students: (1) How many references do I need? (2) How much review of related literature is enough? My typical response is something to the effect of, "Well, I don't really know the body of literature that you're reviewing, so I have no way of knowing." Although they generally do not care for that response, it is usually accurate. Having said that, it is important to recognize that it is often very easy to get bogged down in reviewing literature related to your topic, especially if you are examining a topic that already has a large research base. My recommendation is that you know you have done a reasonably good job of reviewing literature on a given topic when you begin to see the same articles and the same authors being cited in those articles. When you begin to recognize the big names in the field, you can be more confident that you most likely have not missed any substantial information (Schwalbach, 2003). The bottom line is that you must be comfortable with the level of review you have done. Johnson (2008) offers a good rule of thumb with some specific numbers of sources. Master's theses typically call for 25 or more sources, whereas doctoral dissertations require 50 or more. Action research projects designed to be published in journals, presented at conferences, or shared with peers might use anywhere from 2 to 15 sources. Schwalbach (2003) suggests some important questions whose answers may help you better make this determination: Do you understand the current trends in the field? Do you understand the historical context of your topic? Have you uncovered research that examines both—or *all*—sides of the issue? Do you believe that you have enough information to design a good action research project? If you answer yes to these questions, you can probably stop reviewing literature related to your topic.

Sources for Related Literature

Sources for related literature can be broken down into two types: primary sources and secondary sources. **Primary sources** are firsthand accounts of original research. Common primary sources include journal articles, monographs, and papers presented at professional research conferences (Mertler & Charles, 2011). In contrast, **secondary sources** of information are not firsthand accounts; they do not consist of original research. Rather, they are summaries, compilations, analyses, or interpretations of primary information (i.e., original research) made by other individuals. They include such publications as encyclopedias of research, handbooks of research, reviews of research, scholarly books (e.g., a textbook), and perhaps magazine and newspaper articles. As a general rule, it is best to examine secondary sources first, in order to gain some perspective on the body of literature you will be examining in terms of trends and general conclusions (Mertler & Charles, 2011). However, your literature review should focus predominantly on primary sources of information.

Secondary sources are typically found in the reference section or other specific sections of the library and can be located by searching the library's main catalog (Mertler & Charles, 2011). In the past, these catalogs consisted of small index cards located in numerous drawers (hence the name "card catalogs"). However, most libraries now have all of their holdings cataloged electronically and provide computers for you to be able to conduct an efficient search for these various secondary sources. Reference books, such as the *Encyclopedia of Educational Research, Review of Educational Research,* the National Society for the Study of

Education yearbooks, and various handbooks of research, can usually be found in the library's main reference section. Newspaper stories can be located and reviewed through the library's computer system via *Newspaper Abstracts*. The original newspaper articles can then be read in their entirety on microfiche or microfilm. Similarly, magazine articles can be located and reviewed through the use of *Periodical Abstracts*.

Primary sources are most often found by searching specialized indexes or databases (Mertler & Charles, 2011). Most of what you will identify by searching these databases are original research articles, either published in academic journals or presented at professional research conferences. There are literally hundreds of different academic journals published in the field of education. The purpose of academic journals is to inform the field of education or a more specific discipline within the educational field (Johnson, 2008). Most journal articles are written by researchers or other academicians (usually college and university professors). Manuscripts are submitted to the editor of the journal and then sent out for peer review, which means that they are reviewed usually by three to six experts in the field in order to check for quality, accuracy, validity, and overall contribution to the field. Each reviewer provides evaluative comments and makes a recommendation for publication. If the article is accepted for publication, there are typically a couple of rounds of revisions that must be made prior to its appearance in the journal. Some journals have acceptance rates of 50%, whereas others may have acceptance rates as low as 5%.

Although there are numerous electronic databases in operation, the ERIC database is arguably the most popular among education researchers. ERIC, or the **Educational Resources Information Center**, was established in 1966 by the U.S. Department of Education. It is the largest database for locating research in education. However, it is important to be cautious of what you may find. ERIC has historically been a clearinghouse, meaning that the manuscripts submitted are not peer reviewed in the same manner as they are for academic journals; therefore, the quality varies quite a bit (Schwalbach, 2003). On the other hand, ERIC has recently undergone a substantial revamping. The new ERIC digital library opened to the public on September 1, 2004. Now, two advisory panels provide research, technical, and content expertise (Institute of Education Sciences, n.d.a). One of these panels, the advisory panel of content experts, provides recommendations for selecting journals and nonjournal materials for inclusion in the ERIC database (Institute of Education Sciences, n.d.b). Members of the panel of content experts provide expertise in the following areas:

- Adult, career, and vocational education

- Assessment and evaluation

- Community colleges

- Counseling and student services

- Disabilities and gifted education

- Education management

- Elementary and early childhood education

- Higher education

- Information and technology

- Languages and linguistics

- Reading, English, and communication

- Rural education and small schools

- Science, mathematics, and environmental education

- Social studies/social science education

- Teaching and teacher education

- Urban education

The ERIC online system provides the educational community with the capability to search the ERIC bibliographic database of more than 1.3 million citations dating back to 1966. More than 107,000 full-text nonjournal documents, previously available through fee-based services only, are now available free of charge (Institute of Education Sciences, n.d.a). The ERIC database can be searched from its main page, affiliated with the U.S. Department of Education (http://www.eric.ed.gov). The process of searching the ERIC database will be discussed in the next section.

Many, but not all, other databases require the public to pay some sort of subscription or user fee. Searching ERIC is a free service; all you need is access to the Internet. However, it is important that you not limit yourself only to one database or only to full-text articles that are available online. Granted, this is an easier way to gain access to related literature; however, you limit your review of the *entire* body of literature if you use only certain databases or succumb to the lure of not having to leave your computer in order to print copies of articles. All it takes is a little time—and some loose change—to go to your college or university library and make photocopies of articles you locate.

Of course, there exist numerous other searchable, free-of-charge Internet databases. **Google Scholar** is one example. According to the website (http://scholar.google.com/intl/en/scholar/about.html):

Google Scholar provides a simple way to broadly search for scholarly literature. From one place, you can search across many disciplines and sources: articles, theses, books, abstracts and court opinions, from academic publishers, professional societies, online repositories, universities and other web sites. Google Scholar helps you find relevant work across the world of scholarly research. (para. 1)

When you search for a topic in Google Scholar, the database returns to you a list of relevant articles, but also ranks the documents in terms of the full text of each document, where it was published, who wrote it, and how often and how recently it has been cited in other scholarly literature.

ProQuest (http://www.proquest.com/en-US/aboutus/default.shtml *or* http://proquest.umi .com/login) is another searchable database containing not only published articles and conference papers, but also dissertations and theses. ProQuest calls itself "an information partner, creating indispensable research solutions that connect people and information." Many of the articles housed within the database are accessible in full-text format. Although dissertations and theses are not available in full text but only for purchase through the site, you can preview selected pages from them.

Finally, the Internet can be a valuable source for related information, as well as for exploring ideas for research topics. There is a wide variety of search engines available on the web. **Search engines** organize websites by *keywords*. When you search for a specific keyword or words, the results yield a list of related websites and usually an attempt to rank them in terms of relevance to the topic (Mertler & Charles, 2011). Many professional associations also maintain websites and include links to related web pages. These sites are often very useful in identifying or narrowing a topic, as well as for locating related literature and other information. The premier professional association in education is the American Educational Research Association (AERA). AERA (http://www.aera.net) is divided into 12 divisions, based on broad disciplines. In addition, there are numerous special interest groups (SIGs). More information related to search engines and professional associations is provided in the Related Web Sites section later in this chapter.

Searching the ERIC Database Online

ERIC is composed of two indexes, both of which are searchable online. The *Current Index to Journals in Education (CIJE)* cites and presents abstracts of journal articles published in education and closely related fields. *Resources in Education (RIE)* on the other hand cites and abstracts documents that have not appeared in education journals. These include such documents as papers read at conferences, technical reports, reports of evaluations of federally funded programs, and any other original research that has not been published elsewhere (Mertler & Charles, 2011). The main page for this site is shown in Figure 3.2. Under the section titled Search ERIC, users should click on Advanced Search in order to arrive at the ERIC search page, as shown in Figure 3.3.

Notice that, initially, one can search for up to three terms in ERIC. Furthermore, notice that the search can be conducted based on one of several criteria (located in the drop-down menus, or *selection buttons),* including searching by keyword, title, and author. Most searches are conducted by keyword, at least during the initial stages. Let us consider a concrete

| Figure 3.2 | The Main Page for ERIC (http://www.eric.ed.gov) |

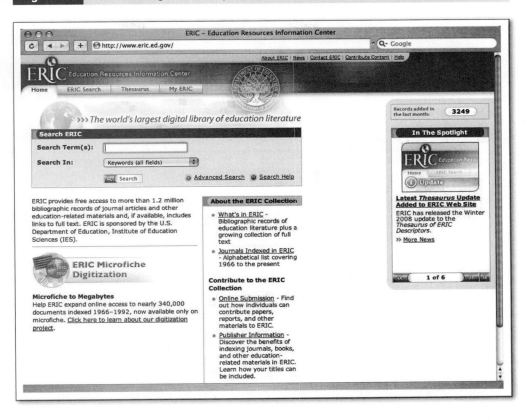

example: Suppose we wanted to locate published research on the topic of teachers' classroom assessment practices. We might search under the terms *educational assessment* and *classroom techniques* (see Figure 3.3). Notice that located beneath the "Search for" button is another set of selection buttons containing Boolean operators. **Boolean operators** are keywords that enable the retrieval of terms in specific combinations. The most common operators are "and" and "or"—if "and" is used, only those documents that contain *both* keywords as descriptors will be retrieved (i.e., a narrower search); if "or" is used, *every* document with *either* of these two keywords as descriptors will be retrieved (i.e., a broader search). We will use "and" for our example—therefore, we are searching for documents that contain both "educational assessment" *and* "classroom techniques." We then click on Submit to begin our search of the database. The results of our search are shown in Figure 3.4.

First, you will notice that ERIC retrieved 2,560 documents containing these two descriptive keywords, entirely too many to search through. By clicking on "Search Within Results," you can reduce the number of citations returned by adding more descriptors or by focusing the years of publication. For the purposes of this search, I narrowed the focus to those

Figure 3.3	The Advanced Search Page for ERIC

documents authored by myself (by entering "mertler" into the keyword box), thus reducing the number of citations returned to five documents. The documents are initially screened by the user for relevance by examining the titles. If you are interested in exploring a given document more closely, this can be accomplished by simply clicking on the title of the document. This will take you to a new page that provides the entire citation information for that document. For example, if you scan down the list, you will notice that a document written by me appears on the list. By clicking on the title (in this case, *Teacher-Centered Fallacies of Classroom Assessment Validity and Reliability*), you are provided with the document's citation (see Figure 3.5).

The ERIC Number (ERIC #, as shown in Figure 3.5) serves as the document's identification within ERIC but also informs you as to whether the document was published in an academic journal (EJ) or exists in one of several unpublished forms (ED). Documents listed as EJ will include the citation information for the journal in which the document appears. This

| Figure 3.4 | Sample of ERIC Search Results |

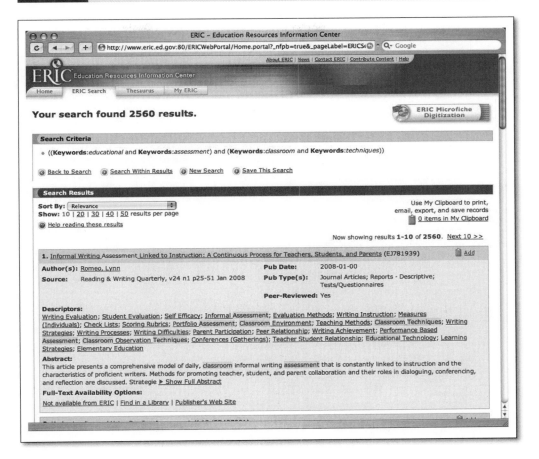

is important information, since you will need it in order to locate the article on the appropriate library shelves.

Documents listed as ED may have originally been written as papers to be presented at academic conferences, position papers, technical reports, research reports, and so on. The Accession Number is again of vital importance here, since all ED documents appear on microfiche and *are cataloged by the six-digit ED number*. This number is the *only* means of locating the correct microfiche in your library's microfiche stacks.

Also of great importance to the researcher is the **abstract**. This is a brief summary of the contents of the document, including the results and conclusions of the study, if appropriate. Only by reading the document abstract can you really be sure if you want to obtain the full document for complete review. It is always best to study the abstract prior to investing the time required to locate the complete article. Finally, all keywords under which this particular document is catalogued within ERIC are provided in the section labeled "Descriptors."

Figure 3.5	Document Citation From ERIC

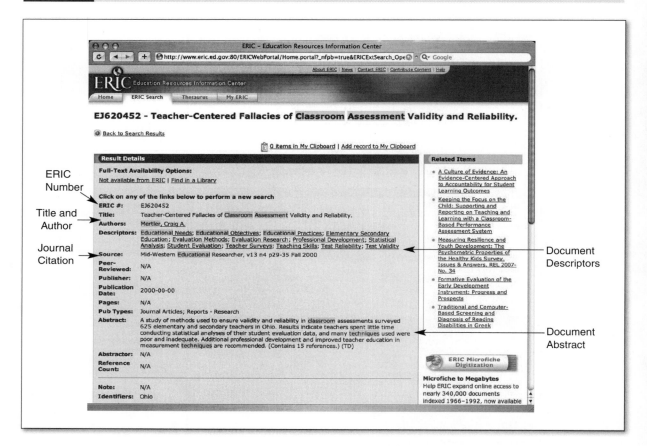

Because of the flexibility of the searchable ERIC database, it takes some practice and experience in order to be able to work with it effectively. The idea of combining keywords in a single search—or even combining keywords with authors' names, and so on—can be a little intimidating to the beginning researcher. However, novice researchers should not hesitate to experiment with searches of ERIC. Online access to the ERIC database is certainly a valuable research tool of which all researchers—at any level of experience—should take advantage.

Writing a Literature Review

Writing a review of related literature is, in my opinion, one of the more difficult aspects of writing up any type of research. What makes it so difficult is that every study is different, and every body of literature is different. Therefore, there is no easy, prescriptive, step-by-step process for writing such a review. One of the best ways to learn how to write a literature review is to examine how others have accomplished the task. With that in mind, I will offer several suggestions that will hopefully help you organize your review and get it down on paper.

It is initially important to keep in mind the purpose to be served by a written review of related literature. Its purpose is to convey to all individuals interested in the particular topic of the action research project the following:

- the historical context of the topic,

- the trends experienced by the topic, and

- how theory has informed practice and vice versa.

For each study that you review, encapsulate it into a brief summary that reflects any aspect of the study that has relevance to your topic (Mills, 2011). This may include the variables studied, the methodology employed, the participants studied, and the conclusions obtained. However, the literature review should emphasize the *findings* of previous research (Pyrczak & Bruce, 2003)—that is, what will influence your study most.

Once you have done this, develop an outline for the review, beginning with an introduction that communicates the organization—often using subheadings—of your review (Pyrczak & Bruce, 2003). Again, your organization and subheadings should focus on the aspects of the body of literature that are relevant to your topic and study. As you begin to use this organizational outline to write the actual review, it is important to keep in mind that it should not be written in the form of an annotated list (i.e., one study summarized in a paragraph, followed by another summarized in the next paragraph) but rather as a cohesive essay that flows smoothly for the reader (Pyrczak & Bruce, 2003). This creates a better view of the trends that your topic has seen over time. All literature related to a given subtopic is cited during the discussion of that topic.

Another key organizational aspect of writing a literature review is how the topics are to be ordered. Essentially, a well-written literature review will begin with the subtopics that are *least* related to your specific proposed study. As you proceed through the development of your literature review, the subtopics begin to focus more and more. In other words, they become *more* closely related to your topic. This "design" somewhat parallels a funneling effect (see Figure 3.6). As you write—and someone reads through—your literature review, the scope of the research being summarized is continually narrowed; in other words, you are "funneling the reader's attention" in the direction of your specific topic. The logic behind this practice is that the final subtopics presented in your literature review will be those most closely related to your study (which you will present next as your study's methodology). For example, a recent study of mine focused on the perceptions held by teachers of the influence that No Child Left Behind (NCLB) has had on their classroom assessment practices. The

Video Clips 3.2 & 3.3 View clips of educator-researchers discussing how to identify a topic and writing a literature review.

subheadings (beginning with the more broad literature and progressing to the more focused) of my literature review were as follows:

- *The Impact of "No Child Left Behind"*

- *Teachers' Perceptions of "No Child Left Behind"*

- *"No Child Left Behind" and Classroom Assessment*

I think you can see how the literature review moves from research that is broadly related (i.e., NCLB, in general) to the research that most closely aligns with what I specifically studied (i.e., the connection of NCLB to actual classroom practice).

A concluding, summary paragraph is extremely useful because it provides a starting point for your study, based on what previous research has found (Mills, 2011). It also provides support for your study by placing it into a relevant context and demonstrating how your study will potentially contribute to that particular body of literature. Finally, it provides a brief overview of the existing research for the benefit of those individuals who have not had the opportunity to review it as thoroughly as you have. More in-depth information related to the act of writing up action research is presented in Chapter 9.

Figure 3.6   Depiction of the Narrowing Focus (Funneling Effect) of a Literature Review

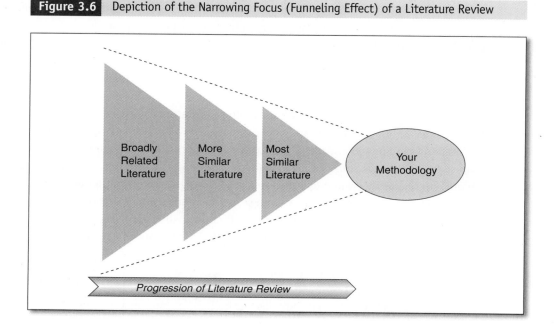

WRITING UP ACTION RESEARCH:
TOPICS AND LITERATURE REVIEWS

In the Writing Up Action Research sections, which begin in this chapter (below) and continue throughout the remainder of the book, excerpts from actual published—or otherwise disseminated—action research studies are presented. These passages demonstrate how to write up the specific section of a research report addressed in the particular chapter. This section in the current chapter includes excerpts from two published articles, illustrating the introduction of the research topic and review of related literature:

Prominent organizations such as the National Council of Teachers of Mathematics (NCTM) and the National Research Council (NRC) have identified aspects of mathematics classroom instruction that must be changed to improve mathematics instruction and increase student achievement (NCTM, 1989, 1991, 2000; NRC, 1989). One is the need to make stronger connections between mathematics and students' lives outside of the mathematics classroom.

Another is a shift from lecture and transmission model, where students are expected to memorize procedure and facts, to a participation model, where students are to actively participate in constructing their own knowledge. According to McNair (2000), both of these reform efforts are supposed to change students' role in the classroom from that of a knowledge consumer to a knowledge producer.

Proponents of mathematics reform have argued that traditional mathematics instruction, the predominant form of instruction in our nation's schools, has been unsuccessful in promoting conceptual understanding and application of mathematics to real-life contexts. Battista (1999) asserts that, "For most students, school mathematics is an endless sequence of memorizing and forgetting facts and procedures that make little sense to them" (p. 426). A major thrust of the current reform movement is to get students actively involved in their study of mathematics and to encourage them to see the big picture (Ross, 1996). Data suggests that most classroom instruction is geared toward the development of rote procedural skills. Existing teaching methods do not develop the high levels of conceptual understanding or the reasoning, problem solving, and communication skills that students will need to be competitive (Silver & Stein, 1996).

From the eighth-grade teacher's perspective, the transmission method of mathematics is a simpler way of teaching, predetermined and more clearly defined. In contrast, a participation-based method is more complex, demanding that he motivate students to participate in developing math concepts; this, he cautions, is not a straightforward matter. He believes successfully motivating all students to participate may depend on the connections made between mathematics and students' experiences outside the classroom, but these connections are highly individualized, mediated by social and cultural elements of the students' environment (Lakoff & Nunez, 1997; Lave, 1988). A "daunting task" faces him in trying to reach every student, especially since there is a wide range of abilities in his classroom. He is concerned that using a reform mathematics curriculum may detract from the quality of his teaching, thus affecting student report card grades; he is troubled that parents and administrators view report card grades as a yardstick to measure the effectiveness of the curriculum and seeks a more objective criterion for making an important curriculum decision in his school district.

(Continued)

(Continued)

There is resistance towards mathematic reform from teachers, parents, administration, and school boards. What are their concerns? One, according to Ross (1996), is that the laudable focus on understanding seems to have led to some decline in mathematical skills. Since it is easier to measure and spot deficiencies in skills than it is to spot deficiencies in understanding, this decline can easily be overemphasized. However, this problem is serious, especially since our future scientists, engineers, and mathematicians must obtain both substantial understanding and fluency in their skills. This study attempts to shed light on the question of how traditional and reform mathematics curricula affect eighth-grade mathematics students' overall mathematics achievement, problem-solving ability, and skill proficiency.

Source: Alsup & Sprigler, 2003.

The purpose of this research was to assess the effectiveness of cloze procedure as an instructional tool in a middle school classroom. The question that the research revolved around was, "Does the use of cloze procedure increase student learning as measured by performance on multiple-choice tests?" For several years I have used a form of cloze procedure as an instructional technique in my seventh grade classroom. Although cloze procedure was originally developed as a way to measure the readability of written material, it has come to be used for a wide range of teaching purposes (Jongsma, 1980). I do not believe a textbook should form the core of classroom curriculum or dictate instructional methods. Yet, textbooks remain an important resource that can contribute to high levels of student learning. Improving the ability to read subject content has been shown to be an effective way of improving student comprehension (Jongsma, 1980).

Cloze procedure, which arose primarily in the field of reading, grew out of the cognitive school of psychology. Cognitive psychology, like earlier Piagetian theory, views learning as an active process that combines the acquisition of new information with prior knowledge and structures. Human behavior is not controlled by stimuli only, but also by how people interpret and react when in contact with the environment. A primary ambition of cloze procedure is to encourage the learner to link new with previously learned material and to initiate questions to be asked. Besides helping the learner to link new information with prior knowledge, cloze sheets also actively involve the learner in thinking about what they are reading. In general, cloze sheets provide opportunities for recall and contribute to better conceptual organization of information (Santa, 1988).

For the purpose of this study, standard cloze procedure will be defined as the random deletion of every nth word in a body of text. A modified method is to purposely delete specific words of text that include key concepts and words. Typically, I construct five or six cloze sheets for a chapter of written material (the number of cloze sheets varies depending upon the length or difficulty of the chapter), selecting lines of text that I think best summarize and highlight key concepts and terms. These teacher-made cloze sheets are completed by students as they read assigned portions of their textbooks. The cloze sheets are then checked, graded, and returned to the students. I have found the quickest and most efficient way for me to grade the sheets is on a "did it" and "did not do it" basis.

I have found two major advantages to using cloze sheets in my classroom. First, the use of cloze sheets increases the likelihood that students will complete reading assignments, and second, completed cloze sheets can be used by the students as a study guide. A majority of my students verbally describe cloze sheets as helpful. Such anecdotal evidence from my students indicates that the use of cloze sheets aids in their learning. However, at the time of the study I was unsure whether the perceived gains justified the amount of time required for teacher preparation and student usage.

One of the developments for the use of cloze procedure has been for aiding student comprehension by creating teacher-made worksheets that summarize key portions of text. These worksheets delete relevant words that the student supplies as he/she reads (Santa, 1988). Several studies (Hayes, 1988; Gauthier, 1990; Andrews, 1991) have found cloze procedure effective in helping students make connections with concepts contained in content material. Fuchs (1988) found cloze procedure to be effective with special education students, while McKenna (1990) found cloze procedure to be marginally effective with upper level elementary students.

Andrews (1991) completed a study in a high school science classroom with emphasis on the use of cloze procedure for creating a reading study guide. This study ascertained that only 28 percent of her students reported completing reading assignments prior to the introduction of cloze sheets. She found that "to complete the individualized reading study guide, students were unable to skim text material, but instead had to read the assignment thoroughly" (p. 11). Also reported was a posttest increase of 16 points in mean test scores. However, others (Kintsch & Yarbrough, 1982; van Dijik & Kintsch, 1983) have found the procedure to have little effect on students in grasping the text as a coherent whole.

Source: Weldon, 1995.

Consideration	Your Response
What is your topic?	
What do you want to learn about this topic?	
What are you planning to do in order to address the topic?	
To whom will the outcome of your study be important?	
How much time do you anticipate the study requiring?	
How difficult do you anticipate it will be to conduct the study?	
Will there be any monetary costs?	
Do you foresee any ethical problems?	

Note: Two Action Research Portraits begin in this chapter. These illustrations of action research projects will describe—in continuing fashion through Chapter 8 of the book—two action research studies from beginning to end, highlighting the related aspect that is addressed in that particular chapter.

❦ ACTION RESEARCH PORTRAIT 1 ❦

Enhancing Academic Performance Through Improved Classroom Assessment

Over the past few years, several members of the faculty at Jones Middle School have become increasingly aware of a problem related to their students' academic performance. The teachers who make up Team North—Susan (language arts), Larry (mathematics), Cathy (science), and John (social studies)—have noticed that although their group of students earn good grades in their coursework, they do not seem to perform well on the statewide proficiency tests given each fall and spring. The teachers believe that their classroom assessments appropriately address the content they are teaching, but ironically, the proficiency tests are also designed to measure the same content, since both are based on the state's curriculum guides and standards in each of the four content areas.

In one of their regular team faculty meetings during the spring, they decided to take a methodical look at this problem. Susan began by sharing that she really wanted to find a way to enable their students to perform better on the proficiency test, especially in the spring, since it is near the end of the school year. However, the others quickly replied that they did not want to simply teach to the proficiency test. Susan responded that she was really talking about trying to find some way to improve their performance, some way for them to actually learn better so that they could demonstrate that mastery on the spring proficiency test. All four teachers agreed but were unsure as to how they should go about accomplishing this.

Cathy shared that she had recently read an article in a teaching journal that talked about how enhancing the quality of teacher-made classroom assessments and the quality of assessment feedback provided to students can actually result in improved student performance on standardized achievement tests. A couple of the teachers expressed skepticism about this relationship, stating that the two types of assessment are very different. Susan explained that if assessments—whether standardized or teacher-made—are done well, they not only provide information about how students are performing, but they also help reinforce student learning for the students themselves.

Cathy then reminded the group of a flyer that had just been posted in the teachers' lounge. The flyer advertised a 2-week workshop being conducted at the university that summer. Its basic purpose was to help teachers improve their classroom assessments. Since all four teachers were thinking about taking a course or two that summer, they decided to take the assessment workshop together. Larry also shared that he was currently taking a research methods course and that he had just learned about action research. The group discussed the feasibility of the four of them designing—once they had completed the assessment workshop—an action research project for next year in order to investigate if improving their classroom assessments would also improve students' performance on standardized tests.

Larry explained that there were some things they would need to do that summer. In addition to the workshop, they would need to gather some information related to their research topic. They all agreed that they needed to formalize their topic before moving on. They decided to state the topic as improving student achievement by improving teachers' assessments. They decided to make a plan for finding research that had already been done on their topic. The four teachers then resolved to spend the first part of the summer looking for research and any other information related to their topic. They planned to meet again just prior to the beginning of the workshop in July.

At the meeting in early July, the teachers met to share what they had found. Although there was not a great deal of research related specifically to their topic, what they did find was very informative. They found several opinion pieces from experts in the field of classroom assessment who supported the original article that Cathy had shared earlier in the spring. In addition, they found numerous empirical research studies related to teachers' classroom assessment practices. The majority of these studies concluded that teachers need and desire more training in the area of assessment and that only then will students be able to better achieve their full potential. The teachers agreed that this provided the motivation they needed to attend the workshop and pursue the investigation beginning in the fall.

❧ ACTION RESEARCH PORTRAIT 2 ❧

Improving Reading Comprehension in a Title I Program

Kathleen is a Title I reading specialist in a small, suburban elementary school. She has always striven to improve her reading instruction but has had trouble targeting a specific area for the upcoming year. She talked with several of her fellow teachers, who reminded her that students in their building have always seemed to have trouble with reading comprehension. Kathleen agreed, noting that in the 5 years she has served as a reading specialist, she has noticed that her intermediate-level (i.e., fourth-, fifth-, and sixth-grade) students struggle most with reading comprehension. She has several sources of evidence for this fact. First, she can tell from the daily observations of her students. Kathleen generally has students read short sections of chapter books aloud and then engages them in several related activities, including having them respond to either written or oral comprehension questions or having them complete a book project. The students seldom answer more than one half of the questions correctly. In addition, the book projects require that extended time be spent on rereading. Second, Kathleen administers diagnostic reading tests on several occasions throughout the school year.

(Continued)

(Continued)

Her students consistently experience their lowest performance on the reading comprehension section. Finally, these diagnostic test results have also been supported by the results of the standardized test administered each spring. Although the reading comprehension section is not lengthy, her students continue to perform low.

Kathleen would like to try something new this year with her students in order to improve their reading comprehension skills. Currently, she relies on both oral and written comprehension questions—asked of students on an individual basis—following a reading assignment, as well as small-group discussions and book projects that focus on comprehension skills. One day, during her planning time, she conducted a brief search of ERIC in the computer lab. She found several articles that provided her with ideas for ways to improve her students' comprehension skills. Several of the techniques showed promise, although she read a number of articles that also criticized the potential effectiveness of those techniques.

A couple of the articles that Kathleen read showed that matching classroom, teacher-made assessments to a format similar to that of a standardized test results in increased student performance on that test. She decided to continue teaching reading comprehension as she typically has in the past but to provide students with additional, different types of assessments. She planned to have students read brief passages taken from reading-level-appropriate books and then provide them with written multiple-choice and extended-response types of items addressing their level of comprehension. She would still teach and assess reading comprehension, but students would additionally become more familiar with the format of items they would see on the standardized reading comprehension test.

Related Websites: Sources for Research Topics and Related Information

Several websites and groups of websites are described below. All provide good suggestions or sources for ideas for research topics, as well as for related research and other information. This list is certainly not intended to be exhaustive.

- **Internet Search Engines**

  You read a bit about Internet search engines earlier in this chapter. Search engines provide an excellent resource for preliminary investigations into a potential research topic. Some of these available search engines, listed with their respective URLs, include the following:

  o Ask **http://www.ask.com**

  o Excite **http://www.excite.com**

  o Go.com **http://www.go.com**

- ○ Google **http://www.google.com**
- ○ WebCrawler **http://www.webcrawler.com**
- ○ Yahoo! **http://www.yahoo.com**

- **Professional Associations**
  You also read about using professional associations to generate ideas for research topics. A sampling of other prominent professional associations is listed below:

  - ○ American Psychological Association **http://www.apa.org**
  - ○ Association for Educational Communications and Technology **http:// www.aect.org**
  - ○ Association for Supervision and Curriculum Development **http://www.ascd.org**
  - ○ Council for Exceptional Children **http://www.cec.sped.org**
  - ○ International Reading Association **http://www.reading.org**
  - ○ International Society for Technology in Education **http://www.iste.org**
  - ○ National Association for the Education of Young Children **http://www.naeyc.org**
  - ○ National Council of Teachers of English **http://www.ncte.org**
  - ○ National Council for the Social Studies **http://www.ncss.org**
  - ○ National Council of Teachers of Mathematics **http://nctm.org**
  - ○ National Education Association **http://www.nea.org**
  - ○ National Science Teachers Association **http://nsta.org**
  - ○ Phi Delta Kappa **http://www.pdkintl.org**
  - ○ Teachers of English to Speakers of Other Languages **http://www.tesol.org**
  - ○ In addition, the U.S. Department of Education maintains a list of professional organizations and links to their websites. The list currently includes more than 25 professional organizations and can be found at **http://www2.ed.gov/about/ contacts/gen/othersites/associations.html**.

- Research to Practice: Guidelines for Planning Action Research Projects **http:// literacy.kent.edu/Oasis/Pubs/0200-08.htm**
  In the section titled "Identify the Question," Nancy and Gary Padak provide a foundational overview of three major characteristics of good research topics and questions.

- Classroom Action Research: Starting Points **http://oldweb.madison.k12.wi.us/ sod/car/carstartingpoints.html**
  This page on the Madison (Wisconsin) Metropolitan School District website offers a process for developing good research topics and questions. Included are several incomplete statements for teachers to consider, such as, "I would like to improve . . . ," "I am really curious about . . . ," and "An idea I would like to try out in my class is. . . ."

SUMMARY

★ Identifying a topic for action research is one of the most important steps in the process.

- Action research topics should address realistic classroom problems or issues.

- Research topics should also be weighed against several practical considerations, including your personal interest in the topic, its potential importance, the amount of time it will require, the anticipated difficulty, potential costs, and any ethical issues.

- Narrowing a topic can be accomplished by addressing practical considerations and also through self-reflective, descriptive, and explanatory activities.

★ Preliminary information related to the topic should be gathered.

- This information can be gathered by talking with other educators, reviewing curricular materials, or examining professional publications.

- Information can also be gathered through reconnaissance, with involved self-reflection, description, and explanation.

★ A literature review is described as a systematic examination of research and other information related to your research topic.

- This information can be gathered by talking with other educators, reviewing curricular materials, or examining professional publication.

- Literature reviews help establish a connection between your given project and what has been done before.

- Literature reviews can provide guidance in helping to identify and narrow a topic, formulate research questions and hypotheses, select appropriate data collection methods, and identify appropriate techniques for data analysis.

- When reviewing related literature, it is important to consider its quality, objectivity, and timeliness.

- When trying to locate related literature, it is best to begin with secondary sources and then move to primary sources. Furthermore, it is best to focus your review on primary sources.

- If it becomes necessary to write a formal review of related literature, bear in mind its purpose: to convey to all individuals interested in the topic the historical context of the topic, the trends experienced by the topic, how theory has informed practice, and vice versa.

- A literature review should not consist of an annotated list of summaries of research, but rather it should flow smoothly for the reader as a cohesive essay.

QUESTIONS AND ACTIVITIES

1. Think of a preliminary topic you are interested in investigating. Complete the table below by addressing the considerations discussed in the chapter.

2. Make a list of ethical considerations with which you might want to be concerned in an action research study.

3. What do you believe might be the most difficult aspect of doing reconnaissance related to a potential action research topic?

4. What do you believe might be the most difficult aspect of conducting a review of literature related to a potential action research topic?

5. Searching databases and the Internet for related literature can sometimes seem a daunting task. Begin small by identifying a preliminary topic of interest and find one of each kind of the following: a published journal article, a paper presented at a professional conference, and an Internet website.

6. Assume that you will write a literature review for only the three items you located in Number 5 above. Draft an outline of your review based on the contents of those three sources.

STUDENT STUDY SITE

Visit the Student Study Site at **www.sagepub.com/mertler3study** for these additional learning tools:

- Video clips
- Web resources
- Self quizzes
- E-flashcards
- PowerPoint slides
- Sample action research reports
- Full-text S AGE journal articles
- Chapter summaries

CHAPTER 4

Developing a Research Plan

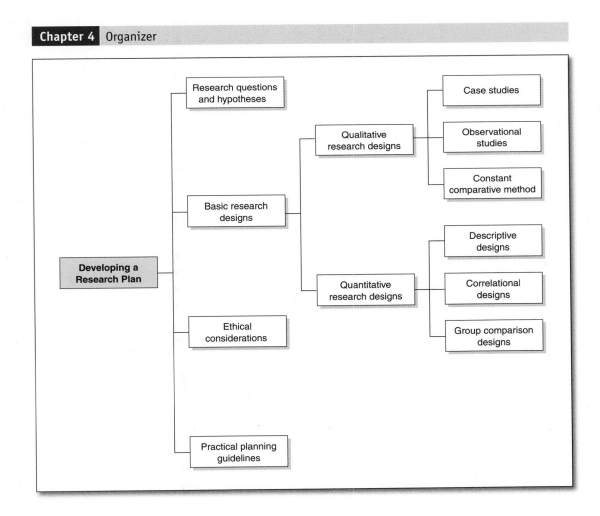

The last step in the initial stage—the planning stage—of conducting action research is the development of a research plan. Once you have decided on an area of focus, narrowed its breadth, and reviewed the literature and other information related to your topic, it is time to develop a concrete plan for actually carrying out the action research study. Developing this research plan necessitates the conversion of your topic into research questions or hypotheses and the selection of an appropriate design for collecting and analyzing your data.

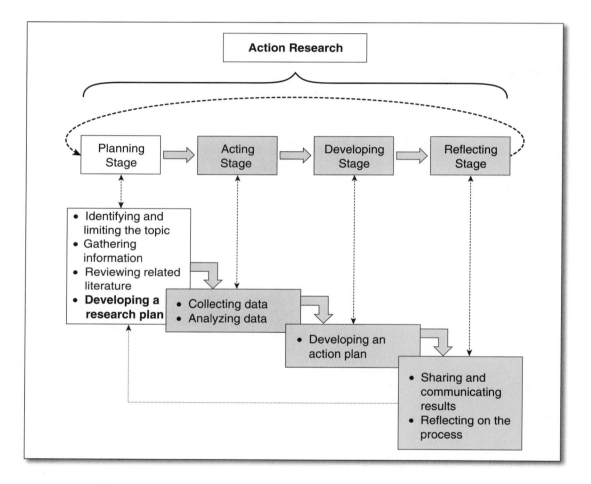

Research Questions

Before actually framing research questions, it is important to decide whether you intend to use qualitative or quantitative methods in your action research study. Formally stating your research questions can help you make this determination regarding research approach. On the other hand, however, it is best to know which approach you intend to use prior to formally stating the questions. Leedy and Ormrod (2005) provide a dichotomous decision-making table, of sorts. Table 4.1 offers an adaptation of their table. The table is designed to help you determine which approach is most appropriate based on several factors, including your beliefs, the nature of your research topic and study, and various types of skills you possess. Of course, one of the benefits of action research is that it lends itself nicely to either approach, as well as to using a mixed-methods approach, combining aspects of both qualitative and quantitative research. Before examining each type, it is important to understand that qualitative research approaches are directed only by research questions, whereas quantitative research approaches may be guided by either research questions or hypotheses.

A research question is defined as the fundamental question inherent in the research topic under investigation (Mertler & Charles, 2011). Its purpose is to guide the research study, for the goal is to be able to answer the research question at the end of the study. These guiding research questions do not offer any speculative answers, as opposed to hypotheses, which, as you will discover shortly, do (Leedy & Ormrod, 2005). Research questions are appropriate for any type of study that uses qualitative, as well as any that use quantitative, approaches to research. Generally speaking, qualitative research questions tend to be more open-ended and holistic in nature than quantitative research questions. The reason for this is to allow for possibilities that the researcher has not imagined or anticipated (Hubbard & Power, 2003). Qualitative research questions are often posed in such a way that they can be answered by detailed description and observations. Keywords that often appear in qualitative research questions include *how* and *what,* which provide the teacher-researcher with the opportunity to

Video Clip 4.1
View a clip of Dr. Mertler discussing the importance of carefully stating a research question.

Table 4.1   Should I Use a Qualitative or a Quantitative Approach?

Use This Approach If	Qualitative	Quantitative
You believe that . . .	There are multiple realities constructed by different individuals.	There is a single reality that can be objectively measured.
Your potential audience is . . .	Familiar with qualitative studies.	Familiar with quantitative studies.
Your research question is . . .	Broad, holistic, and interpretive.	Specific, confirmatory, or predictive.
Your related body of literature is . . .	Limited.	Relatively large.
Your research topic . . .	Involves in-depth study.	Covers a lot of breadth.
Your available time is . . .	Relatively long.	Relatively short.
Your desire for structure is . . .	Low.	High.
You have skills in the areas of . . .	Inductive reasoning and attention to detail.	Deductive reasoning and statistics.
Your writing skills are strongest in the area of . . .	Literary, narrative writing.	Technical, scientific writing.

Source: Adapted from Leedy and Ormrod, 2005.

thoroughly describe the processes and any changes as they occur (Hubbard & Power, 2003). Often, researchers using qualitative methods do not state research questions at the beginning of the study. Rather, they wait until they begin to collect data in order to have a better sense of what it is they are really looking for (Schwalbach, 2003). Even then, they may continue to revise their questions throughout the period of data collection. Quantitative research questions are stated up front and seldom change during the course of a study.

When attempting to convert your research topic into a research question, it is important to keep several important characteristics of research questions in mind (Schwalbach, 2003). These characteristics are listed below; each will be discussed subsequently.

- Qualitative research questions should be stated in more open-ended fashion; quantitative research questions should be more focused.

- Research questions should not be stated in a manner that assumes an answer even before data have been collected.

- Research questions should not be too broad or too specific in scope, especially when conducting quantitative action research.

- Research questions should be based in the body of literature that encompasses the topic.

- Research questions must be able to be answered by collecting available data.

- Research questions must be ethical.

- Research questions should be both important and feasible to answer.

First, qualitative research questions should be stated in more open-ended fashion; quantitative research questions should be more focused. In either case, one should try to avoid questions that require a simple yes or no answer. For example, consider the following research question:

Is there a relationship between students' academic performance and the number of hours spent studying?

The simple answer to this question—in probably every case—would be yes, since some sort of relationship is always likely to exist. However, that is likely not what a researcher would really want to know. Contemplate the following revised version of the question:

What is the nature of the relationship between students' academic performance and the number of hours spent studying?

Notice that this revised version, while still focused on the specific variables of performance and time spent studying, allows the researcher to discover much more about the relationship, other than whether or not one simply exists.

Second, research questions should not be stated in a manner that assumes an answer even before data have been collected. For example:

To what extent will the integration of technology into the writing process improve students' writing skills?

In this example, the researcher has already assumed that the integration of new technologies into the process of teaching students to write will have a *positive* (due to the use of the word *improve*) effect on their actual writing samples. This research question might be restated more objectively as:

To what extent will the integration of technology into the writing process affect students' writing skills?

It is important to remember that the merit and potential value of any research study does not hinge on finding positive results. If results of a study are negative or not what you expected to find, you have still discovered something important (i.e., a technique or approach that does *not* work), answered your research question, and added something beneficial to the body of literature.

Third, it is important to ensure that the research question not be too broad or too specific in scope, especially when conducting quantitative action research. The following question—

What will improve students' critical-thinking skills?

—is entirely too broad; a teacher-researcher probably would not even know where or how to begin collecting data to answer this question. In addition, it does not even suggest any methods or techniques for improving those thinking skills. In contrast, an alternative version provides more structure and focuses on a particular technique:

To what degree will problem-based instruction impact students' critical-thinking skills?

Fourth, research questions should be based in the body of literature that encompasses the topic. Recall that one of the purposes of conducting a review of related literature is to inform the development of research questions. A research question should not consist of a query that you simply develop off the top of your head. It should be well informed by the literature and related information that you have reviewed.

Fifth, a research question must be able to be answered by collecting available data. Consider the following "research" question:

Does God exist?

I honestly have no idea what kind of data to collect and analyze in order to be able to answer this question—it is virtually impossible. There are, of course, numerous variations of this question that could be answered by readily accessible data. For example:

To what extent do people believe that God exists?

I can collect data—for example, by surveying or interviewing individuals—that would allow me to answer this question.

Sixth, you must make sure that your research question is ethical. Recall from the previous chapter that you cannot ethically do anything to participants in a research study that exposes them to risks of any kind. This includes risks that are physical, emotional, and

dif 'hypothesis (handwritten)

psychological in nature. Be especially careful of a research study that would necessitate placing any sort of derogatory labels on students.

Finally, examine your research question to ensure that it is both important and feasible to answer. We have previously discussed these two characteristics in relation to research topics in Chapter 3. Remember, the results of your action research study should make some sort of difference in some aspect of education. Also, it must be feasible to answer the research question in light of the difficulty level of the study and available resources (e.g., time and money).

Video Clips 4.2 & 4.3 View clips of educator-researchers discussing the importance of a carefully-stated research question.

Recall that in Chapter 3 (see Table 3.1), we looked at several sample research topics and narrowed their focus into more researchable topics. Those same examples of research topics and their associated research questions are presented in Table 4.2. You will undoubtedly notice that the research questions characteristically consist of the research topic simply restated in the form of a question.

As a final point, it is important to make sure that your research question truly reflects your topic. In other words, it must clearly represent either the problem or issue you are interested in learning more about or the desired change you are trying to make in your teaching. If this match does not exist, you will end up with not-entirely-meaningful results of your action research study.

In contrast to research questions, hypotheses are tentative, but intelligent and informed, guesses about the findings of a study, made of course before the study begins. They usually make predictions about future events, existing differences between groups, or existing relationships between variables (Mertler & Charles, 2011). They are only used in quantitative research studies but are not appropriate for all types of quantitative research. Hypotheses are appropriate only when the design calls for the use of inferential statistics (you will read more about inferential statistics in Chapter 6), although their use is becoming much less commonplace. For this reason, I will only briefly introduce them here.

null hypothesis (handwritten)

There are three types of hypotheses: null hypotheses, nondirectional research hypotheses, and directional research hypotheses. A **null hypothesis** states that no effect will occur in the study or that no differences between groups or no relationship between variables will be found. Typically, this is not what the researcher expects to find; if it were, most studies would never be conducted. A second type of hypothesis is a **nondirectional research hypothesis**, which essentially states that there will be some sort of effect (or difference or relationship) discovered in the results of the research study, although we cannot comfortably predict the nature or direction of that effect (or difference or relationship). This is probably due, at least in part, to the fact that our review of the literature did not provide us with any overwhelming or compelling evidence to inform us of the specific nature of the effect. The third and final type of hypothesis statement is a **directional research hypothesis**, which not only states that an effect (or difference or relationship) will be found but also specifies the direction or nature of that effect. In all likelihood, we would want to state this type of research hypothesis only if we found overwhelming evidence to support it from our review of literature.

Table 4.2   Examples of Research Topics and Their Associated Research Questions

Research Topic		Research Question
Leisure activities of elementary teachers and the amount of time spent on them	→	What types of leisure activities do elementary teachers engage in? How much time do they spend on them?
Hispanic students' perceptions of factors that make academic success more difficult	→	What are the perceptions held by Hispanic students of factors that make academic success difficult?
Effectiveness of a word processing program in helping students revise drafts of written stories	→	Is there a difference in the quality of written drafts between students who use a word processing program and those who do not? If so, what is the nature of the difference?
Effect of reading practice with fifth-grade "buddies" on the developing reading skills of first-grade students	→	What is the effect of reading practice with fifth-grade "buddies" on the developing reading skills of first-grade students?
Tenth-grade biology students' perceptions of virtual and real animal dissections	→	How do 10th-grade biology students feel about virtual and real animal dissections?

Basic Research Designs

It is imperative to conceptualize the design of a given action research study prior to its initiation (McLean, 1995). Teacher-researchers must carefully consider all aspects of the study to be conducted. These design aspects include not only how data will be collected and analyzed but also primarily how the study will be planned. In other words, a research design is the formal plan for conducting the action research study—it is the "blueprint" that specifies exactly how the study will be carried out. We will examine basic designs for both qualitative and quantitative approaches to conducting action research.

Qualitative Research Designs

The concept of a "qualitative research design" is somewhat of a misnomer, because throughout the literature, the term *research design* has historically, in my opinion, referred almost exclusively to quantitative research studies. That being said, however, teacher-researchers still need to have a plan of attack for conducting a study in which they wish to use qualitative methods. This plan for conducting a qualitatively based study simply tends to be less structured, when compared to quantitative studies. By no means am I implying that it is less valuable or somehow easier to accomplish. Actually, studies using qualitative approaches tend to be more difficult for most people—of course, depending on your natural research skills—since they tend to be broad, holistic, and in-depth studies that are carried out over an extended period. Leedy and Ormrod (2005) have summarized this approach to research by stating, "To answer some research questions . . . we must dig deep to get a complete understanding of the phenomenon we are studying" (p. 133).

Because qualitative research questions tend to be more open-ended, teacher-researchers sometimes have difficulty identifying ahead of time the exact methods they will use (Leedy & Ormrod, 2005). Often, they may select some "preliminary" methods of data collection (usually observations and interviews), and as they learn more about their topic, their plan can become more focused on the specifics (e.g., the *who,* the *what,* and the *where)* of the observations and interviews. As they become more focused on what they really want to learn from their action research study, they have a better idea of exactly *whom* to interview, *what* to observe, and *where* those observations should occur. It is largely for this reason that qualitative approaches to conducting research studies are said to have "emergent" research questions and methodologies.

Leedy and Ormrod (2005) provide an overview of several approaches to qualitative research, including case studies, ethnographies, and phenomenological studies. In *case studies*, a particular individual, program, or event is studied in-depth for a defined period, usually relying on a variety of sources of data, including observations, interviews, and reviews of existing documents. *Ethnographies* involve in-depth study of an entire group, usually focusing on the culture of that group. Site-based observations and interviews are key methods of data collection in this type of qualitative study. Finally, *phenomenological studies* attempt to understand people's perceptions of a particular situation, usually relying heavily on lengthy interviews. For more additional and more specific information related to these and other qualitative research designs, the reader is referred to Leedy and Ormrod (2005) and Schwalbach (2003).

Case Studies

A case study is formally defined as a detailed examination of a single setting, a single subject, or a particular event (Bogdan & Biklen, 2007). Case studies can vary in terms of their complexity, depth, and breadth. Focusing on a single subject is the best way to begin working with case study designs (Bogdan & Biklen, 2007). After experiencing success with single subjects, settings, or events, action researchers may move on to multi-site or multi-subject case studies.

Bogdan and Biklen (2007) describe the general design of a case study as a funnel. The beginning of the study is located at the wide, or open, end of the funnel. The teacher-researcher looks for possible people or places that might serve well as the sources of data for investigating the chosen topic. Once this has been determined, the researcher begins to collect data while concurrently exploring, analyzing, and reviewing those data in order to make decisions about the future direction or next steps for the study. During this process, teacher-researchers may discard old ideas and plans for the study and develop new, more appropriate ones, based on the nature of the data collected to that point in time. The research design and data collection procedures are continually modified and specified (i.e., as in the narrowing of the funnel) as they learn more about their chosen topic of interest. As time progresses, the teacher-researcher makes specific determinations about the focus of the study. Decisions are made about which of the particular aspects of the setting, subject, or data source will serve as the true focus of the study. At this point, specific research questions are formulated, and data collection activities begin to constrict to very precise characteristics or features of the individual site or person.

Observational Case Studies

Observational case studies are perhaps the most common type of case study. They involve the study of a particular organization or some aspect of the organization (Bogdan & Biklen, 2007). The focus of observational case studies might be a particular physical location in the organization (e.g., a classroom, the teachers' lounge, the main office, or the cafeteria), a specific group of people (e.g., teachers in a particular academic department, the cafeteria staff, or the central office staff), or a particular activity within the school (e.g., faculty meetings, assemblies, or the end-of-day dismissal).

It is important to realize that a requirement of observational case studies is to select a focus within the school setting. However, once a focus has been identified for detailed study, it becomes somewhat artificial and no longer authentic (Bogdan & Biklen, 2007). The specific aspect on which the teacher-researcher decides to focus is naturally integrated with other activities throughout the school. For example, a teacher might want to look at the nature of events that take place during faculty meetings. The process of isolating that particular aspect will likely "distort" it. Events, teachers' behaviors, and the nature of discussions that occur at faculty meetings are, out of necessity, influenced by other events, both internal and external to the school. Through the use of data, collected primarily in the form of observations and interviews, the teacher-researcher must take into account the relationship of the focus of the study to the school as a whole. For this reason, it is often best to select an aspect that can be seen as a naturally existing unit.

Bogdan and Biklen (2007) also warn that care must be taken when selecting or identifying groups of people for observational case studies. They caution that the smaller the number of participants or subjects in the group being studied, the more likely you are—as an observer of their behavior—to alter that behavior, simply by your presence. It is important to try to select a setting or a group that is large enough so that you are less obtrusive but small enough so that you are not overwhelmed by the task of data collection across so many individuals.

Observational Studies

Observational studies are similar to observational case studies in that the researcher becomes an integral part of the setting of the study. The primary difference is that the focus may not be on an aspect of the *organization* of a school. The focus of observational studies may be much broader. However, the teacher-researcher must still acquire the status of a "trusted person" in the particular setting (Glesne, 2006). Otherwise, the participants in the study will be unlikely to open up to the researcher in order to share honest feelings, perceptions, or opinions. The act of becoming a trusted person in the setting actually makes the researcher a participant in that setting or group, as well. **Participant observation—** observing as a researcher but also participating in the group or setting as an equal, active member of that group or setting—enables the researcher to learn firsthand how the actions of the participants correspond with their words, to see patterns of behavior, to experience that which was unexpected, and to develop a deeper quality of trust that motivates the participants to share with you what they otherwise might not want to or feel comfortable doing (Glesne, 2006). Participant observation is something that typically occurs throughout data collection in observational studies but is most important during the early stages of that data collection in order to establish this type of trusted relationship.

In observational studies, there are varying levels of researcher participation. As shown in Figure 4.1, levels of researcher participation range from mostly participant on one end to mostly observer on the other end (Glesne, 2006). Participant observation can serve as the sole means of data collection, although it is typically supplemented with individual or small-group interviews. Your participation may fall at any point on this continuum; often, you will find yourself at different points along the continuum during different stages in the data collection process of the study.

At the left end of Figure 4.1, the teacher-researcher acts completely as an observer. In this role, the researcher has little to no interaction with the participants being studied (Glesne, 2006). For example, the teacher-researcher may observe elementary students through a one-way glass. This is not an uncommon method of observing preservice teachers so they do not know they are being observed. At this end of the continuum, those individuals being observed typically do not know they are being observed.

The next defined point on the continuum is **observer as participant**. In this role, the teacher-researcher remains *primarily* an observer but has some level of interaction with the participants (Glesne, 2006). At a minimum, the participants know that they are being observed, so there may be some nonverbal communications occurring between the participants and the observer. Typically, in this role the researcher is seated in the back of a classroom, for example, simply observing and taking notes. The researcher does not teach, offer advice, provide assistance, speak, answer questions, or participate in any other way.

A **participant as observer** actually takes on a much more active role with the context of the particular setting. The researcher continues to observe and take notes on what is

---

Figure 4.1   The Participant-Observer Continuum

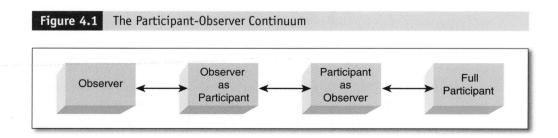

observed but also has the opportunity to interact with the participants in the study. Glesne (2006) notes an interesting paradox that can occur when in this role. The more you function as a participant in the world that you are actively researching, the more you risk losing your "eye of objectivity" (p. 44). However, at the same time, the more you participate, the greater your opportunity to learn firsthand what goes on in that setting.

Finally, at the right end of the continuum, a **full participant** is simultaneously a fully functioning member of the "community" as well as a researcher (Glesne, 2006). In this role, the researcher is first and foremost part of the group—as opposed to being an "outsider"— who also happens to be collecting data on the group.

Glesne (2006) is quick to point out that the location of a researcher on this continuum is not necessarily a conscious decision. It usually depends on the nature of the research questions you are investigating, the context of your study, and the nature of the group of participants you are studying (in other words, how feasible would it be for you to "join" them as a participant?). In most cases, if you are conducting classroom-based action research, you are more likely to be a full participant than if you are conducting more traditional forms of qualitative research (Glesne, 2006).

Constant Comparative Method

multiple data

A final type of qualitative research design that we will discuss is the constant comparative method. In most types of qualitative studies, especially case studies (Bogdan & Biklen, 2007), emerging themes guide the data collection, but formal analysis of data does not occur until after the data collection is near completion. The **constant comparative method** is a research design for studies involving multiple data sources, where data analysis begins early in the study and is nearly completed by the end of data collection (Bogdan & Biklen, 2007). In actuality, data collection typically begins prior to a specific topic or focus of study being identified. According to Bogdan and Biklen (2007), the steps involved in implementing the constant comparative method include the following:

1. Begin collecting data.

2. Examine data for key issues, recurring events, or activities that may become the focus of the study and the basis for categorizing the data.

3. Continue to collect data that provide incidents of the categories of focus.

4. Begin writing about the categories being explored, attempting to describe and explain all the incidents included in the data while at the same time searching for new incidents.

5. Continue to work with the data and the emerging "model" in order to discover the basic social processes and relationships among and between the individuals in the group being studied.

6. Engage in summarizing, coding, and writing as the analysis focuses on the most meaningful categories.

It is important to note that although this process has been described as a series of seemingly linear steps, all the steps actually occur simultaneously in a completely integrated manner. The data collection and analysis continue to double back and revisit more data collection and analysis (Bogdan & Biklen, 2007). In this sense, the constant comparative method epitomizes classroom-based action research with its apparent cyclical nature.

Quantitative Research Designs

When considering a quantitative approach for your research, there are four categories of research designs appropriate for teacher-led action research: descriptive designs, correlational designs, group comparisons, and single-subject designs. These categories and any specific designs are described below.

Descriptive Designs

The purpose of descriptive research is to describe and make interpretations about the current status of individuals, objects, settings, conditions, or events (Mertler & Charles, 2011). Descriptive research simply examines the phenomenon *as it exists*; there is no attempt to artificially manipulate any conditions or situations. Two common descriptive research designs are observational research and survey research. In **observational research**, as a quantitative design, the focus is on a specific aspect of behavior, perhaps a single particular variable (Leedy & Ormrod, 2005). It is important at this point not to confuse this design with its qualitative counterpart. Qualitative observations, as you will recall, are usually recorded in great detail that attempts to capture a holistic portrait of human behavior. Those observation notes are then analyzed, based on their content, and summarized in narrative form. In contrast, *quantitative* observational research focuses on a single variable on which observations are made. The striking difference is that the observations are then *quantified* (Leedy & Ormrod, 2005). In other words, each instance of the targeted behavior is tallied, or otherwise recorded, and then is simply counted in order to determine its overall frequency of occurrence. In other situations, instead of the behavior simply being counted for the number of times it occurred, the behavior might be rated for accuracy, quality, proficiency, or some other dimension. The design itself simply requires that a specific schedule of observations be established and some sort of tally sheet be developed.

As an example of a descriptive observational research study, consider the teacher-researcher with a student who often exhibits disruptive behavior in class, but the behavior is not constant. It seems to occur sporadically throughout the day. The teacher-researcher develops a brief tally sheet that allows her to indicate points in time during the day when the disruptive behaviors occur. In addition, she speculates that the disruptive behaviors may be associated with other students in the classroom. She builds into the tally sheet a section that allows her to indicate with whom the student is interacting when any type of disruptive behavior occurs. At the end of a predetermined period of time, she counts the various tally marks in order to better understand the student's disruptive behavior.

The second type of descriptive research design is survey research. **Survey research** involves acquiring information from individuals representing one or more groups—perhaps about their opinions, attitudes, or characteristics—by specifically asking them questions and then tabulating their responses (Leedy & Ormrod, 2005). The ultimate goal of survey research is to learn more about the current status of a reasonably large population either by surveying a subset (known as a *sample*) from the population or by surveying the entire population, if it is not too large. Although it can be complex, survey research is typically a relatively simple, straightforward design. The researcher poses a series of questions, usually in written form, to participants who are willing to complete the survey. Once the questions have been answered, the responses are aggregated across all the participants or, perhaps, subgroups of participants. The analysis of data usually involves the calculation of frequency counts or percentages of response. Applications of school-based survey research would include a school principal who wants to know what students like and dislike about various aspects of the school. Surveys are given to each student in the building. Upon completion, the data are aggregated, and percentages of response are calculated. The principal may even wish to aggregate and report responses for various subgroups of the school population (e.g., boys and girls, different ethnic groups).

It is important to remember that survey research simply takes a "snapshot" of the phenomenon under investigation. Through the administration of the survey, the researcher captures opinions, and such, during a fleeting moment in time. The results should not be taken as a constant for the group surveyed—actions, perceptions, opinions, and even characteristics can change from one moment to the next.

Correlational Designs — Statistical relationship

A second category of quantitative research designs is correlational research. In a **correlational study**, the action researcher examines whether and to what degree a statistical relationship exists between two or more variables. It is typically used to measure or describe an existing condition or something that has happened in the past (Johnson, 2008). The basic design for correlational research involves a *single* group of people who are measured on *two* things or characteristics (i.e., variables) that have already happened to them. For example, suppose we wanted to know if there was a relationship, and how strong that relationship was, between the numbers of hours that students study independently and their score on a unit test. Realize that at the time that we might collect data, the two "things" (i.e., hours spent studying and the administration of the unit test) have already occurred. Furthermore, the variables studied in a correlational study generally occur naturally. In our example, students would ordinarily study and would ordinarily, or at least likely, take a test upon completion of an instructional unit. When a correlational design is used, there is no manipulation of either of the conditions being measured.

Relationships between variables are measured statistically by calculating a correlation coefficient. **Correlation coefficients** report two aspects of the relationship between given variables: the *direction* of the relationship and the *strength* of the relationship. There are numerous correlation coefficients that can be used to describe the nature of the relationship between two variables, the most common of which is the **Pearson correlation coefficient**, symbolized by *r*. The coefficient itself is reported on a scale that ranges from –1.00 to +1.00. The direction is indicated as either a positive or a negative value on the scale. A **positive correlation** indicates that as the scores or values on one variable increase, the values on the other variable also increase. Similarly, as the values on one decrease, the values on the other also decrease (in other words, the values on the two variables tend to move in the same direction). In contrast, a **negative correlation** means that as the values on one variable increase, the values on the other variable decrease. The relationship between outdoor temperature and sales of lemonade would be an example of a positive correlation (as the temperature increases, lemonade sales also increase); the relationship between outdoor temperature and sales of coffee would be an example of a negative correlation (as the temperature decreases, coffee sales increase). You will learn more about the calculation and interpretation of correlation coefficients in Chapter 6.

The strength of the relationship is indicated by the magnitude of the numerical value of the coefficient. The largest coefficient possible would be equal to 1.00, in either the positive or the negative direction. A correlation coefficient equal to +1.00 indicates a perfect positive correlation. However, it is important to note that in educational settings, a perfect correlation of either type rarely, if ever, occurs between variables. It is not uncommon to obtain *strong* correlations (e.g., correlations that exceed ±0.80) but not perfect ones. The smallest coefficient possible would be equal to 0.00, which means that there is absolutely no relationship between the two variables. Like perfect correlations, rarely, if ever, will you see a correlation equal to 0.00. Again, it is common to find *weak* correlations (e.g., correlations between –0.20 and 0.00 and those between +0.20 and 0.00) but not the complete absence of *any* relationship.

It is important that the results of a correlational study not be misinterpreted. Correlational research only allows the action researcher to conclude that a relationship of a certain magnitude and direction exists between two variables. There is a common misconception that correlational research can also imply causation between the two variables. This could not be farther from the truth. It is critical to remember the following:

Correlation ≠ Causation

Simply because two variables are related, a researcher cannot conclude that one causes the other. Additional variables could likely account for the causal influences but have not been included in the study at hand. For example, recall our example of the relationship between hours spent studying and performance on a unit test. Suppose we discover that there is a strong positive relationship (say, the coefficient is equal to +0.85) between the two variables. It would be inaccurate to conclude that simply studying for a longer period of time (i.e., increase in hours) will cause improved test performance (i.e., increased score)—although students themselves have tried to "prove" this true for years! Many other things could influence test performance, such as the quality of studying that occurred or the level of conceptual understanding of the test material.

Although we cannot use the results of a correlational study to explain causation, we can use them for purposes of future predictions. Based on the nature of the relationship as measured by the correlation coefficient, it is possible to predict future scores on one variable if the value on the other variable is known. If we know that the correlation between hours spent studying and test score is $+0.85$, and if we know the number of hours a certain individual student spent studying, we can predict the test score that student will receive. Only in situations where the relationship is a perfect one (i.e., the coefficient is equal to -1.00 or $+1.00$) can you predict the value on the second variable with 100% accuracy, and we have already discussed how these perfect relationships seldom occur in education. The degree of predictive accuracy is determined by the magnitude of the correlation coefficient. The higher the correlation (i.e., the closer it is to -1.00 or to $+1.00$), the more accurately the value on one variable can be predicted from the other; the lower the correlation (i.e., the closer it is to 0.00), the less accurate the predicted value will be. Keep in mind that this is not a prediction of causation but rather only a prediction of association.

Group Comparison Designs — *Cause + effect*

Group comparison designs attempt to do what correlational designs cannot—investigate cause-and-effect relationships. The general idea behind group comparison designs is that *two or more* groups, which differ on some characteristic or have somehow been exposed to different conditions, are compared on a *single,* common measure in order to see if the differing characteristic or condition may have resulted in different performance. Whenever researchers investigate cause and effect, they examine the extent to which one variable (the *cause*) influences another variable (the *effect*). The variable that is considered to be the cause of something else is called an independent variable. In some instances, this variable may be directly manipulated, or controlled, by the researcher. The variable that is assumed to be influenced by the other variable is called the dependent variable, since its value or score at least in part *depends* on the independent variable. For illustrative purposes, consider a pair of history teachers who want to know if it is more effective for American history to be taught forward (i.e., beginning with the Revolutionary War and progressing to the present) or backward (i.e., beginning with the present and regressing to the Revolutionary War). One teacher volunteers to teach the year using the backward approach, while the other will teach using the standard forward method. Near the end of the year, students of both teachers will take an advanced placement test in American history. Their test scores will be statistically compared to determine if the students taught using one method outperform those taught using the other method. In this example, the independent variable is "approach to teaching American history" (forward versus backward), and the dependent variable is "advanced placement test score." If there is a difference in the test scores for students in the two groups, that difference will *depend* on which type of instruction they received.

When attempting to investigate cause and effect, there really is only one methodology that will definitively show whether one variable causes another. This definitive methodology is experimental research. True *experimental designs* require that a great deal of rigor and control be integrated into the research study. As an example, one of these levels of control is the random assignment of students to treatment groups. This level of rigor and control is simply not attainable, or even realistic, in classroom settings; therefore, experimental designs are typically not appropriate for action research studies. There are, however, three subcategories of group comparison designs that are appropriate for action research in classrooms and schools. These three subgroups are causal-comparative, preexperimental, and quasiexperimental designs.

Causal-Comparative Designs. Causal-comparative research is used to explore reasons behind existing differences between two or more groups. In this sense, it is quite similar to correlational research in that it investigates conditions that have already occurred and collects data in an attempt to determine why one group is different from the other (Johnson, 2008). Causal-comparative designs are also known as ex post facto designs. The term ex post facto literally translates to mean "after the fact." The investigation begins by noticing a difference that exists within a group of people, for example, and then looking back in time in an attempt to determine the conditions that might have resulted in this observed difference. In other words, the action researcher is looking for a cause "after the fact," since the conditions, and their resulting differences, have already occurred. Groups are compared in order to find a cause for differences in some measure or score (Johnson, 2008).

The most common situation for the implementation of causal-comparative designs occurs when the presumed cause, or independent variable, has already occurred. Since it has already occurred, it is not feasible for the researcher to manipulate that particular variable. The conditions that determine group membership of the independent variable, in many cases, are naturally occurring or have occurred as part of some process external to the research study. For example, imagine that a principal has observed a wide range in scores obtained on the annual standardized math test. If she wanted to explore possible causes for these differences—perhaps differences due to gender—she could employ a causal-comparative design. She would begin by collecting the test scores (the effect, also known as the dependent variable) for all students in her school. Then she would need to record for each score the gender (the preexisting and naturally occurring potential cause, also known as the independent variable) of the corresponding student. Males and females would then be grouped together and an average score computed for each respective group. Finally, the group averages would be statistically compared in order to determine if the two groups were different. If so, the principal may conclude that the preexisting condition of gender has influenced math test scores.

As another example, suppose that a guidance counselor wanted to know how effectively a new self-esteem program, which is being pilot tested in half of the district's elementary schools, is working. A causal-comparative design could help the guidance counselor make an informed decision about the future of the program. A self-esteem inventory could be administered to students in schools throughout the district, some of which were pilot testing the program and others of which were not. The students' scores on the inventory would then be compared and analyzed statistically. Again, in this example, the independent variable is the condition that determines group membership—schools with the self-esteem program and schools without the self-esteem program. Realize that this is a preexisting condition—the program was already being implemented in some schools and not in others. That determination was not an aspect of the causal-comparative research design. The dependent variable would be the scores students received on the self-esteem inventory. If the inventory scores for those students who had been exposed to the new program were substantially higher than those for students who had not participated in the program, the guidance counselor would conclude that the new program is effective. On the other hand, if the inventory scores were lower for the students exposed to the new program, or if there was no difference in the scores between the two groups, the counselor would conclude that the new program was detrimental or, at least, ineffective.

Preexperimental Designs. Preexperimental designs are called such because they are "preliminary" experimental designs. They incorporate several aspects of experimental studies but exclude others of substantial importance. For example, in preexperimental designs, the independent "variable" does not vary, largely due to the fact that there is only one group—since all participants in the study belong to the same group, there can be no "group" comparisons. Because of these exclusions, it is not possible to demonstrate in definitive fashion cause-and-effect relationships in preexperimental designs.

As we examine both preexperimental and quasiexperimental designs, note the graphical representations of the designs. In these diagrams, the following abbreviations and symbols are used:

T = Treatment condition

O = Observation or other type of measure

EXP = Experimental group

CTL = Control group

The treatment condition defines the independent variable. Typically, some participants are exposed to the treatment, and others are not. These "levels" of the independent variable are the determining factor for group membership (i.e., experimental group vs. control group). The dependent variable consists of the observation or other measure.

We will consider two common preexperimental designs. The first of these designs is known as the one-shot case study. The **one-shot case study** is a very primitive type of experimental design (Leedy & Ormrod, 2005). In this design, some sort of experimental treatment is introduced and, following the passage of time, a measurement or observation—probably a posttest of some sort—is administered in order to determine the effects of the treatment. This design is depicted diagrammatically as follows:

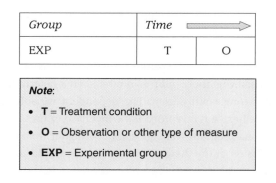

Group	Time	
EXP	T	O

Note:

- **T** = Treatment condition
- **O** = Observation or other type of measure
- **EXP** = Experimental group

For example, a science teacher wants to know if a new lab kit will improve the students' performance in science. The teacher uses the kit with all of her science classes and then administers a practical examination. Exam scores are high, so she concludes that the new lab kits are effective in helping her students learn more. The weakness of this particular design is that so many variables unaccounted for in the study could have influenced the scores on the posttest, when it may be assumed that the treatment caused the desired performance. In our example, perhaps the students would have performed well with another set of lab materials, or even without any lab materials, because they were naturally bright or because they had experienced an enhanced lab setting in last year's science class. In either case, their performance would have been high regardless of the new kits.

The second preexperimental design is known as a **one-group pretest-posttest design**. In this design, we see a good deal of improvement over the previous design. Although there still is no "other" group for comparison purposes, a pretest has been added prior to the introduction of the treatment. This design is illustrated as follows:

Group	Time		
EXP	O	T	O

Note:

- **T** = Treatment condition
- **O** = Observation or other type of measure
- **EXP** = Experimental group

Returning to our previous example, the science teacher administers a pretest practical examination to her students and records the scores. She then implements the lab, using the new lab kits. Upon completion of the lab, she administers a posttest to her students and compares those scores to the scores the students received on the pretest. This design represents an improvement over the one-shot case study because the teacher will, at a *minimum,* know if some sort of change has taken place (Leedy & Ormrod, 2005). However, she still cannot rule out other possible explanations for the change that she did not consider and incorporate into the study.

Quasiexperimental Designs. **Quasiexperimental designs** come the closest to true experiments; however, there still is no random assignment of participants to groups (Johnson, 2008). The notion of random assignment ensures that the groups you are comparing are relatively similar. This is the reason that quasiexperimental designs are quite appropriate for classroom research. In most schools and classrooms, randomly assigning students to different treatments (which might necessitate that they change classrooms, teachers, or even school buildings) is simply not feasible. There are two other methods for ensuring that groups being compared are relatively similar: pretests and matching. When using *pretests* to establish group similarity, a pretest on the variable you are looking to examine is administered prior to the investigation (Johnson, 2008). The groups are then statistically compared on their pretest scores; if they are similar, you can continue with the research. A significant difference between the two groups, however, indicates that the two groups are not comparable. In that case, there are three options: (1) Find another group to compare, (2) rearrange your existing groups so that they are more similar, or (3) take the dissimilarity of the groups into account when describing findings and drawing conclusions (Johnson, 2008). *Matching* is another technique used to create similar groups of participants. Again, a pretest is given to all participants, but it serves a slightly different purpose. Based on the results of the pretest, each participant is matched with another participant who has a relatively similar pretest score. Groups are then created by putting each person in the pair in separate groups (i.e., one into the experimental group and one into the control group) (Johnson, 2008). The end result is two groups that are relatively similar on the variable of interest.

Johnson (2008) is keen to point out that quasiexperimental research requires some intrusion into the educational setting, as you read in the descriptions above. Therefore, quasiexperimental designs should be used with caution in action research settings. In these situations, what you are observing is not an authentic classroom environment but rather one that has been altered in order to be able to examine a particular variable. In this way, quasiexperimental research is also what Johnson refers to as "quasi-action research." It is important to keep in mind that action research does not set out to prove or to disprove any hypothesis, nor is it meant to provide results that can be generalized to larger populations. Quasiexperimental research designs should be used only to provide a description of what is happening in a particular setting or situation.

Although there are numerous quasiexperimental designs, we will examine only one that has practical classroom applications—the **pretest-posttest control group design**. This is very similar to the one-group pretest-posttest design we examined earlier in the section on preexperimental designs. The important difference—as well as improvement—is the addition of a control group, which is not exposed to the treatment condition, for comparison purposes. This design is depicted as follows:

Group	Time		
EXP	O	T	O
CTL	O	–	O

> **Note:**
> - **T** = Treatment condition
> - **O** = Observation or other type of measure
> - **EXP** = Experimental group
> - **CTL** = Control group

The control group allows the researcher to make several comparisons. First, the researcher can compare the experimental group's pretest and posttest scores in order to determine if the treatment had any effect. Second, the pretest and posttest scores from the control group can also be compared in order to see if they are different. If there is a difference between the control group's two test scores, it could not be due to the treatment, since those students did not receive any treatment. If an improvement in scores is found for this group, it may be due to the passage of time and natural maturation. Third, the groups can be compared based on both final posttest scores and gain scores (i.e., not only *if* scores improved from pretest to posttest but by *how much*) from pretest to posttest. The science teacher from our earlier examples could divide her classes into two groups so that one group (perhaps composed of three class periods) was permitted to use the new lab kits and the other group (composed of three different class periods) did not use the kits.

Ethical Considerations in Your Research

Making sure that action research adheres to ethical standards is the responsibility of the educator-researcher. As with other aspects of the job of being a professional educator, ethical treatment of students and colleagues—as well as their respective data—must be a key component of designing your action research study. Most universities and school districts have some sort of review process for ensuring that a proposed research study is conducted in such a manner so as to protect the rights of any human subjects involved. These are typically known as **Human Subjects Review Boards (HSRBs)** or **Institutional Review Boards (IRBs)**. These boards function by reviewing proposed research studies in order to safeguard and protect human subjects involved in a research study. An HSRB or IRB application usually requires the researcher to provide a summary of the proposed study, focusing primarily on the methods that will be used to collect data from participants.

Once you select a research design and begin to draft your research plan, one thing you must remember to factor in is that you will need to get permission from your students and their parents for the data—including audiotapes, videotapes, samples of student work, test scores, and observations in a teaching log—which you will collect. It is important to get permission from individuals because participation in any research study should be strictly *voluntary.* No one—adults or children—should ever feel coerced or compelled to participate.

In determining whether or not you need to get formal permission, Hubbard and Power (2003) suggest that you let your intended audience serve as your guide. If you and other teachers in your school will be the sole audience for your action research work, you may not need to get formal permission for any of the data you will ultimately collect. In this case, the data simply provide *diagnostic* information about a student, several students, or an entire school community. This is information that you and your fellow teachers routinely collect and use to help you make decisions related to teaching. However, if you intend on sharing your action research with a larger audience than yourself and the other educators in your school, you must get permission to use samples of student work, quotes from transcripts of audiotapes or videotapes, or observation notes that you plan to share with others. These "larger audiences" include not only journals where you might try to publish your action research or professional conferences where you might make a presentation but also such activities as presentations for other teachers in your district, to your school board, or to parents and other members of the community or a project for a college course (Hubbard & Power, 2003).

The basic idea of getting permission for conducting action research and collecting data on students is to protect the privacy of both students and their families (Hubbard & Power, 2003). This is typically accomplished by having participants sign an informed consent form. An **informed consent form** describes the nature of the research study, as well as the level of involvement of the participants (Leedy & Ormrod, 2005). In other words, it describes what the study is about and what it is you will be asking participants to do for you, in terms of activities and duration of those activities. This is known as the **principle of accurate disclosure**. One should note the key word "accurate" in the name of this principle. This implies that intentially deceiving your participants should be avoided at all cost; there is no place for deception in action research (Mills, 2011). At a minimum, an informed consent letter should contain the following:

- A description of the research topic and research study

- A description of what participation will involve

- An indication that participation is voluntary and that it can be terminated at any time without penalty

- A guarantee of confidentiality and anonymity

- An offer to provide a summary of the findings to participants

- A place for the participant to sign and date the form (Leedy & Ormrod, 2005)

When adults give you their informed consent by signing the form, they are in essence saying that they understand (a) the nature of the study, (b) what will be asked of them, and (c) that they can opt out of the study at any time without penalty. Furthermore, by signing the form, they are agreeing to participate in the study. A sample informed consent form is presented in Figure 4.2.

In the case of minors (i.e., individuals under the age of 18 in most states), two forms of permission must be obtained. First, since children are not of legal age to give their consent to participate in research studies, permission must be obtained from their parents or legal guardians. They are typically asked to sign a **parental consent form**. An example of a parental consent form is shown in Figure 4.3. Secondly, individuals who do not have the authority to consent to participate in research must still provide their assent. **Assent** is the term given to a child's agreement to participate in research. Assent from a minor must be obtained in a language that is understandable to him or her, and requires use of an age-appropriate (either verbal or written), as opposed to a consent form used to obtain permission from the minor's parents(s) or guardian(s). An example of a child's assent form is presented in Figure 4.4.

The issues of confidentiality and anonymity were mentioned in the requirements for an informed consent letter. There are a couple of ways that maintaining these essential characteristics of action research studies can be accomplished. First, your research plan might call only for the reporting of aggregate data. If you report the average test scores for two groups, for example, neither the names of individual students nor their corresponding test scores will be reported anywhere. Second, another common way to maintain confidentiality and anonymity in cases where data are not aggregated across students is to use fictitious names for individual students. If your research will be presented only locally—for example, within your school building or to a group of community members or the school board—it is necessary to change only the names of individual students. However, if your research will be shared with people throughout the state, region, or nation—in a journal or at a conference— you might also want to change the names of your school building, your school district, or even your town (Hubbard & Power, 2003). This is simply an additional level of protection of your participants.

In addition to the principle of accurate disclosure, as well as respecting the rights of and protecting your research participants, there are a couple of other ethical issues to consider when planning for action research (Mertler & Charles, 2011). The **principle of beneficence** states that research should be done in order to acquire knowledge about human beings and

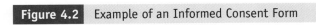

Figure 4.2   Example of an Informed Consent Form

Division of EDFI
School of LPS
Bowling Green, Ohio 43403
(419) 372-7322
FAX: (419) 372-8265

Bowling Green State University
College of Education & Human Development

Informed Consent Form

Principal Investigator (PI): Craig A. Mertler, Ph.D.
Phone: 419-372-9357
Project Title: *Development and Validation of the "Assessment Literacy Inventory"*

Purpose of the study	You are invited to participate with no obligation in a research study which has as its main purpose the development and validation of an instrument designed to measure teachers' assessment literacy. Working with a colleague from Northern Illinois University, it is our intention to develop and validate a new instrument for future research endeavors with K–12 teachers on the topic of classroom assessment literacy.
Description of participation	If you choose to participate in this research study, I would simply like to use the score you receive on a portion of your EDFI 402 final exam (consisting of the 35-item *Assessment Literacy Inventory*, or **ALI**). For purposes of the research study, all identifiers (i.e., names and identification numbers) will be removed from the scores. In addition, I would like to record the percentage of total points you have earned in EDFI 402. *The PI will not know who has or has not agreed to participate until after grades have been turned in at the end of the semester*. The information obtained from this study will be kept confidential and will only be reported in statistical analyses with no specific connections made to individuals. At no point will your identity be revealed. All data will be stored in a locked file cabinet, accessible only by the PI.
Guarantee of confidentiality	Your decision whether or not to participate will not interfere with your course grade, or current or future relationships with your instructor. You may choose to withdraw from the study at any time without penalty, and the PI may choose to cancel your participation at any time.
	Do you have any questions? (Circle one) **NO** **YES**
Voluntary participation	If you circled YES, please contact the PI, Dr. Craig A. Mertler, at the above phone number or by email at mertler@bgnet.bgsu.edu *before signing this form*. If you have questions or concerns regarding your rights as a research participant, you may also contact the Chair of the Human Subjects Review Board at BGSU at 419-372-7716, or at hsrb@bgnet.bgsu.edu. Do not sign this form until these questions have been answered to your satisfaction.
	YOU ARE MAKING A DECISION WHETHER OR NOT TO ALLOW THE PRINCIPAL INVESTIGATOR TO USE THE RESULTS OF A PORTION OF YOUR EDFI 402 FINAL EXAM (CONSISTING OF THE 35-ITEM ASSESSMENT LITERACY INVENTORY) FOR RESEARCH AND PRESENTATION PURPOSES ONLY. YOUR SIGNATURE BELOW ALSO INDICATES THAT YOU ARE OVER THE AGE OF 18.
Formal agreement to participate	I **AGREE** **DO NOT AGREE** (circle one) to participate in this research study.
Signature lines	Participant's Name (please print): _____ Date: _____ Participant's Signature: _____

Figure 4.3	Example of an Parental Consent Form

May 18, 2010

Dear [Parent]:

My name is Dr. Craig A. Mertler. I am a Professor at the University of West Georgia.

I am conducting a research study to examine how middle school teachers assess student learning in their classrooms. Specifically, I am interested in how teachers at these grade levels use scoring rubrics to evaluate samples of writing provided by their students. I plan to interview the teachers regarding ways in which they use rubrics. I am also planning to collect some limited data from middle school students and am asking for your child's participation in this research.

Your child's participation will involve responding to a brief, 10-question survey regarding the type of feedback he or she receives from the teacher in response to a writing sample. I will be asking students questions about the level and type of feedback they receive from their teachers, how meaningful that feedback is, and the extent to which the feedback helps them learn what they did well and where they need to improve. The survey will take approximately 10–15 minutes for students to complete.

Knowing how students feel about the type of feedback they receive from their teachers is important in my efforts to help teachers utilize rubrics more effectively. In addition, discovering how meaningful and helpful students find this feedback may help teachers improve their work in the area of grading student work.

If you or your child chooses not to participate, there will be no penalty. It will not affect your child's grade, treatment, services rendered, etc. to which you or your child may otherwise be entitled. Your child's participation is voluntary and he/she is free to withdraw from participation at any time without suffering any ramifications. The results of the research study may be published, but your child's name will not be used. Data collected will be kept confidential and will not be shared with anyone. I will destroy all data within one year of completing the study.

If you have any questions concerning this study or your child's participation in this study, please feel free to contact me at 678-839-6096 or cmertler@westga.edu.

Sincerely,

Craig A. Mertler

Dr. Craig A. Mertler

Professor and Director

Doctoral Program in School Improvement

By signing below, I give consent for my child to participate in the above-referenced study.

Parent's Name: _____ Child's Name: _____

Parent's Signature: _____

Figure 4.4	Example of an Assent Form

May 18, 2010

Dear [Student]:

My name is Dr. Craig A. Mertler. I am a Professor at the University of West Georgia.

I am conducting a research study to examine how middle school teachers assess student learning in their classrooms. Specifically, I am interested in how teachers in your school use scoring rubrics to grade your writing assignments. I plan to interview some of your teachers regarding ways in which they use rubrics. I also want to collect some data from students and am asking for your participation in this research.

If you agree to participate, I will ask you to fill out a brief, 10-question survey regarding the type of feedback you receive from your teacher after you turn in writing assignments. I will ask you questions about the type of feedback you receive from your teachers, how meaningful you think that feedback is, and how much you think it helps you learn what you did well and where you still need to improve. Responding to this survey will only take about 10–15 minutes and will be given to you during class time.

Knowing how you feel about the type of feedback you receive from your teachers is important in my work to help teachers utilize rubrics more effectively. In addition, discovering how meaningful and helpful you find your teachers' feedback may help them improve their work in the area of grading.

If you do not want to participate in my study, no one will be angry with you and there will be no penalty. It will not affect your grade in any way. Your participation is voluntary, which also means that you can change your mind and stop participating at any time. Your name will not appear anywhere on your data; you will be asked to complete the survey anonymously. Your answers to the survey will not be shared with anyone. Finally, I will shred all student surveys within one year of completing the study.

If you have any questions about my study, you can ask me or your teacher at any time. If you want to contact me with your questions, you may do so at 678-839-6096 or cmertler@westga.edu.

Sincerely,

Craig A. Mertler

Dr. Craig A. Mertler

Professor and Director

Doctoral Program in School Improvement

Please check one of the following:

_____YES. I want to be in the study. I understand the study will be done during class time. I understand that, even if I check "yes" now, I can change my mind later.	_____ **NO**. I do not want to be in the study.

Your name: _____   Signature: _____

the educational process; in other words, it should benefit someone or some group of people. It should never be conducted as a means of doing harm to individuals or groups or to denigrate, find fault, or suppress academic progress. A second principle is the principle of honesty. The **principle of honesty** is absolutely essential when conducting research and should not even seem necessary to mention. Honesty must be exhibited in all aspects of a research study—from the specification of the purpose of the research study to the collection and analysis of data and the ultimate conclusions drawn upon its completion. Action researchers must be honest with participants about the purpose of the study. They must also be honest about what data they collect and how they collect those data. Once collected, data must not be tampered with, altered, or suppressed in any way. If these stipulations cannot be adhered to, the research study should be stopped and, at a minimum, replanned. Finally, the **principle of importance**, similar to the principle of beneficence, indicates that the findings of research should somehow be likely to contribute to human knowledge or be useful elsewhere in the field of education. The potential value of the findings of research should be worth the time, effort, and energy expended, on the part of both the researcher and the participants.

Getting Organized for Your Research

Teachers often feel a bit overwhelmed once plans are in place for conducting an action research study. Narrowing the focus into a manageable topic, formulating research questions, deciding on an appropriate research design, getting permission from participants, collecting data, analyzing data, and writing up a final report may besiege even the most energetic of teachers. Rightfully so, because conducting these kinds of projects admittedly is not the easiest of tasks—if it were, more teachers would do classroom-based action research, not just those dedicated, reflective teachers (like yourself!). An important issue and concern for teachers is how to find the time to actually plan and conduct an action research study. One realistic suggestion is that any given action research project should be integrated within the context of what you typically do in your classroom. It should not be some sort of stand-alone endeavor that you have a difficult time relating to your instructional practices or simply finding the time to do. For example, consider our group of teachers from Action Research Portrait 1. Recall that their topic was to examine the extent to which improving teachers' assessments would improve student achievement. Notice that in this example, the teachers decided to focus their efforts on something they do all the time, something that is integrated throughout their instruction—developing and administering teacher-made classroom assessments. Their action research idea involved taking something that they already do in the form of developing assessments (e.g., written tests, performance assessments), working on improving the quality of those assessments, and determining if doing so has an impact on student achievement. As good, conscientious teachers, this is something they would likely do as part of their classroom practice; they are simply choosing to collectively focus their efforts in this area.

Another important piece of advice that I can offer is to develop a *research schedule*. I construct one of these every time I begin to design a research study or undertake a large-scale project (including writing a textbook) of any kind—in my mind, these schedules are indispensable. I have seen too many researchers and teachers alike fail to complete a study or to maintain a reasonable time frame because they simply are not organized. A schedule helps keep me focused, provides an overview of everything that needs to be done, breaks down big tasks into smaller manageable ones, and provides me with an opportunity to pat myself on the back when I complete a given task. You may not adhere to your schedule precisely; even if you do not, it will still provide you with much-needed structure. An example of a research planning schedule sheet (adapted from Leedy & Ormrod, 2005) is shown in Figure 4.5. Notice that included in the right-hand column is a series of check boxes—an opportunity for you to reward yourself when you complete a task.

Figure 4.5   Sample Research Planning Schedule Sheet

Activity to Be Completed	Estimated Amount of Time Needed	Target Date for Completion	Task Completed? (✓)
			☐
			☐
			☐
			☐
			☐
			☐
			☐
			☐
			☐

Source: Adapted from Leedy and Ormrod, 2005.

Finally, it is important to note that just because you have developed a schedule, you should not be fearful of revising it whenever necessary. Sometimes, teacher-researchers find that, even though they clearly spelled out their research topic and investigative questions, they become interested in different aspects of the topic as they proceed through the study. They may find something that is more problematic, more interesting, or more relevant (Mills, 2011). Action researchers should not feel that they are prohibited from pursuing these new lines of inquiry simply because they did not constitute the original topic. Mills (2011) states:

That is the very nature of action research; it is intimate, openended, and often serendipitous. Being clear about a problem is critical in the beginning, but once teacher-researchers begin to systematically collect their data, the area of focus will become even clearer. (p. 93)

Do not hesitate to alter and refocus your research topic even if you are well into the data collection phase (Mills, 2011). Remember that when you as a teacher engage in classroom-based action research, you are doing it in order to benefit *you* and *your* students in *your* classroom. If your discoveries begin to lead you in a different direction, do not become anxious at the thought of going there. If you unintentionally stumble upon a new idea, a new question, or a different method or technique, simply adjust your research plan and schedule and continue your action research investigation. Ultimately, you and your students will be the beneficiaries of those alterations.

WRITING UP ACTION RESEARCH: THE RESEARCH PLAN

The research design was a posttest-only control group design. In such a design, students were randomly assigned to either the experimental group or the control group. The treatment (cloze sheets) was administered to the experimental group and not to the control group, and both groups were administered a posttest.

The unit of investigation was the individual student. The population of the study included seventh graders in my first four periods (n = 100 students). A list was compiled of the first 100 students in each of my classes, numbering them from 001 to 100 in the order that they appeared in my class rolls. From a table of random numbers, 50 students were placed into the treatment group and 50 students were assigned to the control group. Of the total, 42 students were female and 58 were male. Forty-two of the 100 students participating in the experiment had received all of their schooling within the county, while 58 of the participants had moved into the county after beginning their public school education elsewhere. Nine of the students in the research group were African American.

The experimental treatment consisted of the treatment group completing a set of teacher-made cloze sheets in addition to participating in class lectures and activities in a single unit of instruction. While the treatment group completed cloze sheets, the control group was completing reading assignments without being engaged in the completion of a written product. The treatment group had the cloze sheets graded on a "did it" / "did not do it" basis, and they kept the cloze sheets for use as a study guide.

The potential for the treatment group to be resentful of the control group for not having to do cloze sheets became a concern. This problem was addressed by stating that while only the treatment group did cloze sheets for the second grading period, the control group, exclusively, would be required to do cloze sheets during the third grading period. Neither group was told that only the data collected during the second grading period was used for data analysis.

At the end of the unit of instruction both groups were given a teacher-made multiple choice test that yielded a numerical grade with a potential scoring range from 0 to 100%.

Source: Weldon, 1995.

The qualitative research method that I used most closely resembles an emergent design. At the outset, my research design was not clearly focused. Instead, the questions I asked were broad and exploratory. These questions, however, did provide a strong beginning focus for my study. The idea of choosing a theme like rockets and using it to drive my physical science curriculum for an extended period of time really appealed to me. Then the idea of studying cooperative group learning in the context of an extended thematic unit enabled me to visualize a setting from which I wanted to make a detailed examination. My intention was to allow the research design to evolve as my questions became more focused and my data collection methods became more defined.

Source: DuBois, 1995.

⤙ ACTION RESEARCH PORTRAIT 1 ⤚

Enhancing Academic Performance Through Improved Classroom Assessment

Recall that the purpose of this action research study is to improve teachers' classroom-based assessments in an effort to improve student achievement.

The four teachers making up Team North at Jones Middle School have decided to examine the impact that improving their own classroom assessments will have on their students' performance on standardized tests. They were aware that the problem of students in their middle school earning good course grades but not performing well on the statewide proficiency tests was not unique to just the students in Team North. Teachers on the three other instructional teams—Teams East, West, and South—also reported a similar type of problem. During the summer, the teachers from Team North attended a 2-week workshop on the topic of classroom assessment and searched for literature related to their action research topic—improving student achievement by improving teachers' assessments.

(Continued)

(Continued)

The teachers decided to have one more meeting prior to the beginning of the school year in order to plan their action research study. Larry volunteered to take the lead in the discussion of a research design that the team should use in its study, since he had recently completed a course in educational research methods. He suggested that, since the statewide proficiency test is administered in October and in March, they use a pretest-posttest design. The students would be tested early in the month of October, and then the teachers could begin implementing their new systems of assessment in their respective classrooms. The students would then be tested again in late March. Larry explained that the teachers would then compare the spring test scores with the fall test scores. If the scores were substantially better, they could conclude that the improved assessments that they designed and used with their students resulted in improved test performance.

Susan cautioned the group, stating that that particular conclusion might not be the most accurate one. What if there was something else—not considered in the study—that resulted in improved test performance? Cathy suggested that they use some sort of other group of students as a basis for comparison. Larry suggested that they could use one of the other three teams in the building as a comparison group. They randomly selected Team East, whose students' scores would be used for comparison to Team North scores, and continued making plans for implementing their pretest-posttest control group design. They formally stated their research question as follows:

Research question:

Is there a difference in the scores received on the spring administration of the statewide proficiency test between students who are exposed to systematically improved classroom assessment and those who are not? If there is a difference, which group outperforms the other?

❧ ACTION RESEARCH PORTRAIT 2 ❧

Improving Reading Comprehension in a Title I Program

Recall that the purpose of this action research study is to improve students' reading comprehension skills within a Title I context.

Kathleen wanted to improve the reading comprehension skills of her fourth-, fifth-, and sixth-grade Title I students. She decided she would teach reading comprehension skills, as she typically had in the past, but would assess her students differently. She decided to design her in-class assessments such that the format mirrors that of reading comprehension achievement test is only administered in the spring in her district, she could not rely on that as a dependent measure, especially if she wanted to compare those scores to some sort of "pretest" measure. Although she administers diagnostic tests throughout the year, they differ in format and purpose from the standardized achievement test given annually. She decided to use a pretest-posttest design, where her pretest and posttest measures would consist of repeated administrations of the same diagnostic test, one occurring in September and the other in May. In addition, based on the reading she had completed, she tentatively believed that this intervention treatment condition would improve her students' reading comprehension skills. Therefore, she decided to not withhold the intervention from any of her students; in other words, she would not have a comparison group. She would implement a one-group pretest-posttest design.

Although Kathleen was happy with the plan for her action research study, she was not convinced that the test scores would tell her everything she needed to know about the extent to which her students' comprehension skills had improved. She decided to integrate some qualitative design aspects into the existing plan for her study, thus using more of a mixed-methods research design. She decided to make observational notes regarding what she saw on a daily basis regarding comprehension skills. She wanted to look at the degree to which students were able to correctly answer her oral and written questions immediately following the reading of a passage. In addition, she planned to periodically interview her students, asking them what they thought about their own progress in the comprehension of reading material.

She stated two research questions, one to be addressed with her quantitative data and one to be addressed by her qualitative data. Her research questions were as follows:

Research Question #1:

Is there a difference in students' reading comprehension skills following experience with teacher-developed comprehension items, whose formats mirror items on standardized tests, based on pretest and posttest diagnostic test scores? If so, what is the nature of the difference?

Research Question #2:

What are the perceptions held by students and their teacher regarding the students' reading comprehension skills, especially following experience with teacher-developed comprehension items?

Related Websites: Research Questions and Research Designs

Three related websites are featured in this chapter. The first two address issues related to developing research questions and provide several actual examples. The third site provides a thorough overview of various research designs, their notations, and their applications.

- Guidelines for Developing a Question **http://oldweb.madison.k12.wi.us/sod/ car/cardevelopquestion.html**

This page on the Madison (Wisconsin) Metropolitan School District website offers a list of 12 simple guidelines for taking your research topic and developing from it a research question. Examples of the district's guidelines include "one that hasn't already been answered," "something do-able (in the context of your work)," and "keep it close to your own practice; the further away you go, the more work it is."

- Action Research Questions **http://www.alliance.brown.edu/dnd/ar_quests .shtml**

  The Development and Dissemination Schools Initiative is a 5-year project of the New York City Department of Education's Office of English Language Learners [and the Education Alliance at Brown University. Teachers at schools throughout New York City have developed and implemented action research projects focusing on language and other skills of English-language learners. This particular page features a list of 20 teacher-developed action research questions, which may serve as wonderful examples for the beginning teacher-researcher. Several of the questions are followed by links to summary reports or slide presentations of their action research projects.

- Research Designs **http://www.socialresearchmethods.net/kb/design.htm**

  William Trochim's Research Methods Knowledge Base is a complete electronic research methods textbook. On this particular page, Dr. Trochim provides an overview discussion of various types of research designs; however, much more detailed information is provided on linked pages. In Introduction to Design (http://www .socialresearchmethods .net/kb/desintro.htm), he introduces the idea of research design and explains the various notational symbols. In Types of Designs (http://www .socialresearchmethods .net/kb/destypes.htm), he discusses the basic differences between experimental, quasiexperimental, and nonexperimental research designs. Finally, in Designing Designs for Research (http://www.socialresearchmethods .net/kb/desdes.htm), Dr. Trochim discusses several issues related to the implementation of studies that focus on cause-and-effect relationships. He also discusses what he believes to be the four basic design elements of any research design and includes several very helpful sample notational illustrations.

SUMMARY

★ A research question is the fundamental question inherent in any research topic under investigation.

- Qualitative research questions are typically open-ended, providing for a holistic view; quantitative research questions are more focused, usually on only a few variables.

- Research questions should not be stated in a manner that assumes an answer before data have been collected.

- Research questions should be based in the body of literature related to the topic.

- Research questions must be able to be answered by collecting available data.

- Research questions must be ethical and feasible to answer.

★ Hypotheses are tentative but intelligent, informed predictions about the findings of a study.

- Three types of hypotheses are the null hypothesis, the nondirectional research hypothesis, and the directional research hypothesis.

- The null hypothesis states that no effect, difference, or relationship will be found between variables.

- The nondirectional research hypothesis states that an effect, a difference, or a relationship will be found but does not specify the direction of the effect, the difference, or the relationship.

- The directional research hypothesis also states that an effect, a difference, or a relationship will be found and specifically indicates the direction of the effect, the difference, or the relationship.

★ A research design is the basic blueprint for conducting an action research study.

★ Qualitative research designs are less structured and more holistic in their approach to conducting a study than are quantitative designs.

- A case study focuses on the detailed examination of a single setting, a single subject, or a particular event.

- In observational studies, the researcher may participate as an observer, an observer as participant, a participant as observer, or a full participant.

- The constant comparative method is a qualitative research design for studies involving multiple data sources, where data analysis begins early in the study and is nearly completed by the end of data collection.

★ Quantitative research designs fall into four categories: descriptive designs, correlational designs, group comparisons, and single-subject designs.

- Descriptive designs include observational research and survey research and simply attempt to describe the current status of the phenomenon of interest.

- Correlational designs investigate the extent to which a relationship exists between two or more variables.

- Group comparison designs involve a manipulated independent variable and a dependent variable measured across all groups.

- Group comparison designs include causal-comparative designs (which explore the cause of an effect after the fact), preexperimental designs (which typically involve one group simply being "compared" to itself), and quasiexperimental designs (which involve two groups being compared to each other on a common dependent variable).

QUESTIONS AND ACTIVITIES

1. How would you describe the relationship between a research topic, a research question, and a set of hypotheses?

2. Think of a topic of interest to you and appropriate for an action research study. State the topic, a research question, and all three types of hypotheses for your topic.

3. Think of another research topic of interest to you. Develop a research question for investigating the topic using a qualitative approach and another for using a quantitative approach. Are your questions different? Could they be identical? Explain your answers.

4. Correlational research is a commonly used quantitative research design. The mass media, such as newspapers and television news, often summarize the results of correlational studies. Find and discuss an example of correlational research that has appeared in newspapers or on the news. Are there any misconceptions or misinterpretations evident?

5. For the two research questions you listed in Number 3 above, briefly describe an appropriate research design for each. Remember that one question will necessitate a qualitative research design, while the other will require a quantitative research design.

6. Based on one of the research questions and designs you listed in Number 5 above, draft an informed consent letter for parents or students. Make sure your letter includes all essential components as discussed in the chapter.

STUDENT STUDY SITE

Visit the Student Study Site at **www.sagepub.com/mertler3study** for these additional learning tools:

- Video clips
- Web resources
- Self quizzes
- E-flashcards

- PowerPoint slides
- Sample action research reports
- Full-text SAGE journal articles
- Chapter summaries

"What Do I Do With All These Data?"

Part III of this book exposes you to everything you ever wanted to know about data. In Chapter 5, you will learn about numerous techniques for collecting both qualitative and quantitative data. Several concrete examples (e.g., field notes, interview guides, interview transcripts, focus group interview guides, surveys, checklists, student self-assessments) are also included. In Chapter 6, you will learn techniques for analyzing your qualitative and quantitative data. Discussion of software programs that can assist you in these tasks is also presented. Finally, guidelines and suggestions for writing up the results of your analyses are discussed.

Collecting Data

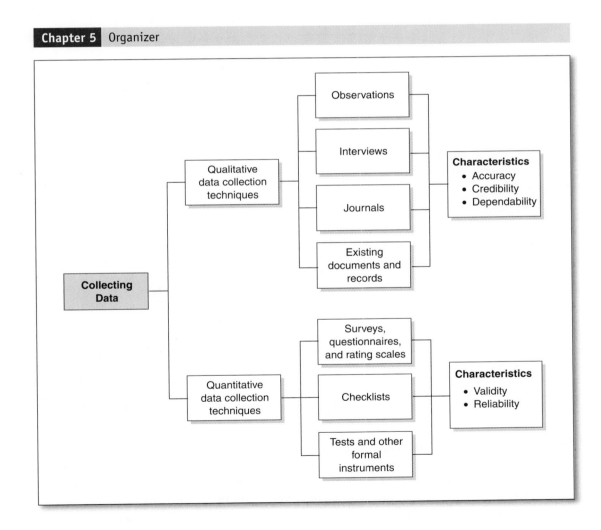

In this chapter, we enter into the second stage—the *acting* stage—of conducting a classroom-based action research project. Recall that the acting stage is composed of data collection, which will be discussed in the present chapter, and data analysis, the topic for Chapter 6. As you will soon learn, there are numerous techniques that can be used to collect both qualitative and quantitative data for your teacher-led action research studies.

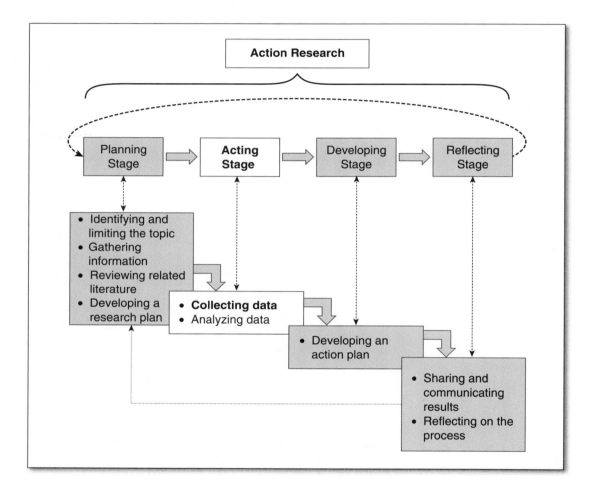

Qualitative Data Collection Techniques

Recall that qualitative data are *narrative;* that is, the data themselves are words. These "words" may appear in the form of interview transcripts, observational notes, journal entries, or transcriptions of audio- or videotapes or as existing documents, records, or reports. They may be collected using a variety of techniques, but it is important to remember that the resulting qualitative data will always consist of descriptive, narrative accounts.

Observations

As human beings, we are constantly observing and taking note of the world around us. Furthermore, as teachers, we are constantly observing our students. However, on a daily basis, we typically observe our surroundings in somewhat of a haphazard manner—something more akin to "watching" than observing. **Observations**, as a means of collecting qualitative data, involve *carefully* watching and *systematically* recording what you see and hear going on in a particular setting (Schmuck, 1997). Observations can be extremely useful in certain situations where other forms of data collection simply will not work, such as when teachers want to check for students' nonverbal reactions to something that is occurring in the classroom or when students are working in small groups in order to better understand how they interact and communicate with one another.

Classroom observations can range from highly structured to semistructured to unstructured (Parsons & Brown, 2002; Schmuck, 1997). **Structured observations** typically require the observer to do nothing else but observe, looking usually for specific behaviors, reactions, or interactions. Because so many other things are going on in a given classroom when observations are being made, it is often difficult to conduct structured observations. Classroom-based action research should never be done at the expense of your teaching (Hubbard & Power, 2003; Johnson, 2008); it should only be done in order to enhance and inform your teaching. **Unstructured** or **semistructured observations** allow the teacher-researcher the flexibility to attend to other events or activities occurring simultaneously in the classroom or to engage in brief, but intense, periods of observation and note taking (Hubbard & Power, 2003). In addition, unstructured observations are more typical of qualitative data collection, since they are "free flowing," allowing the teacher-researcher to shift focus from one event to another as new, and perhaps more interesting, events arise (Leedy & Ormrod, 2005).

Schmuck (1997) discusses several advantages of conducting classroom observations. First, teachers can gather data about *actual* student behaviors, as opposed to asking students to report their perceptions or feelings. Second, this enables the teacher to see some things that students might not be able to report on themselves. Finally, as you will see shortly, such devices as videotape recorders allow teachers to "observe" even more than they would normally be able to with their own eyes.

However, conducting observations also has its limitations (Schmuck, 1997). First, the simple presence of the teacher as a "data collector"—with notebook and pencil, or perhaps a video recorder, in hand—can change student behavior. There is a great potential for them to behave differently or to say different things if they know that they are being watched carefully. Second, in cases where specific behaviors are sought, and since behavior can be adversely affected due to the presence of an observer, the teacher-researcher may have to wait for extended periods of time in order to observe the desired behavior. Still, the desired behavior may never occur, even if it is a normal, everyday occurrence. Finally, if teachers are working together on an action research project, different observers may see different things, even while observing the same event.

Classroom observations are usually recorded in the form of field notes. Field notes are written observations of what you see taking place in your classroom (Johnson, 2008). It can sometimes be overwhelming to try to record everything that you see, especially when trying to determine what is important (and, therefore, worth recording) and what is not. Johnson (2008) advises teacher-researchers to simply "stop thinking and just write what you see" (p. 83). As you observe and record what you see, you will undoubtedly begin to focus on things that are interesting or important. As you make observations over time, patterns will begin to emerge from the data you have collected.

When recording field notes, you may want to consider dividing each page of your notebook into two columns. You should use the left column for recording your actual observations and the right column for noting preliminary interpretations of what has been observed (Leedy & Ormrod, 2005). Bogdan and Biklen (2007) refer to these interpretations as **observer's comments**, or *OCs*. Observer's comments often shed light on the emerging patterns from your observational data. Including observer's comments in your observation notes is also one way to integrate reflection into the process of action research. The separation of these two types of commentaries is critical so that *actual* observations are not confused with what you think the observed event *means*. Teachers conducting action research studies need to remain as objective as possible in the records kept and data collected. As an aside, this need for objectivity also dictates that you not censor what you record in your notes with your "teacher's eyes"—do not hesitate to record something even if it reflects negatively on your teaching (Hubbard & Power, 2003); after all, you are trying to learn about and improve your professional practice. In addition, interpretations of observations may change over time as you collect more data; having a record of these changing interpretations can be invaluable over the course of your study. An example of a page from a book of field notes that I recorded several years ago during a study of positive reinforcement in a preschool setting, depicting this two-column format of actual observations and associated observer's comments, is shown in Figure 5.1.

Written field notes can become problematic, however. They are often insufficient to depict the richness and the details of what one is observing (Leedy & Ormrod, 2005). **Videotapes** can provide assistance as a tool for recording observations, although they are not without their respective limitations, as well. Background noises may prevent you from hearing that on which you were hoping to focus your videotaped observation. Furthermore, video cameras can only capture what is happening in a given direction (i.e., the direction the camera is facing). Leedy and Ormrod (2005) suggest that, prior to beginning any formal observations, researchers should experiment and become familiar with various methods of recording observations in order to find what works best for the particular setting and situation. It is, however, important to remember that whatever mechanism you use to record your observations, you simply cannot physically record everything that you see or that is happening (Mills, 2011); it is best not to put pressure on yourself to try to do so.

On a practical note, several tips may facilitate your observations and the development of your observation skills. If you decide to observe and to record those observations using field notes, you may want to consider carrying a clipboard or legal pad with you for several days

Figure 5.1	A Sample Fieldnote Page, the Left Column Showing Actual Observations and the Right Column Showing Preliminary Interpretations

Obs. #3 June 10 10:15–11:00	< Observations >	< Observer's Comments (OC) >
Time	There were very few forms of interactions between the children and the teachers. The children were playing; behaving, for the most part. One of the teachers was pushing two girls on swings and the other teacher was sitting near the wading pools, watching the children. Carol said several things to certain children. She repeatedly used phrases such as, "Don't do that," "Don't throw water," "Don't throw that in the pool," and "You're gonna break the sprinkler . . . don't do that!"	I don't think that, in the entire time I was there today, I heard one positive comment or saw one positive gesture. It seemed that the teachers were in only a supervisory role. All they appeared to be doing was supervising the behavior and actions of the children in order to prevent accidents or injuries. I'm not saying that this is wrong; on the contrary, it is necessary when conducting an activity of this nature, especially with very young children. I just expected to hear some positive behaviors being praised in addition to the negative being addressed.
	Several children came close to hurting themselves and/or others. One 3-year-old girl tried to pour water over the head of a 1-year-old. Two boys were throwing beach balls into the pool and inadvertently hitting smaller children who were playing in the pool.	I began to wonder if this type of activity (i.e., supervisory in nature) did not permit the use of many positive comments. Maybe these teachers leave those types of positive reinforcement for classroom activities. Perhaps activities that require quicker thought and action on the part of the teachers—in order to prevent children from being hurt, or worse—don't allow for positive comments or identification of children to model positive behaviors.
	The children continued to play in the pools, the sprinkler, and the swings. I observed very little verbal interaction between the teachers and the children. Initially, most of what I heard came from Carol. She made several comments to the children, such as "Don't do that" and "You need to ride that bike over there." Carol's daughter picked up a garden hose and began playing with it. Twice Carol told the girl to stop playing with the hose and put it down, but to no avail. The third time she spoke to her, she said, "You better put that down or it will turn into a snake and bite you."	Carol's comment was not in jest. She said it with a firm tone in her voice. I didn't like hearing this. I was always taught never to threaten children, regardless of their age and regardless of how idle the threat. I find myself expecting to see and hear this kind of behavior from Carol and not from Marilyn, as I have not yet heard her say something of this nature.

prior to beginning your observations and recording any field notes. It is important that the act of recording field notes becomes a part of your daily routine, as opposed to something that "feels" unfamiliar, extraneous, or irrelevant. Similarly, if you decide that you will record your observations through the use of a video camera, you may want to set up the camera several days in advance of your recording. This is important because both you and your students, or other participants, will be more comfortable being videotaped if you and they are accustomed to seeing the camera in the classroom. Again, it becomes part of the daily routine or setting.

Interviews

An alternative to observing people is to directly ask them questions. This can be accomplished in several ways. *Interviews* are conversations between the teacher-researcher and participants in the study in which the teacher poses questions to the participant (Schmuck, 1997). Interviews can be conducted with individuals or with groups. It is best to prepare an **interview guide**, containing either specific or general questions to be asked prior to conducting any interviews.

Similar to observations, interviews are typically classified as being structured, semi-structured, or open-ended. In a **structured interview**, the researcher begins with an interview guide consisting of a specific set of predetermined questions. Those questions—and *only* those questions—are asked of each person being interviewed. This is typically done for the sake of consistency. Interestingly, consistency is usually not a concern when collecting qualitative data; it is typically more desirable for the researcher to have some flexibility and to be able to ask clarifying questions (not initially included on the interview guide), to pursue information not initially planned for, and to seek different information from different people (Leedy & Ormrod, 2005).

When gathering truly qualitative data, interviews are probably best conducted following semistructured or open-ended formats. In **semistructured interviews**, the researcher asks several "base" questions but also has the option of following up a given response with alternative, optional questions that may or may not be used by the researcher, depending on the situation. When developing interview guides, it is best to keep your questions brief, clear, and stated in simple language (Johnson, 2008; Schwalbach, 2003). For example, if we were interviewing students regarding their opinions of our school, we might ask the following questions, where the italicized questions represent the optional, follow-up, probing questions:

- What do you enjoy most about this school?
    - *Why do you enjoy that aspect so much?*
    - *Do you think other schools have this particular benefit?*

- What are your favorite academic subjects?
    - *Why is that your favorite subject?*
    - *Do you have any others?*
    - *What about extracurricular activities? Are there any that you participate in?*
    - *Which are your favorites? Why?*

- What do you like least about this school?
  - *Why do you like that so little?*
  - *Is there anything that the principal or teachers could do to improve that aspect?*

The semistructured interview guide that I used in my positive reinforcement study is shown in Figure 5.2, and a portion of the transcript from one interview that I conducted is shown in Figure 5.3.

Figure 5.2   A Sample Semistructured Interview Guide

Semistructured Interview Guide

Interview With the Director

- What type of training and/or certification is held by your classroom teachers?
- Do you have any advice or suggestions for giving positive reinforcement, as discussed with your teachers? How have those suggestions been received by your teachers? Have they attempted to implement them?
- What do you see as acceptable forms of positive reinforcement for children in your school?
- What do you think the meaning of positive reinforcement is for you? Do you think it is the same for your teachers? Why or why not Do you think it is the same for your students? Why or why not?

Interviews With the Teachers

- Has your director ever provided you with suggestions for giving positive reinforcement? If so, have you used any of them? To what extent have they been successful?
- What do you see as acceptable forms of positive reinforcement for children?
- What do you think the meaning of positive reinforcement is for you? Do you think it is the same for your students? Why or why not?

Figure 5.3   Portion of a Transcript From a Semistructured Interview, Using the Guide Shown in Figure 5.2

CM:	How would you describe positive reinforcement? How would you define that, or what does that mean to you?
"Carol":	Positive reinforcement means not yelling at the children. It means talking to them in a positive way. Sometimes you can lose your temper. I try not to use time-out a whole lot. I give them choices. If you're going to throw the blocks, then you're going to pick them up. If you're going to hit someone in the head with that toy, then you're going to go apologize to them. And tell them the difference between right and wrong instead of . . . take for instance E., who likes to throw toys at everybody. Instead of putting him in the corner and my picking up all the toys he's thrown, I make a game out of it. Instead of "E., pick them up, pick them up," we count them as we put them in. So he's still having to do what he did—you know, having to clean up his mess—but we're making a game out of it. Instead of "this was wrong and you're going to sit in the corner for this."

(Continued)

(Continued)
CM: So they don't see it so much as a punishment. Rather, you try to turn it into something constructive?
"Carol": Right. Like this morning, he punched a little girl in the face, and Gail and I both agreed that he needs to sit out of the group for a little while.
CM: So it really depends on the situation? It would be hard to take that situation and turn it into something positive.
"Carol": Right. It depends on what they've done and if they keep doing it all day long. Then they need time away. That's why we have that carpet out there. If the child needs to leave the room and get away from the other children for 5 minutes, they go out and sit on the quiet rug.

Open-ended interviews provide the respondent with only a few questions, very broad in their nature. The intent is to gather very different kinds of information from different individuals, depending largely on how each interprets the questions. For example, an open-ended series of interview questions about school climate might include the following:

- What does "school" mean to you?
- What do you like about school?
- What do you dislike?

As mentioned earlier, interviews are conducted not only with individuals but also with groups. A **focus group** is the name given to simultaneous interviews of people making up a relatively small group, usually no more than 10 to 12 people (Leedy & Ormrod, 2005). This type of interview typically lasts between 1 and 2 hours. Focus groups are especially useful when time is limited and because people often are more comfortable talking in a small group, as opposed to individually. Furthermore, interactions among the focus group participants may be extremely informative due to the tendency for people to feed off others' comments. However, when conducting a focus group interview, it is important to ensure that each participant is provided with the opportunity to speak and share her or his perspective (Mills, 2011). There can be a tendency for one or two individuals to dominate the discussion; it is the responsibility of the teacher-researcher to closely monitor the discussion in order to prevent this from happening. The set of guiding questions I used for a study incorporating data collected via a focus group is provided in Figure 5.4.

Figure 5.4   Sample of Guiding Questions Used for a Focus Group Interview

1. (a) What were your overall perceptions of the process used to gather student feedback on your teaching?
(b) What aspects of the process did you like?
(c) What aspects did you dislike?
2. (a) How was the feedback you received useful to you?
(b) How was the feedback not useful to you?

3. (a) What changes have you made to any of your teaching behaviors as a result of the student feedback?

   (b) What behaviors, if any, are you considering changing in your teaching as a result of the student feedback?

4. (a) What unanticipated benefits did you experience as a result of this process of collecting student feedback?

   (b) What negative consequences did you experience as a result of this process of collecting student feedback?

5. (a) Is this method, that of using rating scales, the most appropriate way to collect student feedback?

   (b) What method(s) might work better? Why?

6. (a) For what specific school situations or student groups would this method of collecting student feedback not be appropriate?

   (b) What could be changed in order to make it more suitable in this context or to these students?

7. (a) Is this process feasible for teachers to conduct on their own?

   (b) If not, what would need to be changed in order to make it more feasible?

8. (a) How often should this information be collected from students?

9. (a) What specific things could be changed in order to improve this process of collecting student feedback?

10. (a) Based on your experience, will you continue to collect student feedback in this manner?

    (b) If not, will you continue to collect this information but do so by using a different method? Can you describe that method?

Upon completion of the above questions, explain to the participants that the meeting is about to end. Ask them to take a moment and think about what has been discussed. Then, one by one, ask them if they have any additional comments. If necessary, explore relevant or new comments in greater depth.

Qualitative data may also be collected via the use of e-mail interviews (Mills, 2011). With schools becoming increasingly networked, teacher-researchers can easily collect data from colleagues, parents, and students by sending out a series of questions in an e-mail message. One benefit of doing so is that when the respondent replies to your e-mail questions, the transcription of the interview has already been done for you. However, you must be cautious of possible ethical complications and realize that e-mail responses are not necessarily anonymous or confidential (Mills, 2011). Other individuals who may have access to a server may be able to intercept e-mail responses from targeted respondents.

Hubbard and Power (2003) also remind teacher-researchers not to forget about the value of **informal interviews**—that is, those that are spontaneous, that take place throughout the data collection process, and that are typically part of the daily interactions with students in a classroom setting. Teachers are constantly asking students questions, trying to gather various types of information from them.

Schmuck (1997) provides a discussion of the relative advantages and limitations of conducting interviews as part of action research studies. Advantages include the fact that interviews permit the teacher-researcher to probe further and ask for clarification in a participant's response to a given question. In addition, data can be collected—and, therefore, preserved—through the use of audio- and videotapes, although you want to be sure that individuals being interviewed are not made to feel uncomfortable by the presence of an audio or video recorder. Finally, for respondents who cannot or who are unwilling to share their thoughts, feelings, or perceptions in writing, sitting down and carrying on a conversation about them is often a reasonable alternative. On the other hand, interviews can be extremely time-consuming. Not only does it take time to collect data from individuals during a verbal conversation, but before the data can be analyzed, the interviews must be transcribed so that the responses can be read and processed. The general rule of thumb that I learned in my graduate school days is that for every hour of audiotaped interview, you can expect approximately 8 to 9 hours of transcription work, depending on the quality of the recording. Other limitations of interviews include the fact that respondents are not able to retain their anonymity. Many people are simply uncomfortable with a tape recorder lying on the table between them and the interviewer. Finally, respondents often fear that something they have said may be used against them at some point in the future. An additional responsibility of the teacher-researcher is to put the mind of the interviewee at ease about such possibilities.

Journals

Data journals may be kept by both teachers and students and provide valuable information into the workings of a classroom (Mills, 2011). In a way, **student journals** provide information similar to homework to the teacher, in that teachers can gain a sense of students' daily thoughts, perceptions, and experiences in the classroom. **Teacher journals** can similarly provide teacher-researchers with the opportunity to maintain narrative accounts of their professional reflections on practice. They truly become an ongoing attempt by teachers "to systematically reflect on their practice by constructing a narrative that honors the unique and powerful voice of the teachers' language" (Mills, 2011, p. 86) by reflecting not only observations but also the feelings and interpretations associated with those observations.

Class journals are another means of incorporating journaling into your action research data collection. A **class journal** is a less formal version of a student journal. Johnson (2008) suggests that a blank notebook be passed around the class on a periodic basis or put in a learning center for an extended amount of time. Students are encouraged to enter their thoughts, ideas, perceptions, feedback, or other forms of response, such as pictures or diagrams, as they wish. Teachers may want to provide some sort of guidelines for making entries into the class journal so that it does not become a "quasi-teacher-approved" form of graffiti that may be offensive to other students (Johnson, 2008).

Existing Documents and Records

Often, action research necessitates the gathering of data that already exist. Schools and school districts are veritable treasure troves of existing data. These data are essentially anything collected for a reason *other* than the action research study but are now being used as data for the study. These *existing documents and records* might take several forms, including (at the individual student level) curriculum materials, textbooks, instructional manipulatives, attendance records, test scores, previous grades, discipline records, cumulative folders, and (at the school or district level) attendance rates, retention rates, graduation rates, newspaper stories about school events, minutes from faculty or school board meetings, and standardized test scores perhaps disaggregated by grade level, gender, or ethnicity (Johnson, 2008; Mills, 2011; Schmuck, 1997). These various sources and types of data tend to be very *under*-utilized, especially for purposes of conducting action research. However, a word of caution is in order: Whenever using existing data, it is critical to make sure to follow your school district's approved procedures for securing access to these various types of data and that you use and report the results of any analyses in an ethical manner (Johnson, 2008).

Collecting existing data on students can sometimes become overwhelming—there may be *so much* information you want to collect. The dilemma often faced by educator-researchers is how to organize that information. A nice organizational tool that can aid in your organizational efforts is to record data on a common data form. In other words, you develop for your specific purposes and use a single form as a means of compiling various types of information, as opposed to having a conglomeration of loose papers stuffed in a file folder, for example. Several years ago, I was involved in a study that examined student attendance records, reasons for school absences, discipline referrals, and referrals for special programs and social services. That was a good deal of information to collect on each student. However, I designed a data collection form (see Figure 5.5) that allowed us to collect this wide variety of information on a single form, thus organizing and encapsulating it at the same time.

One possible type of existing "data" that should not be overlooked is that of classroom artifacts. **Classroom artifacts** include any written or visual sources of data, contained within the classroom, that contribute to our understanding of what is occurring in classrooms and schools (Mills, 2011). This source of existing data primarily incorporates work done by students as part of their schoolwork but is now used as data for action research purposes (Hubbard & Power, 2003). Such items as student portfolios or products resulting from the administration of a performance-based assessment or such less formal artifacts as students' responses to a teacher's request to explain the solution to a constructed-response mathematics problem can serve as prime examples of student-produced classroom artifacts.

| Figure 5.5 | Sample of a Data Collection Form for Existing Student Data |

Student Name	Days Absent	Reason for Absences Referrals	Number of Discipline Referrals	Reasons for Discipline	Referral for Special Program? (Y/N)	Referral for Social Services? (Y/N)	Retained? (Y/N)

Reflective Teaching

A final source of (usually) qualitative data is a process or instrumentation for examining your own teaching. Reflective practice is a huge theme that undergirds the action research process, so it only makes sense that it can also provide data the for action research cycle. Instrumentation that might help an educator more closely examine his or her actual practice can be immensely helpful in diagnosing areas in need of improvement when it comes to classroom instruction. These types of reflective data can be collected through self-evaluations, peer observations, daily journals or diaries (either individual or collaborative), or videotaping actual lessons. When reflecting on your own teaching, it is important factor in three aspects: (1) the actual event or lesson, (2) the recollection of the event or lesson, and (3) reviewing and

Video Clip 5.1
View a clip of Dr. Mertler discussing important considerations for data collection.

triangulation

responding to what actually occurred during the event or lesson. While all steps are important, this third step is crucial because it is where any follow-up *action* takes place.

Characteristics of Qualitative Data: Accuracy, Credibility, and Dependability

When collecting data for action research studies, it is important for teacher-researchers to ensure the quality of their data. If data collected for the study are imprecise, or if the researcher has actually measured something other than what was intended to be measured, at a minimum the data will be inaccurate and misleading. The larger concern here is that if the action research study is continued to its logical "end," the results of the study will follow suit: They too will be inaccurate and misleading. If that occurs, you have essentially wasted your time—not to mention that of your colleagues, students, parents, and anyone else involved in your study.

Validity of research data deals with the extent to which the data that have been collected accurately measure what they purport to measure (i.e., that which we intended to measure; Mills, 2011). When dealing with the validity of qualitative data, researchers are essentially concerned with the **trustworthiness**—for example, the accuracy and believability—of the data. Trustworthiness is established by examining the credibility and dependability of qualitative data. **Credibility** involves establishing that the results of qualitative research are credible or believable from the perspective of the participant in the research (Trochim, 2002c). On the other hand, the concept of **dependability** emphasizes the need for the researcher to account for the ever-changing context within which research occurs. The researcher is responsible for describing the changes that occur in the setting and how these changes affected the way the researcher approached the study (Trochim, 2002c).

There are three common practices, typical aspects of any qualitative research study, that can help ensure the trustworthiness of your data. The first of these is *triangulation* or the use of multiple data sources, multiple data-collection methods, and perhaps even multiple teacher-researchers in order to support the ultimate findings from the study (Glesne, 2006; Hubbard & Power, 2003). A given finding is supported by showing that independent measures of it tend to agree with each other or at least do not directly contradict each other (Hubbard & Power, 2003). For example, when you observe Susan *actually doing* something that she has *told* you in an interview that she does and that is also indicated on an open-ended questionnaire (see Figure 5.6), you likely will have more confidence in concluding that it is probably an accurate depiction of Susan's practice. In other words, your interview data has been supported by your observation data and by the questionnaire responses. Had any of the three sources of data contradicted each other, you likely would have arrived at a different conclusion, perhaps that Susan was telling you what you wanted to hear, although in reality she did not practice it.

A second practice that can help ensure the quality of your data is known as **member checking**. This procedure involves the sharing of interview transcripts, analytical thoughts (such as observation notes with observer's comments), and drafts with the participants of the

Figure 5.6   Triangulation of Three Sources of Data

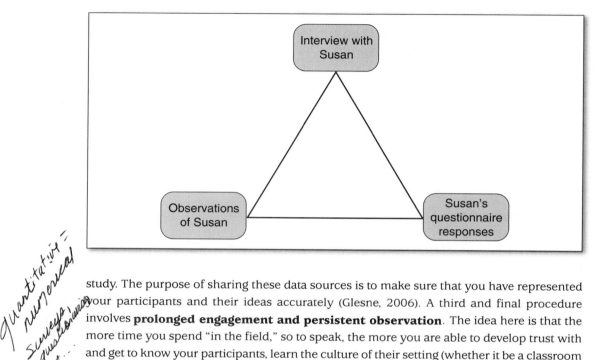

study. The purpose of sharing these data sources is to make sure that you have represented your participants and their ideas accurately (Glesne, 2006). A third and final procedure involves **prolonged engagement and persistent observation**. The idea here is that the more time you spend "in the field," so to speak, the more you are able to develop trust with and get to know your participants, learn the culture of their setting (whether it be a classroom or school building), and observe patterns of behavior to the point of being routine (Glesne, 2006). Observing or interviewing only once or twice will not afford you this luxury.

Quantitative Data Collection Techniques

In contrast to qualitative data, quantitative data are *numerical*. Anything that can be quantified (i.e., counted, calculated, tallied, and rated) can be considered quantitative data. This includes not only items that can be counted but also ratings of one's feelings, attitudes, interests, or perceptions on some sort of numerical scale. Quantitative data collection techniques include surveys, questionnaires, checklists, and rating scales, as well as tests and other more formal types of measurement instruments. Generally speaking, quantitative data collection techniques are more efficient, in that you can collect data from numerous individuals simultaneously. However, the depth of those data does not begin to compare to that resulting from the use of qualitative techniques.

Surveys, Questionnaires, and Rating Scales

The term *survey* refers to a collective group of quantitative data collection techniques that involve the administration of a set of questions or statements to a sample of people.

Surveys may be administered verbally—which then make them a type of interview, although the resulting data are numerical instead of narrative—or in written form. Surveys that are administered in written form, where the researcher asks participants to answer a series of questions or respond to a series of statements and then return their responses to the researcher, are known specifically as questionnaires. Surveys and questionnaires permit the teacher-researcher to gather a lot of—as well as a variety of—information relatively quickly (Johnson, 2008). There is not much that limits your use of surveys and questionnaires. They may be simple or complex; they can be composed of **open-ended questions** (where individuals provide their own responses) or of *closed-response rating scales* (where individuals simply select their response from a set of options provided to them). They may even contain a combination of the two types of questions or statements. Analysis of responses to open-ended items—which are, admittedly, more qualitative in design than are closed-response items—may often reveal unexpected thoughts and feelings from students, the likes of which you may not have been able to anticipate in order to develop closed-response items to address those particular thoughts and feelings (Schmuck, 1997).

A closed-response question or statement provides the respondent with a number of choices from which to select. For example, consider the following item:

What is your favorite subject in school?

☐ English

☐ Mathematics

☐ Science

☐ Social studies

Students would be instructed to select one of the four possible responses. This type of question is easily quantifiable; you simply count the number of students who select each option. Furthermore, it is relatively easy to report the "results" of this item. You might summarize your data and conclude the following:

35% of students responding prefer science.

25% of students responding prefer mathematics.

25% of students responding prefer English.

15% of students responding prefer social studies.

It is important to realize that this type of question may be misleading or controlling (Johnson, 2008). If, in our example, the favorite subject of a given respondent is a foreign language class, how is that person supposed to respond to the question? Any option that person selects will actually provide inaccurate information. One alternative is to anticipate such an occurrence by revising the item to read as follows:

What is your favorite subject in school?

☐ English

☐ Mathematics

☐ Science

☐ Social studies

☐ Other:

Open-ended items allow the respondents to provide a seemingly limitless number of responses. For example, we could have reworded our "favorite subject" question as an open-ended question by simply asking:

What is your favorite subject in school?

Here we might get a wide variety of responses. It is then the responsibility of the researcher to "analyze" the resulting data by grouping similar items together and then tallying the number of responses in each category. The result might look like this:

26% of students responding prefer science.

25% of students responding prefer English.

15% of students responding prefer geometry.

15% of students responding prefer social studies.

10% of students responding prefer mathematics.

5% of students responding prefer art.

2% of students responding prefer physical education or health.

2% responded, "I don't know" or "I don't have a favorite subject."

Obviously, this form of the question provides a more accurate sense of what students really like. The only problem associated with asking open-ended items like this is that you have the sometimes messy task of grouping responses into similar categories before you can count the responses (Johnson, 2008).

The main difference between a survey, or questionnaire, and a rating scale is that surveys are more appropriate for content-based types of questions (similar to our example above), whereas rating scales are appropriate when asking individuals to respond to a set of questions where their response indicates the strength (e.g., the extent of agreement, level of frequency, degree of understanding) of that response (Johnson, 2008). Rating scales can be used very effectively to measure students' attitudes, perceptions, or behaviors. There are two main types of scales that appear in items on a rating scale: Likert and Likert-type scales. A **Likert** (pronounced "lick-ert") **scale** begins with a statement and then asks individuals to respond on an agree/disagree continuum. The Likert scale typically ranges from strongly agree to strongly disagree. I typically recommend using a 5-point scale, with the 5 points defined as follows:

1 = strongly disagree

2 = disagree

3 = no opinion

4 = agree

5 = strongly agree

There tends to be quite a bit of disagreement among those with expertise in conducting research through the use of surveys regarding the appropriateness of including a neutral point on a scale. By including it, you allow your respondents to indicate that they truly are neutral or have no opinion, if in fact that is the case for them. However, if provided with a neutral option, there is a tendency for people *not* to think much about how they truly feel; they simply select the neutral option, which may not represent their true belief (i.e., the data they provide are inaccurate). On the other hand, if individuals *truly* are indifferent or have no opinion and you do not provide this option—because you are operating under the assumption that no one is truly neutral about anything—you "force" them to choose something that they do not really believe, thus providing inaccurate data once again. There is no right or wrong when it comes to deciding on the inclusion of a neutral point on your rating scale. However, you should consider the implications of both including and excluding such a point and then design your scale accordingly. Figure 5.7 presents a portion of a rating scale that I used in a study that focused on students providing their teachers with feedback on their classroom teaching. Notice the format of the Likert-scaled items. Also notice that a higher number corresponds to a higher level of agreement with a given statement.

A similar type of scale is a **Likert-type scale**. This type of scale also exists on a continuum, but something other than extent of agreement is being measured. For example, a Likert-type item might require participants to respond on a scale that examines quality ("excellent . . . poor"), frequency of occurrence ("always . . . never"), or level of comfort ("very comfortable . . . not at all comfortable"; Mertler & Charles, 2011). An example of a Likert-type scale, used in a study of prekindergarten-to-kindergarten transitions, is shown in Figure 5.8.

I want to mention one more thing about using surveys and rating scales with students. Teacher-researchers need to be sure that the various aspects—not just the reading level—of the instrument are appropriate for the age or grade level of students. Although I recommended earlier that a 5-point scale is typically appropriate, one could see how that might create difficulties for young children—they obviously would not be able to discriminate between adjacent points on the scale. However, do not shy away from using such data collection instruments with younger children. You would likely provide fewer options on the scale and perhaps even use graphics for the children to respond to. Several years ago, I was part of a

| Figure 5.7 | Portion of a Rating Scale Instrument Depicting a Likert Scale |

Student Evaluation of Teachers and Teaching Techniques (SE3T)

The purpose of this questionnaire is for you to help your teachers to improve. Several statements about your teacher are listed below. Please circle the number, using the code below, that describes how much you agree with each statement. Your responses will be anonymous; please do not place your name anywhere on this form. Please respond to each statement as honestly as you possibly can and by circling only one number for each statement.

1	2	3	4	5
Strongly Disagree	Disagree	No Opinion	Agree	Strongly Agree

1. My teacher tells me when I do good work.	1	2	3	4	5
2. My teacher encourages me to ask questions when I don't understand what's going on in class.	1	2	3	4	5
3. My teacher tells us why the things we are learning are important.	1	2	3	4	5
4. My teacher makes it clear how grades are determined.	1	2	3	4	5
5. I really pay attention in this class.	1	2	3	4	5
6. My teacher is fair when students misbehave.	1	2	3	4	5
7. My teacher teaches things in an order that makes sense.	1	2	3	4	5
8. My teacher takes time in class to help students.	1	2	3	4	5
9. This class is challenging to me.	1	2	3	4	5
10. My teacher gives fair tests.	1	2	3	4	5
11. It is important to me to learn the material in this class.	1	2	3	4	5
12. My teacher knows how to handle students who disrupt class.	1	2	3	4	5
13. My teacher uses my ideas in class.	1	2	3	4	5
14. My teacher explains assignments well.	1	2	3	4	5
15. My teacher returns tests without much delay.	1	2	3	4	5
16. My teacher has a sense of humor.	1	2	3	4	5
17. I am sometimes confused about what's going on in this class.	1	2	3	4	5
18. My teacher encourages good student behavior in class.	1	2	3	4	5

Figure 5.8   Portion of a Rating Scale Instrument Depicting a Likert-Type Scale

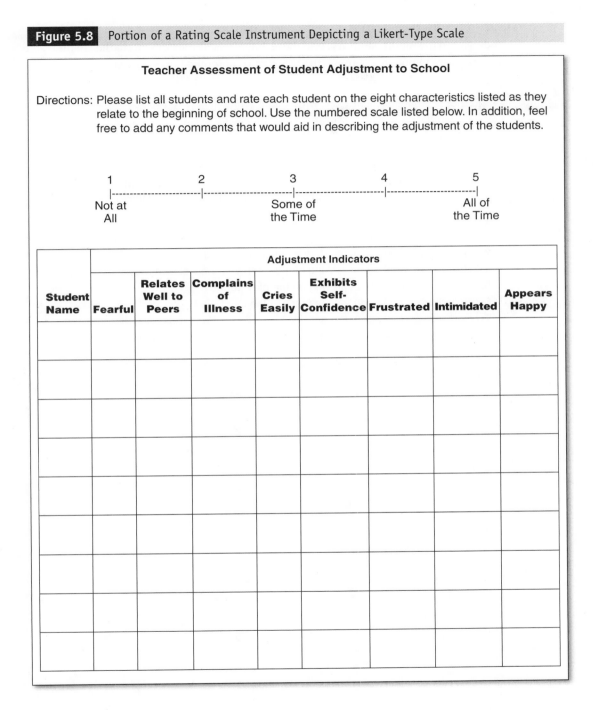

Teacher Assessment of Student Adjustment to School

Directions: Please list all students and rate each student on the eight characteristics listed as they relate to the beginning of school. Use the numbered scale listed below. In addition, feel free to add any comments that would aid in describing the adjustment of the students.

```
        1                   2                   3                   4                   5
        |-------------------|-------------------|-------------------|-------------------|
     Not at                                 Some of                                 All of
      All                                   the Time                               the Time
```

Student Name	Adjustment Indicators							
	Fearful	Relates Well to Peers	Complains of Illness	Cries Easily	Exhibits Self-Confidence	Frustrated	Intimidated	Appears Happy

research team that attempted to "survey" kindergarten students as part of the prekindergarten-to-kindergarten transitions study. We had the teachers read the statements to the children and then asked them to put an *X* through the face that represented how they felt (see Figure 5.9).

Figure 5.9   Rating Scale Instrument Used With Young Children

Student Self-Assessment Survey

Directions: Ask your students to think back to the very first day of Kindergarten. Read each item to your students and instruct them to respond at the appropriate space on the Student Self-Assessment Survey Response Form.

1. How did you feel about the first day of Kindergarten?
2. How did you feel about leaving home on the first day of Kindergarten?
3. How did you feel about meeting a new teacher this year?
4. How did you feel about making friends with your new classmates?
5. How did you feel about playing on the playground?
6. How did you feel about eating lunch in the cafeteria?
7. How did you feel about the activities you did on the first day of school?
8. How did you feel about leaving school at the end of the first day?

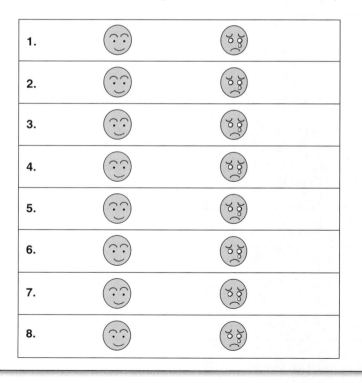

Unfortunately, the children had no idea—and our explanations did not help at all—what the numbers were for. They were instructed to locate the number "1" on their response sheet, as the teacher read the first statement number, and then place their *X* on the appropriate face. After the first few statements, we realized that they were simply placing the *X* over the same faces in the first row. Several of the children had response sheets that looked like this:

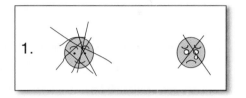

Obviously, you can see the problems that this created with respect to the accuracy of our data! On the spur of the moment, we decided to revise the nature of the response sheet and came up with what you see in Figure 5.10. Using this format, we could direct the children's attention to the box with a certain image in it and have them place their response only in that box.

The advantages of surveys and rating scales include the fact that they are very effective at gathering data concerning students' attitudes, perceptions, or opinions. They are essentially written versions of structured interview guides, where individuals respond to a specific set of questions in writing, as opposed to responding orally. Rating scales and other closed-response items can be answered, and the responses can be tallied or counted quickly. Integrating the use of computer software can make this process of tallying even quicker.

There are, of course, also limitations to the use of surveys for action research projects. Analyzing responses to open-ended items can sometimes be time-consuming, due to the fact that responses may be ambiguous (Schmuck, 1997). This limitation can be overcome by replacing open-ended items with rating scales or other closed-response items. Another limitation is that if the teacher-researcher is not clear about an individual response, there is no opportunity or mechanism for asking respondents to clarify their answers, as with interviews.

At this point, I would like to offer several suggestions—adapted from several sources (Johnson, 2008; Mills, 2011; Schmuck, 1997; Schwalbach, 2003)—regarding the development and use of surveys and rating scales as means of collecting action research data. When developing a new instrument, it is important to apply the following:

- Each item should focus on a single idea or concept.

- Do not use too many questions or questions that are not necessary or are repetitive.

- Keep the length of the survey brief and the reading level relatively easy; failing to do so often results in respondents not completing the instrument or providing you with inaccurate information.

Figure 5.10 Revised Version of Instrument Presented in Figure 5.9

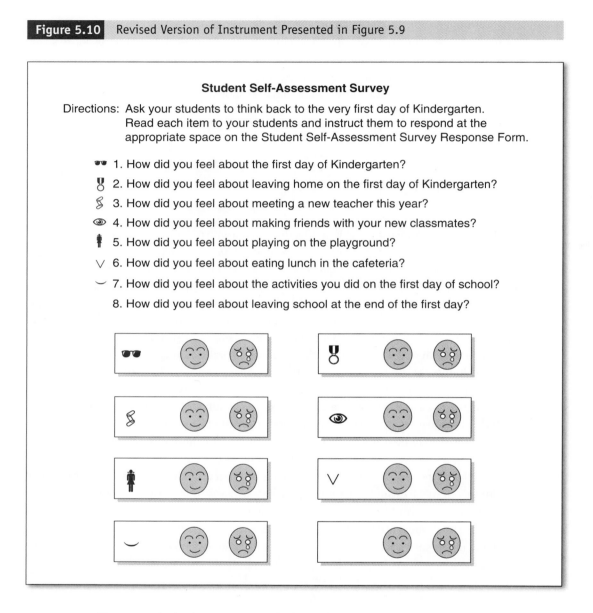

- If you are designing a rating scale, keep the response scale consistent throughout the survey. Otherwise, respondents can become confused or may provide you with inaccurate data.

- Consider using both closed-response and open-ended items, in order to realize the benefits of both.

Summative =
after
instruction.

Formative =
during
instruction

Chapter 5   Collecting Data   **141**

- Do not use leading questions; a good survey or rating scale is one that contains objective items.

- Always proofread your survey—and perhaps have someone else proofread it too—before you administer it to your participants.

Checklists

Video Clips 5.2 & 5.3 View clips of educator-researchers discussing data collection.

A checklist is a list of behaviors, characteristics, skills, or other entities that a researcher is interested in investigating (Johnson, 2008; Leedy & Ormrod, 2005). The primary difference between a checklist and a survey or rating scale is that checklists present only a dichotomous set of response options, as opposed to some sort of continuum. Instead of indicating the extent, degree, or amount of something, checklists enable the teacher-researcher to indicate simply *if* the behavior or characteristic is observed or present or if it is *not* observed or present. Checklists are quicker for the teacher-researcher to use than are surveys and rating scales; however, they provide data that are not nearly as detailed as those resulting from the use of rating scales.

If you are observing students, of any age, and are using a checklist to record behaviors, you will want to keep the list of behaviors or characteristics to a manageable number. Otherwise, you may become overwhelmed with the sheer volume of things you must observe and record on the checklist. A sample student checklist is presented in Figure 5.11.

Formative and Summative Classroom Assessments

When the focus of your action research study is on student learning, multiple sources of data can be utilized to help you answer your research questions. Many of these data are types that are routinely used in the day-to-day process of providing instruction to students and then assessing their mastery of those instructional objectives or units. **Formative classroom assessments** are those assessments that are administered *during* instruction, for the purposes of determining what sort of adjustments should be made to that instruction while it is still ongoing (Mertler, 2003). Formative assessments primarily include those that are informal and often administered spontaneously, such as observations, oral questioning, and student reflections.

Summative classroom assessments are those assessments that are administered *after* a substantial period of instruction (e.g., following completion of an instructional unit, end of a semester, end of a course), for the purposes of making administrative decisions, such as assigning final grades or simply providing a more broad overview of student achievement (Mertler, 2003). Summative assessments are more formal and their administration is usually scheduled in advance. Included here would be chapter tests, unit tests, end-of-course tests, major performance-based projects (e.g., research reports, research-based presentations)—typically any assessment that would measure student achievement and span numerous

Figure 5.11 Sample Student Checklist Looking at Independent Reading at the Elementary Level

Independent Reading Checklist

Student Name: _____

Grade: _____

Date: _____

Independent Reading Trait	Observed?	Not Observed?
Respects others	☐	☐
Stays on task	☐	☐
Chooses appropriate books	☐	☐
Stays focused on the story	☐	☐
Understands various elements of the story	☐	☐
Thinks about the story	☐	☐
Is able to answer questions about the story	☐	☐
Thinks about the characters	☐	☐
Is able to answer questions about the characters	☐	☐

instructional objectives and/or skills. Other formal assessment instruments that might be included here are scores on homework assignments and quizzes and final semester or course grades. If they are included as data in your action research study, it is important that they not be the only source of data (Johnson, 2008).

The advantage of using formative and summative assessments as sources of data in action research studies is that they are typically another type of "existing" data—not at the school- or district-level, but rather at the teacher- or classroom-level—in that they are routinely administered during the teaching-learning process. Therefore, incorporating these sources of data can facilitate conducting the study and make it somewhat more feasible, since designing data collection instruments *specifically*, and *only* for the study is not necessary. However, the disadvantage of using these data is the potential mismatch with the goals of your study. The conscientious and professional educator-researcher must ensure that these instruments will provide the data specifically required to answer the research questions stated at the outset of the study. Otherwise, these data—from the perspective of the action research study—are potentially meaningless.

In addition, there may be instances—depending on the nature of the questions and design of your action research study—where you might design a pretest and posttest specifically to measure changes that (hopefully) occur as a result of exposing students to some sort of instructional "treatment" or intervention. In this case, these may not be considered as existing data, since you designed and administered them with a specific research-related purpose in mind. They do, however, remain an important source of quantitative data.

Standardized Test Scores

Standardized test scores can also be used as sources of quantitative data. It is important to realize that these "formal" data collection instruments would also be considered "existing records," since they are administered to students as a regular part of classroom instruction and district-level accountability. Again, if these types of data are to be included in your action research study, it is advisable that they not be the only source of data; they can be supplemented with more "local" sources of data, such as observations, self-developed surveys, or other forms of existing data.

People in general, but especially educators, tend to have strong opinions when it comes to standardized tests. Regardless of how you might feel about them, they *are* a source of data that can be used to help answer a research question or address an instructional problem with which you might be struggling. I have argued for many years that since we are required to administer these types of assessments to our students, and since we receive their scores (usually as both individual scores and as aggregated scores), why not find a productive way to use them to help us make better-informed decisions about our instruction, curriculum, assessments, etc. The following quote summarizes my sentiments:

> *I honestly don't know anyone who loves standardized testing! But the standardized testing movement is not going away anytime soon. An examination of its impact on this country's educational system over the past 40 years will confirm that. Therefore I approach it from this perspective . . . and I strongly suggest that all professional educators adopt a similar attitude. Anytime we are given the responsibility of making decisions about children, we need as much information as possible in order for those decisions to be as accurate as possible. We ask students questions; we ask them to read to us; we require them to write for us; we test them over units of instruction; we observe them; we encourage them to be creative; we engage them in performance based tasks; etc. The results from standardized tests are just another source of information—about student learning, about our teaching, and about our curriculum. Please use them as such—add them to your long list of various sorts of information about student learning. They can only help improve the accuracy of the decisions that we make about our students, as well as our own instruction. (Mertler, 2007, p. xii)*

Characteristics of Quantitative Data: Validity and Reliability

Validity is an essential quality in quantitative research data and has to do with whether the data are, in fact, what they are believed or purported to be—in other words, did we *actually* measure what we intended to measure, based on the focus of our research? Though any data that you might collect may be entirely accurate, the critical factor is whether or not it is appropriate and accurate *for your purposes* (i.e., does it enable you to accurately answer your research questions?). For example, imagine that a reading teacher uses the results from the reading portion of a standardized test to group her students into above-average, average, and below-average reading groups. Then imagine that a social studies teacher uses those same reading scores to identify students who he believes would be successful in an advanced placement history course. The first interpretation and use of the scores is valid; the second is not. In terms of the social studies teacher's use of the data, it was invalid for the purpose for which it was used. The determination of the validity of data ultimately has a substantial effect on the interpretation of those data, once they have been analyzed, and the subsequent conclusions drawn from those results (Mertler & Charles, 2011).

Currently, validity is seen as a unitary concept (AERA, APA, & NCME, 1999), combining that which has been previously described as four distinct types of validity: content, concurrent, predictive, and construct. It is defined as the "degree to which all the accumulated evidence supports the intended interpretation of test scores for the proposed purpose" (p. 11). Validity of quantitative data can be determined through the examination of various sources of evidence of validity. Although similar to the four outdated types of validity, the five sources of validity evidence are unique in their own right (Mertler & Charles, 2011). These five sources of evidence of validity are based on the following: test (or instrument) content, response processes, internal structure, relations to other variables, and consequences of testing. Many of these sources of validity evidence are more appropriate for large-scale testing programs, especially where it is important for the results to be generalizable to much larger populations than simply those individuals included in a research study. Since this is not a purpose or goal of classroom-based action research, I am suggesting that teacher-researchers be most concerned with evidence of validity *based on instrument content.* This source of evidence is based on the relationship between the content addressed on a test, or on another instrument used for data collection, and the underlying **construct** (or characteristic) it is trying to measure. For example, assume we wanted to survey students to determine their attitudes toward learning mathematics. We would want to ensure that the questions we asked on the survey dealt directly with various aspects of learning math, not learning in any other subject areas or questions that were completely extraneous to the construct of "learning mathematics." As another example, consider a test you might administer to students on their understanding of the process of photosynthesis. If you wanted to be able to draw conclusions *specifically* about their understanding of this scientific process, you would need to be sure to ask only questions related to the process.

If unrelated questions were also asked of students on the test—and provided that they contributed to the overall score on the test—interpreting the scores as an indication of their understanding *only* of photosynthesis would not be a valid, legitimate use of those scores. This type of evidence is typically based on subjective, logical analysis of content coverage on the test and can be established by critical review by teachers, as well as by the judgments of experts in the particular content field. In other words, although it is a subjective process, it is important for teacher-researchers to critically examine the individual items and overall content coverage on a survey, rating scale, checklist, test, or quiz in order to ensure that they are measuring what they intended to measure.

Reliability, a second essential characteristic of quantitative data, refers to the consistency of collected data. If you hear three accounts of a minor car accident from three different individuals, but each account differs as to what happened, who was involved, and what the results were, you will likely have little confidence in any of the versions you have heard. In other words, the accounts (the data) are inconsistent and, therefore, unreliable. If, however, each account is essentially similar, the information you have received is consistent and may be considered reliable. Similarly, if you administer a certain test repeatedly under identical circumstances but find that you get different results each time, you will conclude that the test is unreliable. If, however, you get similar results each time you administer the test, you will consider the results reliable and, therefore, potentially useful for your purposes (Mertler & Charles, 2011).

As with the determination of the validity of quantitative data, there are several methods of determining the reliability of data (Mertler & Charles, 2011), not all of which are appropriate for teachers conducting classroom-based research. Reliability of quantitative data is usually established by correlating the results with themselves or with other quantitative measures. Three different methods are used—test-retest, equivalent forms, and internal consistency. **Internal consistency** is a statistical estimate of the reliability of a test that is administered only once. For this reason, this type of reliability estimate is most useful for classroom teachers conducting research. One of the easiest internal consistency formulas to use is the **Kuder-Richardson formula 21** (also known as KR-21). The resulting statistic will range from 0.00 to 1.00; the closer the value is to 1.00, the more reliable your data are.

We often think of validity and reliability as two distinct concepts, but in fact they share an important relationship (Mertler & Charles, 2011). It is possible for scores obtained from an instrument to be reliable (consistent) but not valid (measuring something other than what was intended). In contrast, scores cannot be both valid and unreliable—if scores measure what was intended to be measured, it is implied that they will do so consistently. Therefore, reliability is a necessary, but not sufficient, condition for validity. When establishing the validity and reliability of your research data, always remember the following adage: *A valid test is always reliable, but a reliable test is not necessarily valid* (Mertler & Charles, 2011).

WRITING UP ACTION RESEARCH: DATA COLLECTION METHODS

I teach eighth grade, comprehensive science (an integrated life, earth/space, and physical science program) at a middle school in a rural North Florida county. I am a member of a four-teacher team, along with one math, one history, and one language arts teacher. We instruct 130 students who make up the academic team (Team E). Although I teach five science classes a day, I targeted my seventh period class for my research.

This class is made up of thirty-one average and above-average science students. I chose this last class of the day for purely logistical reasons. With only one computer in my classroom, I needed to borrow eleven computers daily from neighboring teachers. Seventh period was the most agreeable period to the other teachers. An extra advantage of using the last period of the day was that students could return the computers after the final dismissal bell and not take valuable class time for this task.

My data was generated by comparing these students' attitudes toward learning science at the beginning of the school year, during my study, and at the conclusion of the study period. The students' attitudes and reactions were documented by the students themselves, by their parents, and by my own observations. Collecting data from three sources allowed for triangulation of the findings in this study. Data triangulation helped reduce the likelihood of error in the findings when similar results are reported from two or more of the sources. I surveyed all of the class members and their parents at the beginning and the end of my study.

During the first six weeks of school, I reviewed the scientific method, the metric system, scientific measurement, and laboratory safety. At this point, multimedia technology was not part of the curriculum. Some hands-on activities were used at this time. The students worked both individually and in groups. To determine each student's level of enthusiasm for learning science, during this time I administered a survey which contained the following questions: How do you like learning science? How have you liked learning science so far this year? How enthusiastic are you about exploring science at home? Students were asked to rate their answers to each question using a scale of 1 to 5. The scale was represented by (1) a very un-enthusiastic response, (2) an unenthusiastic response, (3) indifference, (4) an enthusiastic response, and (5) a very enthusiastic response.

Additionally, I sent home parent surveys with each student in order to solicit and record the parents' opinions concerning their child's enthusiasm for learning science. The survey included two questions: How enthusiastic is your child about learning science? How enthusiastically does your child do science activities at home? I used the same rating scale for the parents that I used with the students.

At the beginning of the second six weeks, I introduced a unit on oceanography. Oceanography was used as the unit of study primarily because of the number of resource materials available to the students through the media center. It was during this unit that I began to integrate technology into my curriculum. As the unit was introduced, I asked my students to look through the oceanography chapters in their textbooks and make a prioritized list of the eleven subtopics in physical and biological oceanography they would like to study. Students were grouped according to their interest as much as possible and were assigned to work in groups of two or three to develop a multimedia presentation that would be used as an instructional tool for the other students.

During this period, I began to introduce them to the multimedia computer program, HyperStudio (Wagner, 1994). HyperStudio is a program that allows the user to combine sound, graphics, and animation with text to make creative and entertaining presentations. The introduction of HyperStudio and the development of the student presentations took six weeks to complete.

Throughout the study I observed and made notes as to how the students were working and their reactions to class. These observations were guided by several questions: What problems are the students encountering as they work on their multimedia presentations? Are the students having problems with content? Are there problems working in groups? Are they having problems using the multimedia software? These observations and notes were useful in making sense of any fluctuations I found in the end-of-study student surveys. I was able to discern the source of problems so that content difficulties or friction within groups was not confused with a loss of enthusiasm for technology.

At the end of the oceanography unit I had each group of students share their presentations with the rest of the class. After the presentations, each group was asked to comment to the class on how they enjoyed developing their works. I noted these student comments as they were presented to the class. Each student was also asked to make written, individual comments to me, responding to the following questions: What problems did you encounter while you were developing your presentation? What did you learn about your topic while you were developing your presentations? Did you learn from the other students' presentations? Would you like to do another presentation on some other topic in science? Again, I surveyed the parents of these students to gain information about their child's interest in learning science. I asked the following questions: Is your child talking about science at home? Is your child eager to share what we are doing and learning in science class? Do you feel that your child is learning science? Why or why not? How enthusiastic is your child about learning science? How enthusiastically is your child doing science activities at home? I again surveyed the students asking the same questions that I had asked in the beginning survey.

Source: Hollis, 1995.

Two weeks prior to my starting date, a video camera was placed in my first period classroom and left on so that the students would become comfortable in the presence of the camera in the room. Students were given numbers on construction paper and asked to hold on to them for later use. On day one the first period class was videotaped for the first time. At the close of the period students were asked to complete a four-question survey. They were asked not to use their names, but instead, they were asked to use a number that was given to them earlier. I jotted down notes on how the class session went in a teacher journal.

(Continued)

(Continued)

The week continued with the second taping three days later. Student surveys were filled out for the entire week. Entries were made in the teacher journal whenever I could remember. This turned out to be about three times during that first week.

During the second week, the class was taped on Monday and Thursday. At the end of the second week modifications to the student survey were made on questions 1 and 3 due to mixed responses given by students. The modified student survey questions were:

1. *Did you share something in class today? Yes/No*

2. *If yes, did you share with:*
   a. *students only;*
   b. *teacher only;*
   c. *group of students; or*
   d. *group of students and the teacher.*

3. *Did you ask a question today? Yes/No*

4. *If yes, did you ask a question of:*
   a. *students only;*
   b. *teacher only;*
   c. *group of students only; or*
   d. *group of students and the teacher.*

I continued to tape my first period science class twice a week for a total of 5 weeks. Student surveys were given to all students on a random basis throughout the 5-week period. Journal entries were made daily.

Source: Graham, 1995.

❦ ACTION RESEARCH PORTRAIT 1 ❧

Enhancing Academic Performance Through Improved Classroom Assessment

Recall that the purpose of this action research study is to improve teachers' classroom-based assessments in an effort to improve student achievement.

The teachers who make up Team North at Jones Middle School felt very comfortable about the way in which their data would fit into the pretest-posttest control group design that they selected for their action research study. They developed consent forms that the students in Team North and the students in Team East, as well as their parents, signed.

The forms requested permission for the students' fall (October) and spring (March) test scores, resulting from the two administrations of the statewide proficiency test, to be used for an additional purpose—their action research study.

Approximately 4 weeks after each administration of the test, the individual student test reports came back to the school. For each of the students in the two teams, the four Team North teachers pulled the test report from the student's cumulative folder in the main office. From the test report, they recorded the scaled score (ranging from 200 to 500) for each of the four main subtests: language arts, mathematics, science, and social studies. They recorded the scores for each subtest (where "1" indicated the fall test scores and "2" indicated the spring scores), along with each student's identification number and team membership (where Team North was coded "1" and Team East "2") in a spreadsheet, which looked like this:

student_id	group	la_1	math_1	sci_1	ss_1	la_2	math_2	sci_2	ss_2
00013579	1	355	410	400	450	370	480	410	460
00024680	1	350	250	420	380	370	260	430	420
00012345	2	410	450	460	390	460	440	460	400
00098765	2	380	290	400	430	410	310	380	280

They double-checked each of the students' test scores across the two administrations of the proficiency test for accuracy of entry into the database. When all of the scores had been verified, they prepared their data (and themselves) for the next step—data analysis!

⟨ ACTION RESEARCH PORTRAIT 2 ⟩

Improving Reading Comprehension in a Title I Program

Recall that the purpose of this action research study is to improve students' reading comprehension skills within a Title I context.

In order to address her initial research question—which proposed to examine differences in students' reading comprehension skills following the use of revised teacher-developed comprehension items, based on pretest and posttest diagnostic test scores—Kathleen needed to select an appropriate and valid measure of reading comprehension. After reviewing the various diagnostic tests with which she was familiar and had experience administering, Kathleen selected the Woodcock Reading Mastery Test–Revised (Form H) to administer to her reading students in September and in May. From the resulting

(Continued)

(Continued)

student score reports, she would extract the Reading Comprehension Cluster score, which appears as a percentile rank. An average score on this subtest is the 50th percentile; Kathleen's upper-elementary students typically score near the 35th percentile. She obviously hoped to improve that performance over the course of the school year.

Kathleen's second research question dealt with the perceptions held by both her students and herself regarding the students' reading comprehension skills. She proposed to collect two forms of data to enable her to address the nature of those perceptions. First, she would conduct daily observations of her students and record both what she saw and any analytical thoughts she may have had while conducting the observations. The focus of her observations would be the degree to which the students could answer oral and written questions after having read a passage from a book. Specifically, she would look for how her students used the strategies for reading comprehension that they had been taught. Second, Kathleen also wanted to periodically ask her students direct questions regarding the use of those reading comprehension strategies. She designed a semistructured interview guide for conducting these student interviews. Her interview guide included the following questions:

- What does "reading comprehension" mean to you?
- Do you have trouble understanding what you read?
- Why do you think you have trouble?
- What helps someone understand what he or she has read?
- Do you ever do any of these things?
- What strategies do you use to help you understand what you read?
- Do you enjoy reading?

Kathleen planned to interview each student at least twice at roughly 2-month intervals during the course of her action research project. She anticipated learning more about their perceptions of reading, in general, and reading for understanding. She was also curious as to whether those perceptions would change over time.

Related Websites: Advice and Guidelines About Data Collection

The related websites for this chapter all come from the Action Research Website of the Madison (Wisconsin) Metropolitan School District. They provide several good ideas and suggestions for issues you may very well face when dealing with decisions about collecting data for your action research project.

- Guidelines for Data Collection **http://oldweb.madison.k12.wi.us/sod/car/cardata guidelines.html**

Offered here is a bulleted list of suggestions, or simply things to consider, when planning for your data collection. The page begins with the following statement: "Asking the right questions is the key skill in effective data collection." Guidelines included on this list are "Be clear as to why you are collecting data," "Be clear about how you are going to use the data you collect," "Decide how much data is needed," and "Use multiple sources of data to increase the believability of the findings."

- Techniques for Gathering Data **http://oldweb.madison.k12.wi.us/sod/car/ cartechniques.html**

Fourteen different techniques for collecting data are briefly described. The list includes many that we discussed in this chapter but also includes several additional techniques. These additional techniques include portfolios, still photography, and time-on-task analysis.

- Data Collection: The Five Ws and an H **http://oldweb.madison.k12.wi.us/sod/ car/car5wandh.html**

The authors suggest that, prior to actually collecting data, teachers should ask themselves several questions, listed on this web page. These questions fall under the following broader questions:

Why are we collecting this data?

What exactly are we collecting?

Where are we going to collect data and for how long?

When are we going to collect data and for how long?

Who is going to collect the data?

How will the data be collected and displayed?

SUMMARY

★ Qualitative data are narrative, appearing primarily as words.

- Qualitative data are usually collected through observations, interviews, or journals or by obtaining existing documents or records.

- Observations involve carefully and systematically watching and recording what you see and hear in a given setting.

- Classroom observations may be structured, semistructured, or unstructured.

- Unstructured or semistructured observations allow for the flexibility to attend to other events occurring in the classroom.

- Classroom observations are usually recorded in the form of field notes, which may include observer's comments.

- Interviews are typically formal conversations between individuals.

- Interviews typically follow an interview guide, which may be structured, semistructured, or open-ended.

- Interviews can also be conducted with groups of individuals in an interview known as a focus group.

- Interviews may also be conducted informally or via e-mail.

- Journals may also be kept by both teachers and students in order to provide valuable insights into the workings of a classroom.

- Existing documents and records, originally gathered for reasons other than action research, are abundantly available in schools and may be used as additional sources of information. These include classroom artifacts, such as student work.

- It is important for teacher-researchers to establish the trustworthiness of their data. This includes the accuracy, credibility, and dependability of one's qualitative data.

★ Quantitative data are numerical and include just about anything that can be counted, tallied, or rated.

- Surveys are lists of statements or questions to which participants respond.

- Questionnaires are one specific type of survey involving the administration of questions or statements in written form.

- Items on surveys can consist of open-ended questions or closed-response rating scales.

- A closed-response question or statement provides the respondent with a number of choices from which to select. Analysis of the resulting data involves counting the number of responses for each option.

- Open-ended items allow for a seemingly limitless number of possible responses. Analysis of these data involves categorizing responses into similar groups and then counting them.

- Surveys and rating scales are effective at gathering data simultaneously from numerous individuals, but they can sometimes be time-consuming to analyze.

- Checklists are a simple form of rating scale where only a dichotomy of response options (e.g., present or not present) exists.

- Tests and other formal instruments can be used as quantitative data, provided they are supplemented with other forms of data.

- Validity of quantitative data has to do with the extent to which the data are what they are believed to be.

- Reliability refers to the consistency of quantitative data and is determined statistically.

- Remember the following: A valid test is always reliable, but a reliable test is not necessarily valid.

QUESTIONS AND ACTIVITIES

1. Describe what you might see as the benefits of collecting both qualitative and quantitative data as part of an action research study. Do you envision any potential negative aspects or weaknesses associated with collecting both as part of the same study?

2. Why is it important for researchers in general, and specifically for teacher-researchers, to take measures to ensure the quality of their collected data?

3. Making good, sound observations typically requires some training, or at least practice. Find a location with numerous people (e.g., a shopping mall, your student union) and spend 30 minutes observing and making field notes on what you see and hear. Include any observer's comments as you deem appropriate during your period of observation. After the 30 minutes of observation, reflect on the experience. What did you think, and how did you feel? How could you improve your observation and note-taking skills for your next observation session?

4. Think of a topic of interest to you and appropriate for an action research study. Develop a semi-structured interview guide for a 15-minute interview with an individual. Be sure to include in your guide any "optional" probing questions. Next, interview someone using your guide. Afterward, reflect on your experience as an interviewer. What did you think, and how did you feel? How could you improve your skills for your next interview?

5. Using the same topic you identified for Number 4 above, develop a 15-item survey or rating scale that targets a specific audience, paying close attention to the guidelines presented in the chapter. Remember that a rating scale will use either a Likert or a Likert-type scale. Administer your instrument to at least five individuals. Afterward, ask them to provide you with feedback on the instrument. Reflect on the process of instrument development and administration.

6. Can you think of any existing documents or records that would support an investigation of your topic? What are they? How difficult would it be to gain access to them?

STUDENT STUDY SITE

Visit the Student Study Site at **www.sagepub.com/mertler3study** for these additional learning tools:

- Video clips
- Web resources
- Self quizzes
- E-flashcards

- PowerPoint slides
- Sample action research reports
- Full-text SAGE journal articles
- Chapter summaries

CHAPTER 6

Analyzing Data

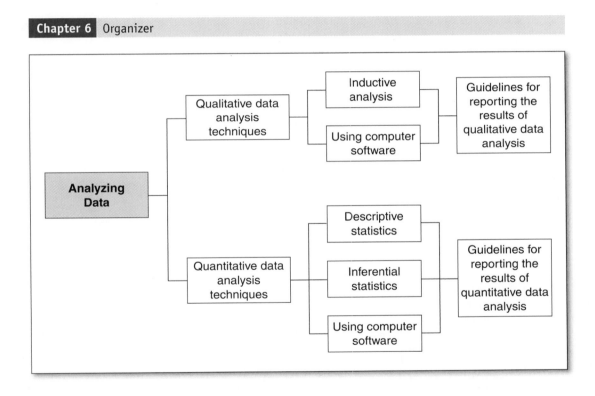

The second step in the acting phase of action research involves the analysis of all these data we have collected. Regardless of whether the study has relied on the use of qualitative data, quantitative data, or both, this is probably the step during which inexperienced researchers encounter the most anxiety. This may be due in part to the vast amount of narrative data that must be read, analyzed, coded, grouped, and summarized or to the fact that statistical analyses may be necessary. In any case, it is absolutely critical to remember that you must use analytical techniques that will provide you with the appropriate information in order to enable you to answer your research questions—in other words, your questions guide the decisions you make regarding data analysis. Your data analysis techniques must be aligned with your research questions. It is also important to remember that the primary goal of data analysis is to reduce vast amounts of data into smaller, more manageable sets of information.

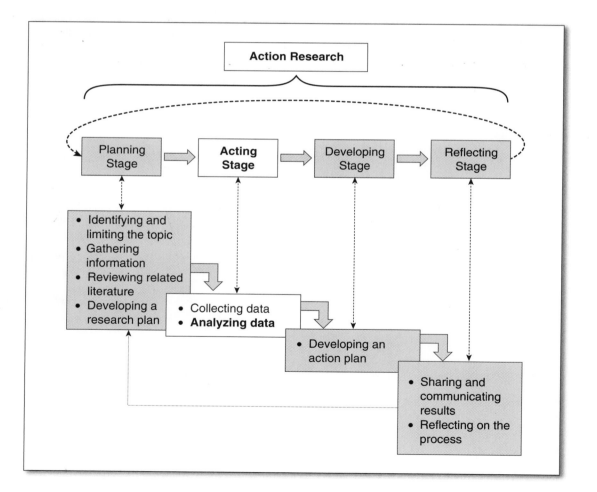

Qualitative Data Analysis Techniques

Recall from our introductory discussion of qualitative research methods in Chapter 1 that the analysis of qualitative data involves a process of inductive analysis. That is, when conducting qualitative data analysis, the researcher begins with specific observations (i.e., data), notes any patterns in those data, formulates one or more tentative hypotheses, and finally develops general conclusions and theories. Also worth reiterating is the fact that the process of analyzing qualitative data attempts to view the phenomenon of interest from a holistic perspective (Parsons & Brown, 2002), factoring in not only the data themselves but also the setting, the participants, and anything else that contributes to the uniqueness of the specific context under investigation.

qualitative

Inductive Analysis

After having gathered potentially voluminous amounts of qualitative data, the teacher-researcher may feel a bit overwhelmed with the task that lies ahead, as it can seem a monumental undertaking (Parsons & Brown, 2002). The real challenge in conducting an **inductive analysis** of qualitative data is to remember that you are trying to reduce the volume of information that you have collected, thereby identifying and organizing the data into important patterns and themes in order to construct some sort of framework for presenting the key findings of the action research study (Johnson, 2008). However, you want to be sure that, during this process of data reduction, you do not *minimize,* distort, oversimplify, or misinterpret any of your data (Schwalbach, 2003). Parsons and Brown (2002) describe the process of qualitative analysis as a means of "systematically organizing and presenting the findings of the action research in ways that facilitate the understanding of these data" (p. 55). They further describe a three-step process for conducting this analysis: organization, description, and interpretation.

The organizational step of inductive analysis involves the *reduction* of the potentially massive amounts of narrative data in the form of interview transcripts, observational field notes, and any existing documents or records that you have collected. This is accomplished through the development of a system of categorization, often referred to as a **coding scheme**, which is used to group data that provide similar types of information (Parsons & Brown, 2002). As you read through your transcripts, field notes, and documents looking for patterns and themes, you will notice categories of narrative information that begin to appear. You should make note of each category as it appears and code your narrative data accordingly. This is accomplished by searching for words or phrases that reflect specific events or observations and that begin to repeat themselves throughout your data (Mills, 2011; Parsons & Brown, 2002). Some researchers will do this with different colored markers or by organizing them on 3" × 5" index cards; others may actually use scissors to cut apart the pages of transcripts and field notes in order to physically group them together. It is important to find some mechanism for coding that works for you (Mills, 2011; Schwalbach, 2003).

In Chapter 5, I shared aspects of a study that I conducted on the use of positive reinforcement in a preschool setting. I conducted numerous field observations and interviews with staff members at the preschool that I visited. Once I had completed my data collection, I began to wade through my field notes, complete with observer's comments, and interview transcripts. As I read through my data, I developed the coding scheme that appears in Figure 6.1. Obviously, some categories contained much more data than others. However, at the time, I believed that all the categories had an important connection to my research questions.

After developing the categories, I began rereading my data in order to code the passages contained in my field notes and transcripts. I have presented brief passages from one observation session (see Figure 6.2) and one interview transcript (see Figure 6.3) demonstrating

Figure 6.1	Sample Coding Scheme Resulting From Data Collected as Part of a Study of Positive Reinforcement

Coding Categories Used in the Analysis of the Data	
Desc	Description of Site
TChar	Teacher Characteristics
TQual	Teacher Qualifications
Meth	Methodology
CAct	Child Activity
TBeh	Teacher Behavior
PInt	Positive Verbal Interactions
NInt	Negative Verbal Interactions
ObsAct	Observer's Actions
Res	Results of My Presence
CBeh	Child Behavior
MO	Missed Opportunity
Modl	Modeling
TCRel	Teacher/Child Relationship
Act	Academic/Social Activities
Sup	Supervisory Role
PR	Positive Reinforcement
NR	Negative Reinforcement
ChBel	Child Beliefs/Interpretations
TBel	Teacher Beliefs
TTrng	Teacher Training

how I coded these samples of my data. As you can see from the examples provided, some passages may be coded with one or more of the categories, depending on what is seen or heard, as well as what is *not* seen or heard.

Often, this process of coding data necessitates reading, rereading, and rereading again all of your narrative data. You will get to "know" your qualitative data very well during the process of inductive analysis. Be aware that this process of coding your data is not an easy one; coding schemes are not automatic, nor are they necessarily overtly apparent in your data (Parsons & Brown, 2002). It is truly necessary to spend a good deal of time reviewing the data, both during and following the development of your coding scheme.

The second step in the process of inductive analysis is to *describe* the main features or characteristics of the categories resulting from the coding of the data (Parsons & Brown, 2002). This is the stage of the analysis process where the teacher-researcher begins to make

Figure 6.2	Sample Page From Fieldnotes, With Passages Coded Using the Scheme Shown in Figure 6.1

One boy asked Carol to push him on the swing and Carol said, "What do you say? What's the magic word?" The boy responded appropriately by saying "Please," and Carol proceeded to push him.   **CAct TBeh CBeh**

O/C: *Why didn't Carol say anything in response to his correct answer? Especially when he gave it after being asked only once? What a perfect opportunity to say, "Very good!" or something. She seems to let many "golden opportunities" for giving praise pass her by. I have observed her miss these chances on many occasions.*   **MO**

Next, I observed Carol's daughter (the girl who has a tendency to misbehave). She wanted to push a bike across the sand, but was having some difficulty. The sand was too deep and the wheels kept getting stuck. She got Marilyn's attention and told her to push the bike for her. Marilyn replied by saying, "Why don't you help me push it?" The girl quickly agreed and they did it together.   **CAct PR**

O/C: *I was very impressed with this brief exchange. Marilyn didn't talk down to the little girl. Instead, she tried to work with her.*   **Modl**

Immediately after this, I noticed Carol playing catch with one of the older boys. They were standing about 15 feet apart. Carol threw the football and the boy made a great catch. Carol turned her attention to other children who were nearby.   **CAct TBeh CBeh MO**

O/C: *ARGHHH! She didn't even say, "Nice catch." This is frustrating to watch. A short comment like that might have meant a lot to that boy. Yet another apparent missed opportunity.*

Figure 6.3	Sample Excerpt From Interview Transcript, With Passages Coded Using the Scheme Shown in Figure 6.1

CM: Can you give me some examples of what you think are acceptable forms of positive behavior, at least as far as you're concerned—things that you would think would be acceptable for you to use with your children?

TBeh

"Marilyn": That's a hard one. [Laugh] Probably just talk to them.

CM: So, you see positive reinforcement as being mostly a verbal type of thing?

TBeh
PInt

"Marilyn": Yeah.

CM: Can you give me an example of something that you, like a concrete example of how or when you would use a verbal type of positive reinforcement and what specifically you might say?

"Marilyn": Well, I would talk like what I used all throughout the play period that we're going to. You're always telling them that maybe they shouldn't – well, not exactly shouldn't do something – but, you know . . . I can't explain it. I'm used to talking to 2-year-olds! [Laugh] Like I said, you go through that all day long, you know, telling them what to do and what not to do. Like to pick the toys up, pick this up before you go and get something else.

CAct
TBeh
CBeh

CM: Well, using that as an example, let's say that you asked the child to do that, to pick up that toy and put it back. Let's take both cases. Let's say first they didn't do it. What would you say in response to that child if they didn't do what you asked them to do?

TBeh
CBeh
PInt

"Marilyn": I would ask them twice, and if they don't do it, I will go and say, "I'm going to pick them up. Why don't you help me do this?"

CM: So, you're kind of modeling for them what you want them to do?

TBeh
Modl

"Marilyn": Yeah.

connections between the data and the original, or emerging, research questions. The categories need to be reflected upon (once again) and described in terms of their connection to or ability to answer the research questions. At this point, teacher-researchers should ask themselves the following question: How does the information in this category help me understand my research topic and answer my research question?

As you address the issues of connectedness of your data to your research questions, it is important to also look for information in your data that *contradicts* or *conflicts with* the patterns or trends that have emerged (Schwalbach, 2003). These discrepant pieces of information often tend to make your interpretations more difficult, but including them in the process will make your findings more accurate and meaningful to your future teaching.

The final step is to *interpret* that which has been simplified and organized. During this step, the teacher-researcher examines events, behaviors, or others' observations—as represented in the coded categories—for relationships, similarities, contradictions, and so on (Parsons & Brown, 2002). The key is to look for aspects of the data that answer your research questions, that provide challenges to current or future practice, or that actually may guide future practice. Because the teacher-researcher's background, experiences, and expertise will affect the ways in which the data are interpreted, descriptions—or, in some cases, concrete examples—should accompany the interpretations offered (Parsons & Brown, 2002). I have provided, in Figure 6.4, an excerpt from the final written report of the positive reinforcement study. Notice the discussion of negative comments provided by the teachers toward the children and the frequency of missed opportunities for offering positive feedback to them (which you saw earlier in the coded data appearing in Figures 6.2 and 6.3). Also, you should be aware of the way in which actual data (in the form of interview and observation quotes) that supported the interpretations were incorporated into the written discussion.

As you work through this process of inductive analysis, it is important to periodically step back from the data, your categorization scheme, and any interpretations you have begun to make (Schwalbach, 2003). This process of *introspection*—yet another way that *reflective practice* is integrated into the action research process—is important in order to ensure that you remain objective and "emotionally unattached" to your data (Schwalbach, 2003). This will permit you to inspect and interpret your data from a more open-minded perspective. Take your time conducting the analysis of your qualitative data—it will pay off in the end with more accurate and meaningful findings.

There are variations of the inductive analytic process. You read about one of these variations in Chapter 4, as it was specifically discussed as a qualitative research design. However, it is also appropriate to discuss the *constant comparative method* as a means of analyzing qualitative data. This method of analysis incorporates the main processes of inductive analysis—namely, the reduction and organization of the volume of information that has been collected in order to construct a framework for presenting key findings—but at the same time it incorporates a complex, iterative process of data collection and coding. In a manner of speaking, the constant comparative method of analysis is a means of applying inductive analysis to multidata sources within a given study, as well as perhaps multisite studies. As was described in Chapter 4, this technique is complex and requires the ability to think analytically. However, it is an important method of controlling the scope of data collection and analysis and for making multisite studies relevant and feasible (Bogdan & Biklen, 2007).

Video Clip 6.1
View a clip of Dr. Mertler discussing analysis of data.

Figure 6.4	Excerpt From the Final Research Report Documenting the "Negative Comments" and "Missed Opportunities" for Positive Reinforcement

Unfortunately, as she became preoccupied with disruptive, off-task behavior, Carol seemed to forget about those children who were on-task. One of the boys finished his painting and held it up to show Carol. He exclaimed, "Look what I did!" He seemed very proud of himself. Carol replied, "What is it?" The boy looked away and did not answer. She appeared to let opportunities to offer positive reinforcement pass her by—truly a "missed opportunity." For example, she might have responded to the boy's prideful comment by saying something like, "Oh, that's very nice! Can you tell me what you painted?" From my own experience, I know that in situations dealing with disruptive behaviors it is often difficult to remember to do the "little things."

Although many of Carol's comments directed at the children were negative, most of the time they were not made with a harsh tone of voice. Sometimes, they were spoken in an almost "pleasant" tone of voice. It was difficult to understand what she meant when she said something negative but in a positive tone. I found myself wondering if, subconsciously, the children were having the same difficulty (i.e., is she unhappy or not?).

Circle time is an activity where everyone sits on the floor in a circle and discusses daily events, including the day of the week, the month and year, projects they will be working on that day, and any special events occurring that day. During my observation of Carol's circle time activity, many of the children exhibited negative, off-task behaviors. In nearly every case, Carol responded with negative statements or actions. During the discussion of the day of the week, for example, Carol's daughter began taking things off the calendar. Carol's initial response to the girl was to threaten to send her to time-out. I do not know if Carol would have actually sent her to time-out, but again the situation was dealt with in a negative fashion and with a threat directed toward the child.

It was during circle time that I began to notice something about Carol. She seemed to be focusing only on the negative behaviors exhibited by the children, and doing so consistently. For each one that was misbehaving, there were two or three who were following directions. I expected Carol to identify those who were behaving and complement their actions, perhaps even single them out as models for the others. Unfortunately, I never saw her do this. She only concentrated on the negative displays—more "missed opportunities."

Using Computer Software to Assist With Qualitative Data Analysis

More and more computer software is being developed to assist with the analysis of qualitative data. As Mills (2011) is quick to point out, the key word here is *assist*. There is a typical misconception that qualitative data analysis software will actually "do" the analysis for you. Unfortunately, it will not. Remember that qualitative data analysis requires the use of inductive logic, which can only occur in the human brain. Even advanced technologies cannot take the place of human logic.

What qualitative analysis software will do is help you store and organize your data, once it has been formally typed up using a word processing program. In addition, these software programs provide a system for developing a coding scheme and then electronically (as opposed to the use of colored markers or 3" × 5" index cards) coding and categorizing large amounts of word-processed data in the form of observation field notes, interview transcripts, and even open-ended survey responses. Once you have electronically coded all of your data, the analysis software allows you to search for specific terms or phrases and then collates all coded passages that are related to similar themes. The interpretation of those related themes must still be done by the individual teacher-researcher.

The use of qualitative analysis software is really only advantageous when you have a great deal of qualitative data. Mills (2011) considers "large amounts of data" to be those in excess of 500 pages of typed field notes and transcripts. This is typically not the case for the "average" teacher-researcher. In addition, if you are not somehow affiliated with a university, it is unlikely that you will have access to the software and the expertise of someone who can support you in its use (Mills, 2011). You can, of course, purchase the software yourself, but some programs can be relatively expensive, ranging from approximately $300 to $500. There are also several different analysis programs available online and free of charge, as well as others that offer free, downloadable trial versions (see the section titled Related websites: Guidelines and Resources for Data Analysis later in this chapter for the websites of several qualitative data analysis software programs).

Quantitative Data Analysis Techniques

When I first introduced the notion of quantitative research methods, I discussed the analysis of numerical data as being a *deductive process*. The quantitative researcher begins by identifying a given topic of interest that is then narrowed down to more specific questions that could be answered or hypotheses that could be tested. This process of narrowing down goes even further when data are collected and analyzed and conclusions about the research questions or hypotheses are derived. Depending on the nature of the investigation, teacher-researchers will utilize either *descriptive* or *inferential* statistics or perhaps a combination of the two.

Using Descriptive Statistics

Descriptive statistics are simple mathematical procedures that serve to simplify, summarize, and organize relatively large amounts of numerical data. There are three basic categories of descriptive statistics, all of which are frequently used by teacher-researchers. These categories are:

1. Measures of central tendency

2. Measures of dispersion

3. Measures of relationship

Following is a discussion of each of these three categories and the specific statistical procedures that comprise them.

Measures of central tendency are statistical procedures that indicate, with a single score, what is typical or standard about a group of individuals. These indices are commonly used when trying to describe the *collective* level of performance, attitude, or opinion of a group of study participants. In other words, a teacher-researcher might be interested not only in knowing how well individual students performed on a test following the implementation of an instructional innovation but also—and, perhaps, more generally—in knowing how a given class *as a whole* performed. There are three measures of central tendency: the mean, the median, and the mode. The **mean** is defined as the arithmetic average of a set of scores. To calculate the mean, one simply adds all scores in a set of data and then divides by the number of scores in the set. When the mean is calculated, the actual value of each individual score is taken into account. The mean is the most commonly used measure of central tendency, although sometimes its use is not appropriate. One situation where the use of the mean is misleading, and therefore inappropriate, occurs when there are extreme scores (commonly known as "outliers") included in a data set. Outliers are scores that are quite different, in that they are extremely high or extremely low when compared to the rest of the scores in the set of data. For example, suppose we had the following set of 10 scores:

Sample Data Set 1:

15, 16, 16, 22, 25, 28, 28, 28, 30, 32

The mean of this set of scores is calculated as 240/10 = 24. We would probably all agree that the value of 24 is fairly representative of the set of 10 scores. However, imagine that the 10th score in our data set above was not 32 but rather 132. The resulting data would look like this:

Sample Data Set 2:

15, 16, 16, 22, 25, 28, 28, 28, 30, 132

Although this scenario is a bit extreme, I believe that it makes a relevant point. In this case, the mean would be calculated as 340/10 = 34. Now, we could probably expect some argument if we tried to say that a mean of 34 represented what was typical for that group. How could a score of 34 be typical if only one person in the group even scored that high? In this situation, the mean is not a good—or at least not an *appropriate*—measure of central tendency.

Another situation where the mean may not be the most appropriate measure of central tendency is when Likert or Likert-type scales are being used to collect data. Imagine that we collected data using the scale first introduced in Figure 5.7, where the scale and Item #1 were as follows:

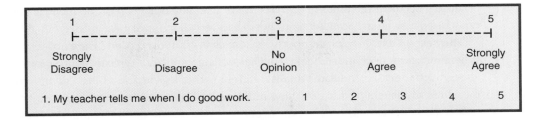

Further imagine that we begin to analyze our data by calculating the mean for Item #1. We received responses across the entire scale (i.e., ranging from 1 to 5). We sum all of the ratings and divide by the number of students who completed the instrument. We find that the average score for Item #1 is equal to 3.25. What does this score tell us about the extent to which the teacher tells students when they have done good work? How do we interpret that score? We cannot conclude that the average rating was "agree," nor can we conclude that students had "no opinion." This average rating is essentially worthless when we try to interpret its meaning.

In such situations as the two described above, the median may be a more appropriate measure of central tendency. The **median** is defined as the specific score in the set of data that separates the entire distribution in equal halves; that is, it is the score at which 50% of all scores fall below and 50% are located above. The median is obtained by first rank ordering all scores from lowest (on the left) to highest (on the right). If we have an odd number of scores in the set (see Sample Data Set 3, which has 11 scores), the median is simply the middle score in the series.

> Sample Data Set 3:
>
> 15, 15, 16, 16, 22, 25, 28, 28, 28, 30, 32

In this data set, the median value is equal to 25. There are five scores below this value and five scores above it.

However, if a data set contains an even number of scores, the median is determined by first rank ordering the scores, finding the two scores in the middle of the series, and calculating the midpoint (or mean) between the two scores. If we take another look at Sample Data Set 1, you can see that the two middle scores are 25 and 28. The midpoint (or mean) of these two scores is equal to $(25 + 28)/2 = 53/2 = 26.5$. Interestingly, we obtain the identical value for the median when we calculate it for Sample Data Set 2. The advantage of the median over the mean in this case is that the actual value of the outlier (i.e., the score of 132) does not have any influence over the value of the resulting median; it is simply one score higher than the midpoint.

The final measure of central tendency is the **mode** or the most frequently occurring score in the overall set of scores. In Sample Data Sets 1, 2, and 3, the mode is 28, simply because it occurs three times in each set, more than any other score. The mode is not used or reported very often because it tends not to be a very descriptive measure of group typicality.

The second category of descriptive statistics is composed of measures of dispersion. Where measures of central tendency indicate what is similar or typical about a group, **measures of dispersion** indicate what is different within a group of scores. Put another way, measures of dispersion indicate how much spread or diversity exists within a group of scores. There are two primary measures of dispersion: the range and the standard deviation. The **range** is calculated by simply subtracting the lowest score in a set of data from the highest score. The calculated range for Sample Data Set 1 is 32–15 = 17. The range for Sample Data Set 2 is 132–15 = 117. You can see how the range, similar to the mean, can be strongly influenced by outlying scores.

One way to address the issue of influential outliers is to calculate the **standard deviation**, which is formally defined as the average distance of scores away from the mean. The calculation of a standard deviation can be accomplished by hand, but the ease with which it can be determined through the use of statistical software—as you will see later in this chapter—makes its hand calculation essentially unnecessary. It is still important to remember that, since the value of each individual score is factored into the calculation, a standard deviation can be adversely impacted by extreme scores. However, since all distances from the mean are in essence averaged, the amount of influence is typically substantially smaller than it would be in the calculation of a range. It is important to note that measures of central tendency and measures of dispersion are used as the means of analyzing data that result from descriptive research designs (see Chapter 4).

The third category of descriptive statistics measures *relationships* between variables. There are numerous types of *correlation coefficients,* the name given to these various measures of the direction and degree of relationship between two variables. Obviously, correlation coefficients are calculated when analyzing data from studies using correlational designs (see Chapter 4). Recall from our lengthy discussion of correlation coefficients in Chapter 4 that correlation coefficients report the *direction* and the *strength* of the relationship between two variables. The coefficient ranges in value from –1.00 to +1.00. The direction is indicated as either a positive or a negative value on the scale. The strength of the relationship is indicated by the magnitude of the numerical value of the coefficient, where strong correlations are typically considered as those whose values exceed ±0.80, and weak correlations are those whose values tend to fall between –0.20 and 0.00 and between +0.20 and 0.00. A general rule of thumb for interpreting correlation coefficients is presented in Figure 6.5. Correlation coefficients can also be computed by hand, but statistical software makes this calculation fairly painless, so formulas calculating this measure will not be shown here. I would be remiss if I did not remind you of an important characteristic of any measure of relationship: correlation does *not* imply causation (see Chapter 4). Therefore, you must exhibit caution when interpreting these results and drawing conclusions based on correlational analyses.

| Figure 6.5 | General Rule of Thumb for Interpreting Correlation Coefficients |

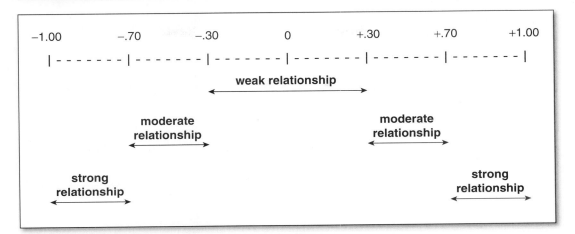

A final method for describing data is not really a statistical procedure, which is why it was not included among the original categories of descriptive statistical procedures. Data can also be displayed visually through the use of frequency distribution tables or through the use of graphs, such as histograms, bar charts, or pie charts. In a **frequency distribution table**, scores are arranged from highest to lowest, moving down the table. In a second column, labeled "Frequency," the number of individuals who received each score is listed; this is known as the frequency with which each score was earned. Finally, a third column presents the frequency value in terms of the percentage of total number of individuals at each score value. An example of a frequency distribution table is shown in Figure 6.6. **Histograms** can present the same frequency distribution information in a more visual manner. Presented in Figure 6.7 are the same data shown in the table appearing in Figure 6.6 but as a histogram. Notice that the height of each bar indicates the frequency of each score category.

Video Clips 6.2 & 6.3 View clips of educator-researchers discussing analysis of data.

When data appear in categories (as when Likert scales are used) as opposed to falling on a continuous scale (e.g., test scores), bar graphs and pie charts may be used. **Bar charts** are quite similar to histograms, except for the fact that adjacent bars do not touch (since the scale is not continuous). **Pie charts** can also be used to visually present categorical data. Figures 6.8 and 6.9 show a bar graph and a pie chart, respectively, for the same set of data.

Using Inferential Statistics

The goal of *inferential statistics* is to determine how likely a given statistical result is for an entire population based on a smaller subset, or **sample,** of that population. Inferential statistical procedures are typically used as the means of analysis for research designs that focus

Figure 6.6 Sample Frequency Distribution Table

Total Score	Frequency	Percentage
8	4	1.1
11	1	.3
12	3	.8
13	2	.5
14	6	1.6
15	9	2.4
16	15	4.0
17	16	4.3
18	17	4.6
19	21	5.6
20	22	5.9
21	23	6.2
22	37	9.9
23	28	7.5
24	20	5.4
25	31	8.3
26	29	7.8
27	24	6.5
28	16	4.3
29	17	4.6
30	16	4.3
31	3	.8
32	5	1.3
33	5	1.3
34	2	.5
Total	**372**	**100.0**

Figure 6.7	Sample Histogram for the Same Data Appearing in Figure 6.6

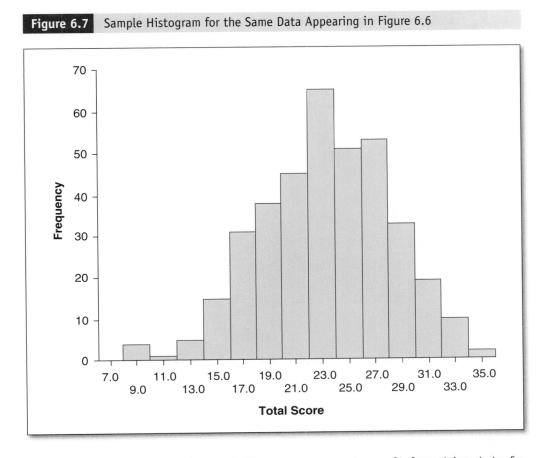

on group comparisons (see Chapter 4). The most common types of inferential statistics for these types of designs are the independent-measures *t* test, repeated-measures *t* test, analysis of variance, and chi-square test.

An **independent-measures** *t* **test** is appropriate for research designs where two groups—usually a *treatment* group, which has been exposed to some sort of new condition, and a *control* group, which has not—are compared to one another on a common dependent variable, such as a test score, for example (in other words, this design consists of *two* groups, each measured *once*). The mean scores for each group are calculated and then statistically compared in order to see if the difference between the means is statistically significant. If a difference between means is *statistically significant,* it is very unlikely that the difference could be attributed to chance. In other words, if the difference is large enough to be significant, it likely represents a *true* difference between those who received the treatment condition and those who did not. In contrast, if the mean values are fairly similar and the difference between them is small, we cannot be sure why they are different. Mills (2011)

Figure 6.8   Sample Bar Graph

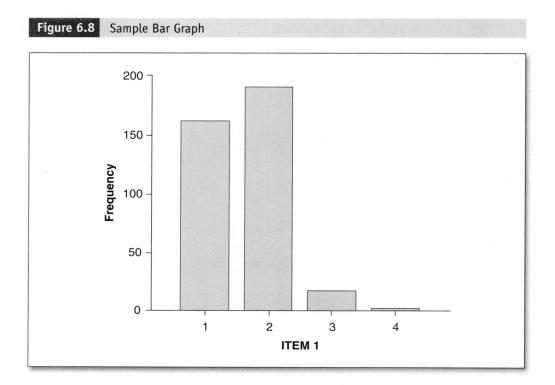

Figure 6.9   Sample Pie Chart for the Same Data Appearing in Figure 6.8

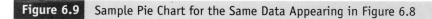
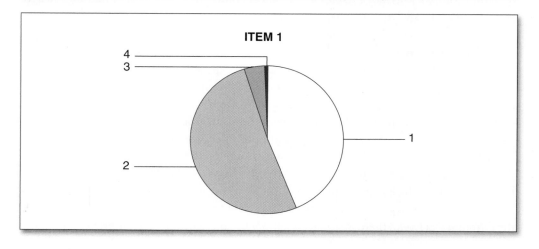

also points out the important distinction between statistical significance and **practical significance**. Statistical significance is determined statistically, while practical significance involves a subjective decision. Simply because a difference between two means is statistically significant does not mean that the difference will have practical importance. For example, there may be a difference between the mean test scores for two groups, but if one mean corresponded to a B+ grade on a letter-grading scale and the other corresponded to a B, there would be no real practical significance between the two (Mills, 2011).

At this point, you might be asking yourself how we go about determining if a difference is statistically significant. As a result of conducting the analysis, we obtain a numerical index known as a p-value. The **p-value** that we obtain from our analysis indicates the probability of chance occurrences in our actual study. The p-value that we obtain must be compared to the **alpha level** (symbolized with a Greek letter α and often seen in print as the "α-level"), which is typically set at 0.05 in educational research studies. An α-level equal to 0.05 indicates that we can be reasonably certain that only 5% of the time would the differences we obtain actually be due to chance, thus representing no real difference between the two groups. The rule of thumb for comparing the obtained p-value with the α-level and thus determining statistical significance is as follows:

> If $p < \alpha$, the difference is statistically significant.
>
> If $p > \alpha$, the difference is not statistically significant.

While the independent-measures t test compares the difference between two different groups of people, the **repeated-measures t test** compares two measures taken on the same individuals. This test is appropriate for designs where, for example, students are pretested, exposed to some intervention, and then posttested (in other words, this design consists of *one* group, measured *twice*). In this situation, the pretest mean is compared to the posttest mean for the same group of students. **Analysis of variance** (or **ANOVA**) is a variation of the independent-measures t test. The only difference is that it is appropriately applied in research designs where there are more than two groups (for example, *three* groups, each measured *once*). Whether there are three, four, five, or more groups does not matter—analysis of variance is still the appropriate statistical procedure to use for analysis. The three preceding types of analysis for comparing groups (i.e., independent-measures t test, repeated-measures t test, and analysis of variance) are compared in Figure 6.10.

Finally, there are times when the data you have collected are frequency counts with categories (e.g., the number of girls versus the number of boys who prefer a part method of reviewing for a classroom test), as opposed to scores resulting from another type of inventory. In this situation, a **chi-square test** would be used to statistically compare the number of students who liked the method to did not like it, for both girls and boys.

Figure 6.10	Contrasts Between Designs for Group Comparison Analyses

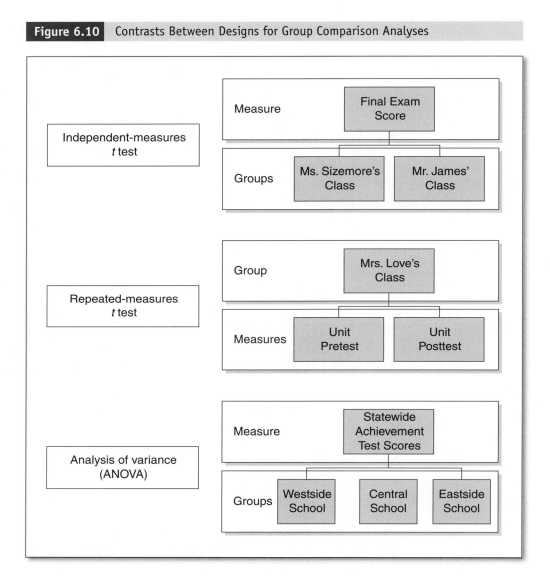

What you have just read represents an extremely quick overview of inferential statistics. Please note that I chose not to inundate you with statistical formulas for any of these inferential statistical procedures. Although both types of t tests, analysis of variance, and chi-square analysis can all be conducted by hand (with the use of a calculator), the advent of relatively user-friendly statistical software makes these analytical procedures much more feasible, as you will see in a later section of this chapter.

A Note About "Analyzing" Standardized Test Data

In Chapter 5, I discussed using standardized test scores as a possible source of data for action research studies. While the notion of "analyzing" standardized test scores is not really accurate, there is a science to *interpreting* them. Since test reports are typically returned to schools already having been "analyzed," the key—and, perhaps, the challenge—is for educators to be able to interpret the scores so they may be used for improving instruction, aligning curriculum, etc.

Most standardized test reports provide both **norm-referenced** test results, which allow performance comparisons with other groups of students taking the test, and **criterion-referenced** information, which provides data such as how many questions students attempted and how many correct answers they gave for each category of question. Language skills might, for example, involve subtests of spelling, capitalization, punctuation, and usage; while mathematics might break down to concepts, problem solving, data interpretation, and computation. Sometimes you will also be able to see the number of questions devoted to each area within a subtest (e.g., in the area of mathematics concepts, how many questions deal with number properties, with algebra, with geometry, with measurement, and with estimation). Typical scores reported might also include the following:

- *Standard (or "scale") score (SS):* A score that has been transformed mathematically and put on a scale to allow comparisons with different forms and levels of a test.

- *Grade equivalent (GE) score:* A norm-referenced score that indicates the grade and month of the school year for which a score is average. The average score for a fifth grader being tested in the seventh month of the school year would be 5.7. If a child has a GE score well above his or her grade in school—a fifth grader with a GE of 9.1 on a reading subtest, for example—it does not mean that the child can do ninth-grade work, but rather, that he or she scored the same as an average entering ninth grader would *if the ninth grader took the fifth-grade test.*

- *National percentile rank (NPR):* The percentage of students in the norm group that performed at or below a particular performance level. It is important to note the group to which students are being compared. Some test publishers provide separate norms for, say, large urban school districts across the country, or Catholic schools, while also providing norms based on a representative sample of testtakers across the country, and/or other groups taking the test in the state.

- *Normal curve equivalent (NCE):* A normalized standardized score with a mean of 50 and a standard deviation of 21.06, resulting in a near equal interval scale from 0 to 99. The NCE was developed by RMC Research Corporation in 1976 to measure the effectiveness of the Title I Program across the United States and is often used to measure gains over time.

- *National stanine (NS)*: Stanine scores range from 1 to 9, with a score of 5 representing an average range. The percentage of scores at each stanine level in a normalized standard score scale is 4, 7, 12, 17, 20, 17, 12, 7, and 4, respectively. Percentile rank scores provide similar, though more precise, information. For example, a percentile rank near the middle of the distribution (e.g., 45 to 55) will be roughly equivalent to a stanine score of 5. A class test report might also present a graphic illustrating *confidence bands,* which represent the margins of error for individual subtests. Studying them will permit a teacher to get a quick overview of class performance because non-overlapping bands indicate that scores are truly or significantly different from each other. For example, the students in a class might perform significantly lower on "Vocabulary" than on "Reading Comprehension."

Educators can learn to use empirical test data to assist in instructional decision-making for their classes or for individual students. To avoid being overwhelmed by data, especially since much of the information provided on test reports is analogous, it is sometimes beneficial to begin by focusing on such scores as national percentile ranks and their associated confidence bands. Interpreting standardized test data for use in making instructional decisions *does* take some practice. Limiting the data to be interpreted—and understanding what those scores really mean—makes the process more efficient and allows educators to make valuable use of their students' standardized test data to bring about increased achievement (Mertler, 2002). Those interested in learning more about interpreting standardized test data are directed to *Interpreting Standardized Test Scores: Strategies for Data-Driven Instructional Decision Making* (Mertler, 2007).

Using Computer Software to Assist With Statistical Analysis

As I have mentioned a couple of times over the past few pages, statistical software to assist researchers in conducting an analysis of quantitative data has become readily available. Programs such as the Statistical Package for the Social Sciences (SPSS) and SYSTAT are available, and both offer free trial versions from their websites (see Related websites: Guidelines and Resources for Data Analysis later in this chapter for the URLs and related information). They can be expensive, although both of these programs offer discounts if you are affiliated with an educational institution of any kind. Another caveat about these programs is that they can be somewhat complex, in that they are designed for use by more experienced researchers and may not be the most appropriate software for the more novice teacher-researcher. However, the trial versions will provide some exposure to the programs and help you decide if you want to pursue their use further.

Although statistical software packages have become much more user-friendly over the past 10 years, their high cost and lack of availability continue to limit their access to educators at the K–12 level. This fact, along with the aforementioned caveat, appears to sometimes limit the use of quantitative designs and related analytical techniques by teacher-researchers. There is, however, a wonderful statistical analysis program available online (and for a nominal charge) to anyone wanting to use it. This alternative is StatCrunch (formerly known as WebStat). StatCrunch (available at http://www.stat crunch.com) is a web-based data analysis software system developed by the Department of Statistics at the University of South Carolina. It works in similar fashion to any statistical software that you might purchase and install on your home or office computer, although there is nothing to download or install. You must subscribe and create a login name and password for yourself, for purposes of future access to any data or results you wish to save on the StatCrunch server. Once you have logged in, you simply click on "Open StatCrunch" to begin the program.

The resulting window—an interactive Java window—is shown in Figure 6.11. Analyses are run on StatCrunch by first simply entering data directly into this window. As with most any statistical analysis program, the columns represent variables, and the rows represent cases, subjects, or participants. By clicking on the column headings, you can name the variables in your data set.

Let us take a look at a simple example. Assume we have a random sample of students from three schools that we want to compare with respect to scores on some dependent measure. We would enter the data for our three variables—scores in School 1 (school*1*), scores in School 2 (school*2*), and scores in School 3 (school*3*)—into the StatCrunch data window (see Figure 6.12).

Once your data have been entered into the data window, you can run both descriptive and inferential analyses. You can also obtain a variety of types of graphs. First, for our example, I wanted to run descriptive analyses on my data in order to see the means and standard deviations for each school on the dependent variable. By clicking on

Stat → Summary Stats → Columns

(see Figure 6.13) and following the directions in the resulting dialog boxes, I obtain the results shown in Figure 6.14. Notice that I get not only the means and standard deviations (abbreviated "Std. Dev." in the table) for each school but also numerous additional descriptive statistics.

I can also obtain a histogram in order to show the distributions of scores for each school by clicking on the following (see Figure 6.15):

Graphics → Histogram

A new window opens, showing me a histogram for school*1* (see Figure 6.16). By clicking on the "Next →" button, I can view the histogram for school*2* and then the one for school*3*.

| Figure 6.11 | Data Entry Window for StatCrunch |

Finally, as I mentioned, I can also run inferential analyses. Suppose I wanted to compare the three schools in order to see if they were statistically different from one another. To do this, I first click on the following sequence of options (see Figure 6.17):

Stat→ANOVA→One Way

Holding down the SHIFT key on my computer keyboard, I then click on each variable in order to move it to the analysis box, located on the right-hand side (see Figure 6.18). I then click the Calculate button.

A new window is opened, containing the results shown in Figure 6.19. Do not be over-whelmed by everything contained in the tables. Remember, first and foremost, we want to compare our obtained p-value to the preestablished α-level of 0.05 in order to establish any statistical significance. Our p-value is equal to 0.0456, which is less than 0.05, indicating that our three schools are significantly different from one another.

Although StatCrunch is not as comprehensive as commercially available statistical software packages, it certainly does overcome the problems of high cost and lack of availability (since all you need to use it is Internet access, once you have subscribed for the nominal

Figure 6.12 Sample Data File Created in StatCrunch

Row	school1	school2	school3	var4	var5	var6
1	25	24	22			
2	10	27	24			
3	15	24	27			
4	21	19	25			
5	23	28	30			
6	25	26	26			
7	18	25	25			
8	24	20	21			
9	22	23	23			
10	21	20	22			
11						
12						
13						
14						
15						
16						
17						
18						
19						
20						
21						
22						

Dr.Craig A. Mertler – StatCrunch 4.0

My StatCrunch   Data   Stat   Graphics   Results   Help

fee). Furthermore, it will typically accomplish most, if not all, of the quantitative analysis needs of most teacher-led, classroom-based action research projects. Give it a try!

Reporting the Results of Data Analysis

Although we will look closely at the skills and techniques used in writing up action research in Chapter 9, an examination of the process of writing up research specifically as it pertains to writing up the results of data analysis is warranted here. The main reason for including this topic here is that the activity of writing up the results of analysis is often one of the most—if not *the* most—frustrating aspects of writing up the results of an action research study for teacher-researchers, thus deserving some special attention.

| Figure 6.13 | StatCrunch Procedure for Running Descriptive Analyses |

Dr.Craig A. Mertler – StatCrunch 4.0								
My StatCrunch	Data	Stat	Graphics	Results	Help			
Row	school1	sch	Summary Stats ▶		Columns			var6
1	25		Tables ▶		Rows			
2	10		Z statistics ▶		Correlation			
3	15		Proportions ▶		Covariance			
4	21		T statistics ▶					
5	23		Variance ▶					
6	25		Regressior ▶					
7	18		ANOVA ▶					
8	24		Nonparametrics ▶					
9	22		Goodness–of–fit ▶					
10	21		Control Charts ▶					
11			Calculators ▶					
12								
13								
14								
15								
16								
17								
18								
19								
20								
21								
22								

| Figure 6.14 | Descriptive Analysis Results Obtained in StatCrunch |

Column Statistics

Options

Summary statistics:

Column	Mean	Variance	Std. Dev.	Std. Err.	Median	Range	Min	Max	Q1	Q3	n	Variance
school1	20.4	23.155556	4.812022	1.521695	21.5	15	10	25	18	24	10	23.155556
school2	23.6	9.6	3.0983868	0.9797959	24	9	19	28	20	26	10	9.6
school3	24.5	7.388889	2.718251	0.8595865	24.5	9	21	30	22	26	10	7.388889

| Figure 6.15 | StatCrunch Procedure for Obtaining a Histogram |

Dr.Craig A. Mertler – StatCrunch 4.0

My StatCrunch   **Data**   **Stat**   **Graphics**   **Results**   **Help**

Row	school1	school2		var5	var6
			Bar Plot ▶		
			Pie Chart ▶		
1	25	24	Histogram		
2	10	27	Stem and Leaf		
3	15	24	Boxplot		
4	21	19	Dotplot		
5	23	28	Means Plot		
6	25	26	Scatter Plot		
7	18	25	Multi Plot		
8	24	20	QQ Plot		
9	22	23	Index Plot		
10	21	20	Chart Group Stats		
11			Parallel Coordinates		
12			Pairs Plot		
13			3D Rotating Plot		
14			Stars Plot		
15					
16			Color Schemes		
17					
18					
19					
20					
21					
22					

Guidelines for Reporting the Results of Qualitative Data Analysis

One of the aspects of writing up research that tends to frustrate researchers of all types—and perhaps even impede their writing productivity—is how to most effectively or efficiently present the results of their analyses. Depending on the type of data you have collected, the results section may comprise the majority of your research report. When reporting the results of the analysis of qualitative data, it is important to realize that you are attempting to create a picture for your readers of what you have discovered (Johnson, 2008). You must try to take all that you have collected in the form of field notes, interview transcripts, journal entries, and so on and convert them into something that can be easily digested by your readers (Johnson, 2008). It is of primary importance that you try not

Figure 6.16 Resulting Histogram Obtained in StatCrunch

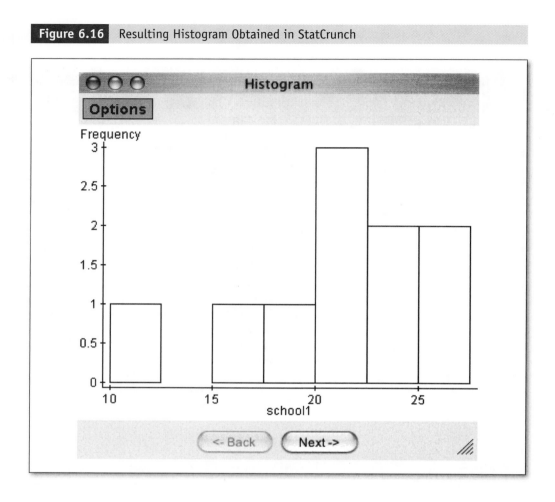

to report every bit of data collected; this will only overwhelm your readers. Instead, your goal is to describe the most meaningful trends or patterns that you saw emerge from your analyses.

Later, in Chapter 9, I provide several general suggestions for writing up research that also apply specifically to writing up the results of your qualitative analyses. These include such recommendations as the discriminate use of *tentative and definitive statements,* writing the results in a *clear and consistent manner,* using *simple language and terminology,* and using various conventions of format, including the judicious and appropriate use of *headings* throughout your results section. In addition to these recommendations, Johnson (2008) also suggests several more guidelines for specifically reporting the results of analyses of your qualitative data. The following five guidelines can help make your action research report clearer and more effective for your readers.

| Figure 6.17 | StatCrunch Procedure for Running Analysis of Variance |

1. *Make every effort to be impartial in your write-up.* It is important for teacher-researchers to realize that it is not possible to be totally impartial and objective; human nature simply does not allow it. However, it is essential that teacher-researchers represent all aspects of their action research studies as fairly, accurately, and objectively *as possible.* Johnson (2008) stresses that you try to steer clear of the "letter-to-the-editor syndrome" (p. 198). You are trying to describe your study and what you discovered during its duration. It is critical that you avoid the inclusion of value-laden statements in your research report. Excessive inclusion of your biases or partiality will likely be viewed by your audience in a negative light. A statement such as:

> It was clear that the teachers involved in this study did not value in any way the professional development opportunities presented to them, as they consciously chose not to participate in them.

Figure 6.18 Variable Selection Procedure in Conducting Analysis of Variance in StatCrunch

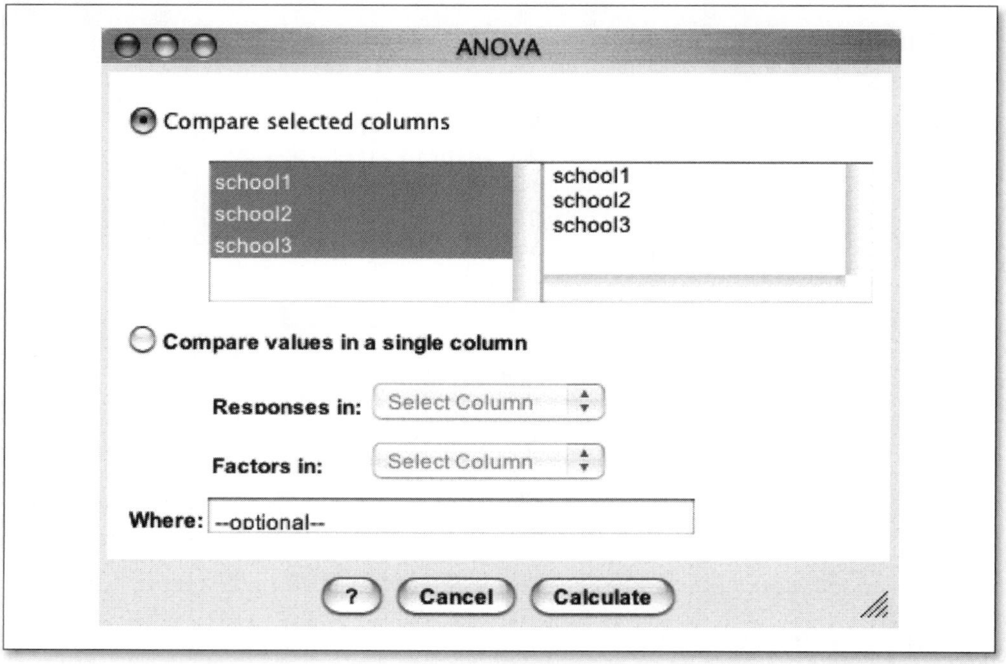

Figure 6.19 Analysis of Variance Results Obtained in StatCrunch

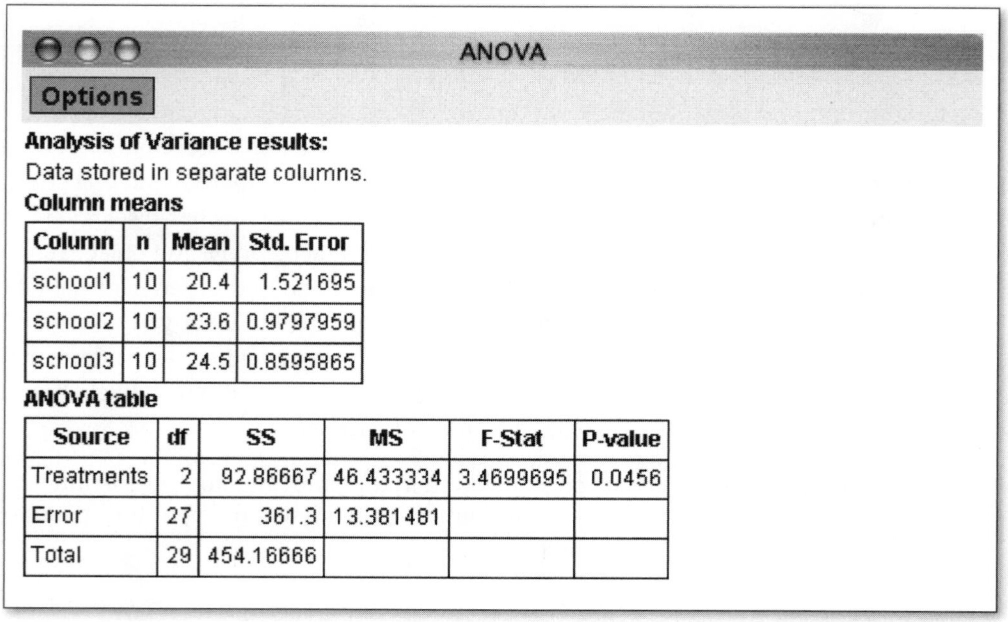
ANOVA

Options

Analysis of Variance results:

Data stored in separate columns.

Column means

Column	n	Mean	Std. Error
school1	10	20.4	1.521695
school2	10	23.6	0.9797959
school3	10	24.5	0.8595865

ANOVA table

Source	df	SS	MS	F-Stat	P-value
Treatments	2	92.86667	46.433334	3.4699695	0.0456
Error	27	361.3	13.381481		
Total	29	454.16666			

might be better written as:

> Observations of the teachers indicated that they did not participate in the professional development opportunities, perhaps because they did not see their value.

2. *Include references to yourself where they are warranted*. When writing your research reports, it is completely acceptable to use first-person pronouns—such as "I," "my," and "me"—when describing something that you did in the context of your action research study. For example, it would be appropriate to write the following:

> During this study, I collected data by observing and interviewing 14 students.

Since you played an active role in the study, it is awkward to refer to yourself using less personal forms of reference, such as "the researcher" or "the author." In addition, it becomes more cumbersome for the readers of your report. However, with this in mind, try not to overuse these types of references. You are still writing a scientific research report; you do not want it to read like a personal journal or diary.

3. *Take your readers along on all aspects of your study*. Allow your readers to see the study through your own eyes. Do not leave out any details of what you did and why you did it. It is important that you follow the suggested outline below:

Introduction

Review of Related Literature

Description of the Intervention or Innovation

Data Collection and Considerations

Data Analysis and Interpretation

Conclusions

Reflection and Action Plan

Even if you decide not to label your sections using these specific headings, you should still include all of these integral aspects to your study. The basic rule of thumb is that someone reading your research report should be able to *replicate* exactly what you did (i.e., your exact procedures) simply by reading your account of the study.

4. *Include representative samples when they enhance your presentation*. Anytime you incorporate actual samples of students' works, verbatim quotes, or word-for-word excerpts from your reflective journal, your data will come alive for the reader (Johnson, 2008). Your data, as well as your analyses of those data and your interpretations, will become much more interesting. It creates for readers a true sense of being there, as if they can *actually observe* the students working or *hear* their comments during an interview session. The following is a passage from the discussion section of my report on my positive reinforcement study:

Initially, Carol stated that positive reinforcement means not yelling at children. It means talking to them in a positive way. She revealed that giving children choices is central to her beliefs. Instead of punishing them (e.g., by placing them in time-out), she tries to turn displays of negative behavior into something constructive. As an example, Carol mentioned Ethan, who "likes to throw toys at everybody. Instead of putting him in the corner and me picking up all the toys he's thrown, I make a game out of it. Instead of 'Ethan, pick them up, pick them up,' we count them as we put them in. So he's still having to do what he did, you know, having to clean up his mess, but we're making a game out of it, instead of 'this was wrong and you're going to sit in the corner for this.'"

Notice how the inclusion of Carol's actual, verbatim statement reads in a much more interesting fashion than if I had simply summarized what she had said in my own words.

5. *Include interesting, but nonessential, information in appendices, if appropriate.* Often, you will have information that you think might be interesting to your readers but that, if included in your report, would interrupt the flow of the report. Readers might get bogged down with the details of this type of information. For example, members of your audience might appreciate and enjoy reading the actual transcripts from your interviews or your complete field notes from observation sessions—in their entirety. These types of information would most certainly be too lengthy to include in the body of your actual research report. However, if you believe that your readers might be interested in seeing them, you can include them in *appendices* at the end of your report. These sections of research reports are quite appropriate for reports presented in local venues or at professional conferences. Conversely, they will likely not be appropriate for reports submitted to journals for possible publication; their inclusion results in the creation of a document that is simply too lengthy to publish. For example, the complete, final report from my positive reinforcement study was 88 pages in length—36 pages made up the body of the report, and 52 were composed of appendices.

Guidelines for Reporting the Results of Quantitative Data Analysis

Although there are more options for reporting the results of quantitative data analyses, the task is no simpler. You can present the results of analyses of numerical data in narrative form or in graphical, visual form. Similar to the presentation of qualitative data analyses, many of the general suggestions for writing up research also apply to the reporting of quantitative analyses. Johnson (2008) has also provided several additional guidelines for reporting the results of quantitative data analysis. The following six guidelines will also help make the presentation of quantitative results clearer and more understandable.

1. *Suggestions for expressing quantifiable data using numerals:.* There are specific guidelines for presenting numerical data, according to the *Publication Manual of the American*

Psychological Association (APA Manual). Numerals (e.g., 1, 14, 251) should be used to express quantifiable information in the following cases:

- Any value greater than or equal to 10 (e.g., a total of 24 interviews were conducted)

- Specifying dates, ages, or time (e.g., the study began on September 10, 2004, and lasted 12 weeks)

- Reporting the number of participants in a study (e.g., there were 57 students who participated in the program)

- Indication of grade level (e.g., most children learn how to read in Grades 1 and 2)

- Reporting scores or ratings (e.g., Thomas received a score of 25 out of a possible 35 points on the instrument)

2. *Suggestions for expressing quantifiable data using words*: The APA Manual also provides guidelines for presenting numerical information using words (e.g., one, fourteen, two hundred fifty-one). Words should be used to represent numerical data in the following situations:

- Values less than 10 (e.g., for the collection of data, six observations and three interviews were conducted)

- Numbers that begin sentences (e.g., Fifty-seven students participated in the program); due to the awkward nature of sentences structured in this manner, my blanket suggestion is to try to avoid starting any sentence with numbers.

3. *Numerical data should be reported in descending order (from greatest to least).* Presenting numerical data in quantifiable order makes more sense and is easier for most people to read and understand. Consider the following statement:

> When asked to indicate their favorite subject, 65 students preferred science, 35 preferred language arts, 28 indicated social studies, and 19 preferred math.

This seems to be more easily understandable than a variation organized alphabetically:

> When asked to indicate their favorite subject, 35 students preferred language arts, 19 preferred math, 65 preferred science, and 28 indicated social studies.

4. *Report the total number involved before reporting numbers in categories.* In an effort to improve the clarity of the previous example, we should report the total number of students who responded to the question prior to reporting the numbers in individual categories:

> Students were asked to indicate their favorite subject. Of the 147 responses, 65 students preferred science, 35 preferred language arts, 28 indicated social studies, and 19 preferred math.

5. *Use tables to organize larger amounts of numerical data.* Tables are very efficient ways to organize lots of numerical data in a nonrepetitive, condensed manner. Tables are meant to take the place of information written in the text of a report. The information provided in a table complements that which is written in the text, but the table itself can also stand on its own. Often, when making formal presentations of research at a conference, for example, researchers will show tables to the audience and use them as the basis for discussing the results. Consider the following paragraph and the accompanying table from a paper I recently presented:

A second phase of pilot testing with the revised ALI was conducted during spring 2004 with 250 preservice teachers. It is important to note that similarity between the two institutions was established by examining the means, standard deviations, and reliability coefficients, as well as statistically comparing the total scores on the ALI across the two groups (see Table 1). [stet] After deleting outliers with standardized total scores (i.e., z-scores) exceeding ±3.00 (of which there was only one case), the total scores were compared for the first (M = 24.50, SD = 4.92) and second (M = 22.98, SD = 4.05). No significant difference was found between total ALI scores for the two institutions, $t(247)$ = 2.558, p > .01, two-tailed.

Table 1   Descriptive Statistics for the Total ALI Scores for the Two Institutions Studied

Institution	N	Mean	Standard Deviation	r_{Kr20}
Institution #1	150	24.50	4.92	.78
Institution #2	99	22.98	4.05	.62
Total	249	23.90	4.64	.74

Notice how the two components mirror each other; they do not present identical information. Also, realize that the table could be used as a visual aid and as a mechanism for discussing the results during a presentation of my study. Note the stylistic formatting for the table.

The table is referenced parenthetically in the text—that is, "(see Table 1)." The word *Table* is capitalized since it is a title. The table number appears to the right of the word *Table*. The title of the table appears on the next line in italics and is set directly above the actual table. The title should be brief but also highly descriptive of the content of the table.

6. *Figures can also be used to organize and present numerical data, largely without numbers.* Figures can also be used to visually and graphically show the results of data analysis. Various types of visuals that can be used as figures were presented earlier in this chapter. Figures are not labeled in the same manner as tables. The word *Figure* is again capitalized but also italicized, and the figure number appears below the actual figure. The title of the figure appears on the same line as the figure number. Below is an example of a histogram from the same research paper as the previous example of the table:

Examination of the item analysis results from this phase revealed a value similar to that resulting from the first phase for instrument reliability, $r_{Kr20} = 0.74$. Across the 35 items appearing on the ALI, item difficulty values ranged from a low of 0.212 to a high of 0.992; the mean item difficulty was equal to 0.681. The entire distribution of difficulty values is presented in Figure 1.

Figure 1   Distribution of ALI Item Difficulty Values

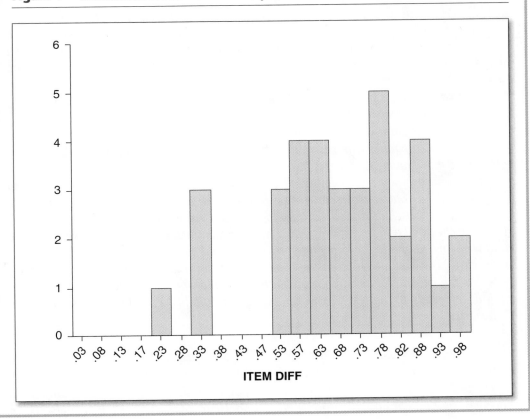

Since figures are not the same as tables, each is numbered sequentially. In other words, tables are numbered sequentially beginning with Table 1, and figures are also numbered sequentially beginning with Figure 1. Imagine you had both tables and figures appearing in your report in this order: table—table—figure—table—figure. The sequence of tables and figures would be numbered in the following manner:

Table 1

Table 2

Figure 1

Table 3

Figure 2

WRITING UP ACTION RESEARCH: DATA ANALYSIS

Data from the focus groups in Phases 1 and 3 were analyzed using the constant comparative method (Glaser & Strauss, 1967) to code, classify, and compare emerging categories as a means to generate themes. The research team was composed of four researchers who met regularly to develop interview questions, debrief after focus groups, discuss key emerging issues, and generate initial conceptual coding categories based on the issues forming in the data. Data analysis was guided by acknowledged qualitative procedures to identify emerging themes (Bogdan & Biklen, 1992; Tesch, 1990).

A graduate assistant working on the project transcribed all transcripts in entirety. A preliminary list of categories emerged from initial reading of the transcripts. Each of the four researchers individually reread the transcripts and identified and coded statements. The research team then met and reviewed all coded statements and discussed agreements and disagreements in order to reach consensus on categories. When disagreements occurred, the team reviewed transcripts and survey data to reach consensus on the categories and themes. As a final check, all transcripts were reread with the identified categories to make certain no data were missed and to see if any interpretations could be clarified.

Several steps were taken to ensure that the data collected and interpreted accurately reflected the experiences of the participants. The following verification procedures were used in this study to address trustworthiness and credibility of findings (Creswell, 1998; Guba, 1981).

Triangulation. *Triangulation was accomplished by using multiple researchers and multiple methods (focus groups and surveys) to increase understanding of the issues that elementary principals face. Collectively, the researchers had backgrounds in early childhood, early childhood special education, education policy, and Head Start, as well as experience in delivering inclusive programs in early childhood special education and training school administrators in local school districts. Also, one of the researchers was the parent of two young children with disabilities who were integrated into an ECE program.*

Peer Debriefings. *Peer debriefings were extremely important to understanding and interpreting the data and allowed for exploration of different researchers' perceptions and interpretations. The research team met regularly to solicit input from elementary school principals, to plan data collection procedures, to discuss issues of data collection, to debrief after conducting focus groups, to discuss emerging themes, to prepare preliminary results for discussion, and to clarify data interpretations and implications. The research team reviewed interpretations to ensure they were consistent and supported in the data.*

Member Checks. *To further ensure that the interpretations accurately reflected the principals and their experiences, six elementary school principals involved in the study were brought together for a day of discussions and feedback on the accuracy and clarity of the data and results. These principals confirmed the accuracy of the data collected and made additional comments regarding family support and future action. In addition, two elementary principals reviewed and provided feedback on a draft of the manuscript. Both principals indicated agreement with the manuscript and reported that these were findings "principals definitely need to think about."*

Survey. *The survey data was used as a secondary data source to enrich the understanding of the qualitative data gathered in focus groups. This article cannot present those findings in detail (separate manuscript in preparation); however, the survey did support the salience and understanding of the six themes. For the data collected in the survey, phase two of the study, Dillman's (1978) procedures were used to mail questionnaires and follow-up reminders. Returned questionnaires were assigned consecutive identification numbers and entered into a computer database. All entries for all items were checked for accuracy. A total of 916 surveys were sent to all elementary school principals in Iowa. A total of 693 surveys were returned for a total return rate of 75.6%. Of these, 655 (71.5%) were usable and were coded. Means and standard deviations were calculated on the 37 items to enrich the understanding of the six themes identified in the first round of focus groups. Means ranged from 2.59 to 4.54 and standard deviations ranged from .59 to 1.23.*

Source: Brotherson, Sheriff, Milburn, and Schertz, 2001.

Individual student SAT scores were recorded for each student who attended the researcher's eighth-grade general mathematics class during the 1997–1998, 1998–1999, and 1999–2000 school years. The Houghton-Mifflin series was used in the first year of the study, the Cord Applied Math in the second, and a combination of both curricula in the third year. The yearly SAT scores were analyzed using an ANOVA with a 0.05 level of significance to determine if there were differences between the scores of the three school years.

Source: Alsup, and Sprigler, 2003.

⇇ ACTION RESEARCH PORTRAIT 1 ⇉

Enhancing Academic Performance Through Improved Classroom Assessment

Recall that the purpose of this action research study is to improve teachers' classroom-based assessments in an effort to improve student achievement.

In order to answer their research question (is there a difference in the scores received on the spring administration of the statewide proficiency test between students who are exposed to systematically improved classroom assessment and those who are not? If there is a difference, which group outperforms the other?) and address their null hypothesis (there will be no difference between the scores received on the spring administration of the statewide proficiency test by students who are exposed to systematically improved classroom assessment and those who are not), the four teachers comprising Team North needed to make decisions about selecting appropriate statistical analyses. They knew that since they had given a set of hypothesis statements, they needed to use inferential statistical procedures. Since their question and null hypothesis dealt with the comparison between two separate groups (i.e., Team North and Team East), they determined that they would conduct independent-measures *t* tests on each of the four spring subtest scores (i.e., language arts, mathematics, science, and social studies). Prior to conducting the analyses, they further specified that they would test their hypothesis at an α-level equal to 0.05.

The teachers conducted four separate *t* tests, one for each of the subtest-posttest scores. The results of both the descriptive and the inferential analyses appear in the tables below.

Upon examining their results, the teachers were thrilled to see that there were significant differences between the two groups of students on two of the subtests—namely the language arts and mathematic tests. Cathy was unsure about the interpretation of these results, and Larry reminded her that they were really just comparing the *p*-values to 0.05. Analysis of the language arts test resulted in a *p*-value equal to 0.001, and that for the mathematics test was equal to 0.045, both of which were less than 0.05. When Cathy noted that the science scores were "almost significant," Larry was quick to point out that they would not be able to talk about results that were almost significant—either the differences are large enough to be significant, or they are not.

Susan then asked one very important question. Sure, they knew that the results showed that the two groups were significantly different on two of the tests, but how could they tell which group scored higher? Certainly, they wanted to be able to show that Team North had performed better than Team East, but what if it had turned out the other way? Larry replied that if it turned out the other way, that is what they would have to report. However, he calmed their anxieties when he suggested that they review the descriptive results table once again. From that table, the teachers could clearly see that Team North had scored higher—and significantly so—than Team East on the language arts and mathematics tests. In fact, the students in their team scored higher on all four subtests, although only two resulted in significant differences.

Descriptive Statistics

SUBTEST	GROUP	N	Mean	Std. Deviation
LA_2	1	30	447.8333	38.85613
	2	32	413.7500	37.13532
MATH_2	1	30	399.6667	76.54088
	2	32	358.7500	80.67258
SCI_2	1	30	436.6667	31.33064
	2	32	422.8125	33.33451
SS_2	1	30	400.3333	53.14154
	2	32	381.2500	61.63106

Independent Samples *t* Test Results

SUBTEST	Mean Difference (Gp. 1–Gp. 2)	*t* test Value	*df*	*p*-value
LA_2	34.0833	3.532	60	.001
MATH_2	40.9167	2.046	60	.045
SCI_2	13.8542	1.684	60	.097
SS_2	19.0833	1.302	60	.198

⪻ ACTION RESEARCH PORTRAIT 2 ⪼

Improving Reading Comprehension in a Title I Program

Recall that the purpose of this action research study is to improve students' reading comprehension skills within a Title I context.

After collecting the final test scores in May, Kathleen prepared to analyze the quantitative data in her action research study. She subjected her students' test scores to a repeated-measures t test, since the same students were measured twice in her one-group pretest-posttest design. The results of her statistical analyses appear in the tables below: comprehension."

Repeated-Measures Statistics

		N	**Mean**	**Std. Deviation**
Pair 1	RC_SEPT	25	35.76	7.897
	RC_MAY	25	39.04	8.825

Paired Samples t Test

		Paired Differences Mean	**Std. Deviation**	**t-value**	**df**	**p-value**
Pair 1	RC_SEPT - RC_MAY	−3.28	7.220	−2.272	24	.032

From the descriptive-statistics table, Kathleen could see that, across her 25 students, the mean score in May (39.04) was clearly higher than the September mean score (35.76). Therefore, she could conclude that her students had improved, but was that improvement substantial enough to be statistically significant?

She proceeded to examine the results of her repeated-measures analysis, noting that the obtained p-value from the t test was equal to 0.032, clearly less than 0.05. Therefore, she could answer her first research question by concluding that there had been significant improvement in her students' reading comprehension skills over the course of the school year and as a result of her intervention efforts.

In order to address her second research question, Kathleen relied on her observation field notes and transcripts from the interviews that she periodically conducted with her students. During the initial interviews with the students, Kathleen discovered that they had a wide variety of ideas about what is meant by "reading comprehension."

One student believed reading comprehension is simply learning how to read. Several others indicated that it had to do with being able to answer questions about what you have read. Still others said that it was about "reading to myself and asking myself questions about what I've read." Most students indicated that they believed that they had trouble reading for various reasons. These reasons included the fact that the students could not understand big words contained in the stories, that they simply did not understand the story in its entirety, that they read a story too fast, and that they made mistakes on new or complex words.

At various times throughout the year, Kathleen asked her students to identify strategies that help people better understand what they are reading. Early in the year, the students could only identify a few strategies, such as looking back in the book, practicing reading, or using picture clues. However, as the year progressed, they were able to list many more techniques for improving reading comprehension. These additional strategies included slowing down when reading, listening to what you are reading, highlighting important information, rereading sections of a story, visualizing what is going on in a story, drawing pictures, and retelling or rewriting a story that has been read. It became clear to Kathleen that her students knew what strategies could help them become better readers, but were her students actually using any of them?

Kathleen's formal observation sessions and accompanying field notes revealed some of the most interesting data in her study. Reflected in her field notes was the fact that as the year progressed and her students' skills were supposed to be improving, she observed substantial growth in her students and their abilities to apply and use various strategies that she had taught them to improve their reading comprehension. Her observations strongly supported her interview data in that early in the school year, her students had limited knowledge of various comprehension strategies and were not able to demonstrate their application very frequently. As the year progressed, however, she saw her students making independent decisions about applying a variety of reading comprehension skills that they previously could only identify to her orally. Interestingly, at points later in the school year, several students identified that Kathleen's oral and written questions—those designed as the teacher-developed intervention for her study and to mirror the format that the students would see on formal tests of reading comprehension—were a very helpful technique for helping them retain what they had read. As a final bright spot in her action research study, Kathleen asked each student at the beginning and near the end of the school year the following question: Do you enjoy reading? Early in the year, roughly half of her students indicated that they did not really like to read; they saw it as something that they just had to do for school. However, by the end of the year, all but one of her students indicated that they really enjoyed reading.

Related Websites: Guidelines and Resources for Data Analysis

This annotated list of related websites presents both guidelines and procedures for analyzing your data by hand and, in the next section, resources for software programs to assist you in your analytical endeavors. You may want to check out the sites with free trial, or demo, versions of some of the programs.

- Guidelines for Analyzing Your Data **http://oldweb.madison.k12.wi.us/sod/car/caranalyzingdata.html**
  This page, from the Madison (Wisconsin) Metropolitan School District's "Classroom Action Research" site, offers a bulleted list of suggestions to keep in mind when beginning the analysis of your qualitative data.

- A Process for Analyzing Your Data **http://oldweb.madison.k12.wi.us/sod/car/caranalyzeprocess.html**
  This page, also from the Madison School District site, provides a step-by-step procedure for analyzing qualitative data. Even if you feel comfortable with the idea of analyzing qualitative data, this brief page offers a good review of the process.

Software Programs for Analyzing Qualitative Data

The following is a list of websites for several qualitative analysis software programs. Descriptions of some of the features of the programs and their sites have been included. If you are interested in learning more about these software programs, I urge you to investigate them further. Be sure to check the computer system requirements before downloading any complete or trial version of a program.

- AnSWR—Analysis Software for Word-based Records **http://www.cdc.gov/hiv/software/answr.htm**
  AnSWR, developed by the Centers for Disease Control and Prevention (CDC), Division of HIV/AIDS Prevention, is a software system for coordinating and conducting large-scale, team-based analysis projects that integrate qualitative and quantitative techniques. AnSWR is downloadable, free of charge, in a variety of PC formats.

- EZ-Text **http://www.cdc.gov/hiv/software/ez-text.htm**
  EZ-Text, also developed by the CDC, is a software program developed to help researchers create, manage, and analyze semistructured qualitative databases, especially those resulting from the use of open-ended surveys. Copies of the EZ-Text software and user documentation can be downloaded free of charge from this website.

- Qualrus **http://www.ideaworks.com/qualrus/index.html**
  Qualrus, developed by Idea Works Inc., advertises itself as "the intelligent qualitative analysis program." The complete program costs $399, but there is a free, downloadable trial available at: http://www.ideaworks.com/qualrus/demo.html

- NVivo8 **http://www.qsrinternational.com/products_nvivo.aspx**
  QSR International has developed this widely used qualitative analysis program . NVivo8 sells for $595, although a student version is also available for $199. In addition, a free trial version is available at: http://www.qsrinternational.com/products_ nvivo_free-trial-software.aspx

- HyperRESEARCH **http://www.researchware.com**
  HyperRESEARCH, developed by ResearchWare Inc., bills itself as "an easy-to-use qualitative data analysis software package enabling you to code and retrieve, build the- ories, and conduct analyses of your data." The current version permits the integration of advanced multimedia capabilities, allowing you to work with text, graphics, audio, and video sources of data. This is one of the only qualitative analysis programs avail- able in Macintosh formats. HyperRESEARCH sells for $370 but is available in a free trial version (which limits the user to 75 codes and seven cases) at: http://www.research ware.com/hr/downloads.html

Software Programs for Analyzing Quantitative Data

The following is a list of websites for several quantitative analysis software programs. Descriptions of some of the features of the programs and their sites have been included.

- SPSS—Statistical Package for the Social Sciences **http://www.spss.com**
  SPSS comes in both Windows (v. 18) and Mac (v. 18 for OS X) versions; both are avail- able for purchase through SPSS's website. More information about both platforms is available at http://spss.com/statistics. Both versions currently retail for about $700, although there is a free downloadable trial version of the Windows edition available for a 14-day trial.

- SYSTAT **http://www.systat.com**
  Part of a larger family of software, more specific information about the statistical soft- ware package SYSTAT is available at http://www.systat.com/products/Systat. SYSTAT13 retails for $1,299 but is available at the educator's discounted price of $599. Version 13 of the program is only available for Windows operating systems. A downloadable trial version (available at http://www.systat.com/Login.aspx?ReturnUrl = %2fDown loads%2fSYSTAT_Trial_Download.aspx) is good for 30 days. However, a "scaled-down" version of SYSTAT, called MYSTAT, is available free-of-charge for students. It can be downloaded at http://www.systat.com/Login.aspx?ReturnUrl = %2fDownloads %2fMYSTAT_Download.aspx

Below are several interactive, web-based statistics calculators. I invite you to check them out; they can certainly assist you with your quantitative analyses.

- Daniel Soper's Statistics Calculator **http://www.danielsoper.com/statcalc**
  This site includes calculators for 21 categories of analyses.

- GraphPad QuickCalcs **http://graphpad.com/quickcalcs/CImean1.cfm**
  This site provides quick calculations of some descriptive statistics. There is also a page (http://graphpad.com/quickcalcs/ttest1.cfm) for performing *t* tests.

- Statistical Applets **http://www1.assumption.edu:80/users/avadum/applets/applets.html**
  This website provides quick and easy calculations for *t* tests (both types) and ANOVAs.

- Online Stats Calculators **http://www.physics.csbsju.edu/stats/Index.html**
  Indexed on this site are calculators for descriptive statistics, graphs, *t* tests, chi-square tests, and ANOVAs.

- VassarStats **http://faculty.vassar.edu/lowry/VassarStats.html**
  Using the navigation bar on the left-hand side, you can select from a variety of statistics modules.

SUMMARY

★ Analyzing qualitative data is an inductive process, involving the reduction of information that has been collected by organizing it into important themes and patterns.

- The reduction of qualitative data is typically accomplished through the development of a coding scheme, which is used to group data that provide similar types of information.

- The process of coding narrative data often necessitates rereading your data numerous times.

- Once all narrative data have been coded, the main features of each of the categories must be described.

- The final step of analyzing qualitative data involves the interpretation of the data that have been coded into categories.

- Reflection throughout the process of inductive analysis is an essential component to remaining objective and open-minded while gaining a better understanding of your data.

- Numerous computer software programs can aid the researcher with the organization and categorization of narrative data.

★ Analysis of quantitative data is a deductive process, using descriptive or inferential statistics.

★ Descriptive statistics are relatively simple mathematical procedures used to simplify, summarize, and organize large amounts of numerical data.

- Three categories of descriptive statistics include measures of central tendency, dispersion, and relationship.

- Three measures of central tendency, which describe what is typical about a group, are the mean, the median, and the mode.

- Two measures of dispersion, which indicate how much spread or diversity exists within a group of scores, are the range and the standard deviation.

- A correlation coefficient is used to measure the degree of relationship that exists between two variables.

- Data can also be "described" visually through the use of frequency distribution tables and such graphs as histograms, bar charts, and pie charts.

★ Inferential statistics are used to determine how likely a given statistical result is for an entire population, based on data collected from a smaller sample from that population.

- The most common types of inferential statistical tests are the independent-measures t test, the repeated-measures t test, analysis of variance, and the chi-square test.

- An independent-measures t test is appropriate for designs where two groups are compared on a common dependent variable.

- A repeated-measures t test is appropriate for designs involving two measures (such as a pretest and a posttest) on the same group.

- Analysis of variance (or ANOVA) is appropriate for designs where more than two groups are being compared on a common dependent variable.

- Chi-square analysis is used when data exist as frequency counts within categories.

- Inferential statistics help the researcher determine statistical significance, which indicates a true difference between groups being compared, as opposed to differences due only to chance.

- Statistical significance is determined by comparing the obtained p-value to the preestablished α-level, usually 0.05 in educational research studies.

- When the p-value is less than the α-level, the results are said to be statistically significant.

- There are numerous computer software programs available to assist in the analysis of numerical data.

QUESTIONS AND ACTIVITIES

1. What are the main steps in the analysis of qualitative data? Summarize the process used to analyze this type of data.

2. Compare and contrast descriptive and inferential statistics, focusing on the main goal and the types of conclusions one is able to draw from each type of statistical analysis.

3. Analyzing qualitative data requires some practice. In order to gain some exposure to this type of analysis, first think of an educational topic of interest to you. Conduct one or two brief observation sessions, taking field notes while you observe. In addition, conduct one or two brief interviews with people on this same topic. Finally, sit down with your narrative data and attempt to reduce it by coding similar categories; then summarize it by identifying the main features of each resulting category.

4. Although a very different process, analyzing quantitative data also takes some practice. Conduct the following analysis using StatCrunch (see the answers below):

Open the "Home Runs" data file by clicking:

> Data→Load data→Sample data→Home Runs

Obtain the descriptive statistics (following the instructions provided in the chapter) by clicking:

> Stat→SummaryStats→Columns

Conduct an analysis of variance (following the instructions provided in the chapter) by clicking:

Is there a significant difference in the number of home runs hit by each player?

> Stat→ANOVA→One Way

Answers to #4: Summary statistics:

ANOVA Table

Source	df	SS	MS	F-Stat	p-value
Treatments	3	2313.296	771.09863	3.531202	0.0227
Error	42	9171.422	218.36717		
Total	45	11484.718			

Yes, since 0.0227 < 0.05, the number of home runs hit is significantly different.

STUDENT STUDY SITE

Visit the Student Study Site at **www.sagepub.com/mertler3study** for these additional learning tools:

- Video clips
- Web resources
- Self quizzes
- E-flashcards

- PowerPoint slides
- Sample action research reports
- Full-text SAGE journal articles
- Chapter summaries

"I've Got Results! . . . Now What?"

Part IV of this book discusses activities involved in the action research process at the "conclusion" of your study. In Chapter 7, you will learn about how to develop an action plan, which essentially is a plan for your next steps in the cyclical process of action research. These plans might be individually, team-, or school-oriented in nature. Reflecting on the experience is also a critical aspect of this step. In Chapter 8, you will learn more about formal methods of sharing the results of your action research projects. Again, professional reflection is a key part of this process. Finally, in Chapter 9, should you be interested in formally publishing or otherwise writing up your results, you will learn about various conventions and practical guidelines for academic writing.

CHAPTER 7

Developing an Action Plan

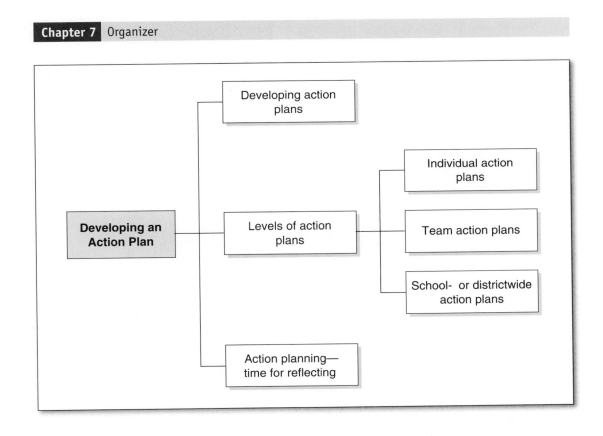

The **developing stage** of the action research process is the focus of this chapter. This stage consists primarily of taking the results of your data analysis, your interpretations of those results, and the final conclusions drawn from the interpretations and formulating a plan of action for the future. This action plan may consist of strategies for the future implementation of the treatments, interventions, revisions and improvements to your instructional methods, and other items that were incorporated into your study and also may consist of designs and proposals for future action research cycles, or perhaps a combination of both.

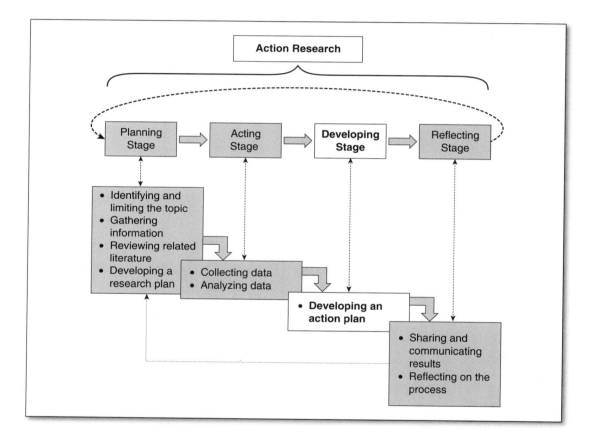

Developing Action Plans

Action research is built on the premise that some type of action will result from your action research project (Johnson, 2008). **Action plans** resulting from action research studies may be informal or formal (Creswell, 2005). This often is dependent on the nature and purpose of your action research project (Johnson, 2008). Action plans may consist of brief statements or simple descriptions about the implementation of a new educational practice; a plan to reflect on alternative approaches to addressing the problem; a plan to share what you have learned with others interested in the topic, such as other teachers, administrators, boards of education, or other schools or districts; or any other "next steps" you might take (Creswell, 2005; Johnson, 2008). The action plan may be more formally written, as an outline for presentation or even as a complete report of your research project that you might submit for possible publication in a professional journal (Creswell, 2005). As Creswell (2005) and Fraenkel and Wallen (2003) point out, the important aspect of developing an action plan is that the teacher-researcher now has some sort of strategy for trying out, carrying out, or otherwise putting into practice the changes resulting from the findings of an action research project.

At the risk of sounding repetitive, developing and implementing an *action* plan is the aspect of conducting the type of research that really puts the *action* into *action* research. In most cases, developing an action plan means that you will be doing something different in the future. There are rare cases where teacher-researchers may discover from their results that everything is fine and nothing needs to be changed (Johnson, 2008). In such cases, the action plan is to do nothing. However, Johnson (2008) has outlined five possible—and common—outcomes of action research studies:

1. A greater understanding of the situation or child under investigation, or of students in general, is developed.

2. A new problem is discovered.

3. A plan, a program, or an instructional method is found to be effective.

4. A plan, a program, or an instructional method is found to need modification.

5. A plan, a program, or an instructional method is found to be ineffective. (pp. 136–137)

During this phase of the action research process, the teacher-researcher is basically trying to answer the following question: Based on what I have learned from my study, what should I do now (Mills, 2011)? Many people consider this phase to be the most important part of an action research project (Johnson, 2008). Once again, professional *reflection* is an important component to this step in the process. Developing an action plan takes some time and thought, looking back across the entire study, starting with the initial need or topic idea, the strategies for research design, data collection, and data analysis. Of course, the focus will typically fall on the findings of the study. Organization is also key during this particular phase of the study. Mills (2011) suggests that the teacher-researcher develop a "Steps to Action Chart." This chart delineates, in concise form, the following components of the study for the teacher-researcher:

• What was learned from the study

• Recommendations for actions, related to specific research questions

• Who is responsible for those actions

- Who needs to be consulted, informed, or approached for permission for the implementation of future actions

- Who will monitor or collect future data

- A timeline for implementing the actions

- Specification of any needed resources (p. 155)

A sample Steps to Action Chart (which has been adapted from Mills, 2011) is shown in Figure 7.1.

Looking across the column headings in Figure 7.1, you will probably notice that the components of the chart seem to somewhat parallel the action research process itself. Beginning with the research questions and moving forward to the collection—and, although not stated, the analysis—of data, the Steps to Action Chart in essence outlines the next action research cycle (Mills, 2011). Continuing this process of planning for action research, conducting action research, and then developing action plans (which incorporates future action research), exemplifies that which was discussed in Chapter 1. Namely, this demonstrates the fact that action research never really ends; the professional educator continues to move through subsequent cycles throughout his or her career, always searching for ways to improve educational and instructional practice.

| Figure 7.1 | Sample Steps to Action Chart |

Summary of Research Questions and Findings	Recommended Actions	Who Is Responsible? T = Teacher/s S = Students P = Principal PA = Parent/s O = Others	Who Needs to Be Consulted, etc.?	Who Will Collect Data?	Time Line	Resources Necessary

Source: Adapted from Mills, 2011.

Levels of Action Plans

Video Clip 7.1
View a clip of
Dr. Mertler
discussing
action planning
and reflection.

Action planning can occur at several different levels within educational settings. Action plans can be developed at the *individual, team,* and *school* or *district* levels (Mills, 2011). The determination of the appropriate level is based initially on the scope of the action research project. In addition, it is important to realize that both action research and action planning can occur at more than one level during a single action research project (Mills, 2011). For example, a given topic under investigation may have a districtwide focus but may also have a substantial impact on individual classroom instruction. As you will see later in this chapter in Action Research Portrait 1, our teachers developed action plans not only for themselves but also for the school as a whole. Let us take a look at each of these three levels of action planning: individual, team, and school/district.

Individual

Often, **individual action planning** results from individual teacher-researchers who have conducted an action research study for a course, to renew certification or licensure, or as part of a grant-funded program or by teachers who have incorporated action research as a regular, integrative part of their classroom practice (Mills, 2011). It is important to note that the primary audience for this type of action research and planning is the individual classroom teacher. Not only has the teacher conducted the research, but that particular teacher is also the target of the action plan. However, that does not mean that other educators would not be interested in the outcome of a given action research study. It is still important to communicate the results of your research to other interested educators, as you will see in the next chapter.

Team

Similar to individual action planning, action research projects can also be conducted and subsequent action planning formulated by teams of teachers. Like individual planning, **team action planning** may also result from networks of teachers, formed as a result of a graduate-level or professional development course, with similar school improvement interests (Mills, 2011). It may also stem from groups of teachers working collaboratively on grant-funded projects. In order for the team to function as such, the teachers will likely share a common focus or area of interest, which serves as the mechanism to jump-start the action research process (Mills, 2011). Team action planning is sometimes easier to facilitate due to the fact that the labor—that is, the various responsibilities related to the research project and resulting action planning—can be divided among several team members. However, be aware that this advantage of team planning can also become a stumbling block at times. The more educational professionals and other individuals—whether they be teachers, administrators, counselors, or parents—who are involved in the process, the more difficult it may become to accomplish the variety of tasks that must be completed. For example, it may become increasingly difficult to arrange times for everyone on the team to meet, due to the number of schedules that must be coordinated. In addition, you may have to address the issue of the team member who has not pulled his or her own weight and completed assigned tasks by the deadline established in the timeline—which can obviously affect subsequent activities related to the action research project or action planning. It is essential that the team possess flexibility in planning and carrying out various research-related activities, as well as that individual team members each make a genuine and sincere commitment to the action research project.

School-Level or Districtwide

Extending the idea of team planning even broader, action research and its ensuing action planning can also be conducted at the school or district levels. Typically, **school-level** or **districtwide action research** and planning engages all members of the particular level in a communitywide research endeavor. Mills (2011) provides an example of a common focus for schoolwide action research at the elementary level consisting of an emphasis on improving reading, writing, or mathematics skills. Another example at the secondary level—and perhaps even as a districtwide initiative—might be an investigation of the effects of a new drug and alcohol abuse curriculum on students' attitudes and behaviors. The important and distinguishing factor in school- or district-level action research is that the *entire* community—whether it be a complete school or an intact district—agrees on the focus for a particular school improvement initiative. As Mills notes, cooperation, collaboration, and communication are principal factors vital to the success of such efforts.

This common focus for school improvement has another potentially important benefit. School building or districtwide—in the case of smaller districts—action research projects can also serve as the basis for professional development, where all members of the particular community engage in not only a common professional development program but one that is also research-based. This is an important and effective form of professional development, since all teachers—and, perhaps, all school staff—are actively involved in the action research program and, as a result, experience practical and applicable professional growth.

Action Planning: A Time for Reflection

As I mentioned earlier in this chapter, action planning is an extremely appropriate time for professional reflection. It provides opportunities for reflecting on where you have been, what you have learned, and where you are going from here (Mills, 2011). This type of reflection may lead to the identification of individual or collective, in the case of team or school-level action research, professional development needs. This process often involves a *re*review of the literature on your research topic in association with the findings from your study. In this manner, you can begin to see not only how your study was fueled by the existing literature but also how your study now fits with and contributes to that body of literature. This practice of incorporating your findings into existing research tends to shed even more light on your topic of interest, thus providing a stronger foundation of knowledge for the next cycle of your research. Mills (2011) suggests that as part of this process, you consider the following questions in an effort to help you make these types of connections:

1. What were the intended and unintended effects of your actions?

2. What educational issues arise from what you have learned about your practice? (p. 160)

These questions require you to take some time in order to look back at your classroom instructional practice from a new, more enlightened perspective. This new perspective is one that has resulted from a *systematic inquiry* into *your* own practice.

Action planning is also an appropriate time to reflect on your action research study itself. No research study—regardless of who has conducted it—is perfect. There are always ways to improve any given research study; as the saying goes, *hindsight is 20/20!* After completing your study by drawing your conclusions and any recommendations, it is often beneficial to formally reexamine your entire study. During this retrospective examination, educator-researchers should look at the various logistical aspects of the action research study, focusing on anything they might want to do differently next time. For example, begin by reviewing your research questions and answering the following:

Video Clips 7.2 & 7.3 View clips of educator-researchers discussing action planning and reflection.

- Did I really ask what I wanted to ask?
- Was I able to sufficiently answer my research questions?
- Might it be necessary for me to change the questions for the next cycle of my research and data collection?

Next, move on to your methodology and address such questions as:

- Did my research design end up being appropriate for what I wanted to address or answer with my research questions?
- If not, is there another design that might work better?
- Were the data that I collected the most appropriate for enabling me to answer my research questions?
- If so, are there additional sources of data that I might want to include next time?
- If not, what sources might I use in place of them?
- Do I need to alter my choices for analyzing my data, based on my answers to the previous questions?

Remember that there is no such thing as a perfect research study, but you can always make revisions to your action research plans for the purposes of improving implementations of your research in subsequent cycles. In all likelihood, this will make your data stronger (i.e., more valid), thereby making your conclusions stronger and more meaningful.

WRITING UP ACTION RESEARCH: ACTION PLANS

The results of this study support the notion that the level of enthusiasm for learning science was increased through the incorporation of computers and multimedia software into the middle school science curriculum. The integration of technology will be an ongoing pursuit in my classroom. The enthusiasm it brought to my students has been infectious. Students and parents of students in my other four classes have asked when they would have an opportunity to work with computers. Teachers throughout the school have become interested in integrating technology into their curriculum. Through the insistence of my coworkers, I have taught two HyperStudio training sessions for twenty-one teachers and teacher aides from all academic disciplines as well as areas such as special education and the media center. Seventeen of my study group students volunteered to assist me with these teacher training sessions.

I believe that multimedia computer technology could enhance all of the core curricula. In English, it could be used to illustrate creative writing assignments. Social studies classes could use multimedia to develop geography or history presentations. One of my study group students used HyperStudio to develop an award-winning math fair project. Adding enthusiasm to learning in any discipline through the use of technology is limited only by the ability of a school to provide funding for the equipment, adequate software, and teacher training. The availability of equipment when doing class projects involving technology is critical.

This active research study was made possible through the cooperation of my fellow teachers. By borrowing computers from neighboring classrooms, each group of students that developed a presentation had a computer to use throughout the study period. Ideally, computers and software should be made available to students and teachers for checkout and use at home as well as at school through the school's media center. The difficulties encountered in this study (all of which involved the logistics of accessing the equipment needed) were far outweighed by the academic benefit to my students.

This active research study not only increased my students' enthusiasm for learning science, but it also rekindled my excitement for teaching. During the prestudy period, I was extremely apprehensive and began to question the feasibility of the study. Once I began, however, I found myself looking forward to the hectic pace and the commotion that resulted from eleven groups of middle school students using sound, animation, and graphics to develop multimedia computer presentations.

Source: Hollis, 1995.

From the eighth-grade classroom teacher's perspective, these results question the cost and time being spent by teachers and his school district to implement reform math. A reform mathematics curriculum is expensive to implement; teachers must be trained and supplementary kits must be purchased. Such expenses, in his opinion, are questionable, since a reform mathematics curriculum did not promote an increase in student achievement. In his classroom a traditional mathematics curriculum was superior with regard to teaching skills and procedural competency and, thus, would help students at the high school level, since success in high school math courses in his school district is "built upon the foundation of facts and procedures." He summarizes the results of his study in the following manner: "Over the decades educators have tried to develop more effective methods to teach mathematics. Though most educators agree that mathematics achievement needs to improve, the current reform trend does not appear to be the answer. Further, it appears to be detrimental to procedural knowledge."

Source: Alsup and Sprigler, 2003.

❧ ACTION RESEARCH PORTRAIT 1 ❧

Enhancing Academic Performance Through Improved Classroom Assessment

Recall that the purpose of this action research study is to improve teachers' classroom-based assessments in an effort to improve student achievement.

The four teachers making up Team North at Jones Middle School were very excited about the results of their action research study. They wanted to share them with the other teachers in their building—and perhaps elsewhere—simply because they believed that there would be some interest in their findings. But first, however, they needed to make some decisions about the next steps for their study. They needed to develop a plan of action for implementing the results and for determining the direction that the next cycle in their research would take. Larry shared with the others a format for developing an action plan. It consisted of a relatively simple table that would outline their research question, relevant findings, and the specifics about the next steps in their process. The group decided to meet on a Thursday afternoon to complete their action planning table.

After everyone in the group had contributed their ideas in a brainstorming session, they completed the action planning table. The finished plan appeared as follows:

Summary of Research Question and Findings (What Happened?)	Recommended Actions (What's Next?)	Who Will Collect Data? (Who?)	Time Line (When?)	Resources Necessary (How Much?)
1. Is there a difference in the scores received on the spring proficiency test between students who are exposed to systematically improved classroom assessment and those who are not? Yes!	1. Team North continues with collaboratively improving classroom assessments. 2. Recommend to principal that other teams	One person from each team will serve as collector for respective students: North–Larry East–Sharon	1. Training will occur in summer. 2. Study replicated next school year.	1. $$$ for professional development? –Contact principal

(Continued)

(Continued)

Summary of Research Question and Findings (What Happened?)	Recommended Actions (What's Next?)	Who Will Collect Data? (Who?)	Time Line (When?)	Resources Necessary (How Much?)
2. If there is a difference, which group outperforms the other? Experimental group outscored control on all subtests.	receive training in assessment. 3. Repeat study next year, with more (all?) teams.	West– Robert South– David Central– Cynthia	3. Results reported in June.	–Contact district administration –Look into any grant opportunities

As shown in their action plan, the teachers decided to continue their efforts to improve the quality of their classroom assessments by continuing to engage in professional development and working collaboratively to assist each other in developing new and more appropriate classroom assessments. They also decided that they would share their results with their principal and recommend that the other teachers at Jones receive similar training in the development of classroom assessments. With her support, the teachers thought that everyone in the school could receive this training, and perhaps the next cycle of the study could involve the entire school. The team's final recommended action was to replicate the study next year, focusing on trying to improve the subtest scores in science and social studies (by improving the assessments that they develop for those classes) while maintaining the improved level of performance in language arts and mathematics.

The data would be collected by everyone on the team, but one individual would be identified to serve as the coordinator for each team. Those five individuals would be Larry (Team North), Sharon (Team East), Robert (Team West), David (Team South), and Cynthia (Team Central). The professional development training would occur during the summer, as it had during the first cycle of the project. The study would be replicated during the next school year, with the final results being reported and shared in June. Finally, as a possible incentive for other teachers in their building to participate in the project, they decided to pursue opportunities for funding the professional development training. They would contact both their principal and district administrators about any available funds. In addition, they would seek out any grants that might be used for such training.

⫷ ACTION RESEARCH PORTRAIT 2 ⫸

Improving Reading Comprehension in a Title I Program

Recall that the purpose of this action research study is to improve students' reading comprehension skills within a Title I context.

Kathleen's efforts to systematically improve her Title I students' reading comprehension skills seemed to have paid off. Her students' scores on the Reading Comprehension Cluster of the Woodcock Reading Mastery Test improved significantly over the course of the school year due to her instructional efforts. In addition, the results of the analysis of her qualitative data resulting from observations and interviews supported this fact. She observed students beginning to use—and then consistently using—the reading comprehension skills she taught to them.

For her next step, Kathleen decided that she would continue to use these same procedures next year with some of the same returning students, as well as some new students. She would continue to collect the same types of data—namely diagnostic test scores—and interviews with and observations of students. However, upon reflecting on her study, she became concerned that her biases—specifically due to the fact that she was the teacher as well as the data collector—may have confounded some of her results.

She was concerned that she only saw what she wanted to see. Because of this fact, she decided to make a few additions to her data collection next year. First, she decided that she would invite at least two other Title I reading teachers to come into her classroom and conduct their own observations of the students, asking them to focus their observations on the students' abilities to answer oral and written questions after having read a book. As Kathleen had done with her observations, she would have them look for how her students used the strategies for reading comprehension that they were being taught. Second, she decided to also interview selected parents of her students. She was concerned that her students may have been using the strategies only while in her class and that they were not using them when reading at home, whether they were reading homework assignments or were reading for leisure. Kathleen believed that the parents' perceptions of their children's reading practices at home would add a very beneficial piece to her data collection. This would also let her know if her students were extending their learning of reading comprehension skills beyond the four walls of her classroom.

Related Website: Action Plans

- Action Research: A Strategy for Instructional Improvement **http://www.education oasis.com/resources/Articles/action_research.htm**
  In her article, Carol Reed provides several brief scenarios of classroom-, school-, or district-based action research studies. Included in her descriptions are numerous

samples of action plans that follow directly and logically, first from the stated question guiding the investigation, followed by the collection of data and the ultimate findings. This article provides a beneficial and succinct way to see the connection between research questions, collected data, and resulting action plans.

SUMMARY

★ Action planning is the *action* part of action research.

- Action plans can be informal (e.g., brief statements about the implementation of a new practice or a plan to reflect or share what has been learned) or formal (e.g., a presentation outline or a complete research report).

- There are five "typical" outcomes from action research: (a) developing a greater understanding of an educational situation, (b) discovering a new problem, (c) finding a program to be effective, (d) finding a program to need modification, or (e) finding a program to be ineffective.

- Organization of your action planning can be accomplished through the use of a Steps to Action Chart.

- Action planning can occur at the individual, team, school, or district level.

★ Practicing professional reflection is an important component of the action planning phase.

- Teacher-researchers should reflect on intended, as well as unintended, outcomes of the study for the purpose of planning future professional development.

- Teacher-researchers should also reflect on the action research study itself, focusing primarily on the methodology employed.

QUESTIONS AND ACTIVITIES

1. Describe the purposes of action planning as an integral step in the action research process.

2. Why is professional reflection an essential component of action planning? Describe the two main ways that teacher-researchers should engage in reflective practice as part of their action planning.

3. Although you will be somewhat limited in terms of details, use the excerpts from the two studies appearing in Chapter 6 (in the Writing Up Action Research section) to create a brief action plan for future cycles of action research, as well as for instructional or other educational practice.

STUDENT STUDY SITE

Visit the Student Study Site at **www.sagepub.com/mertler3study** for these additional learning tools:

- Video clips
- Web resources
- Self quizzes
- E-flashcards

- PowerPoint slides
- Sample action research reports
- Full-text SAGE journal articles
- Chapter summaries

CHAPTER 8

Sharing and Reflecting

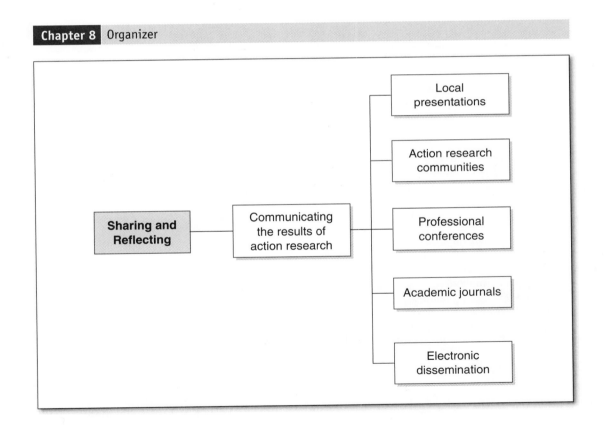

In Chapter 1, we discussed the gap that exists between what is learned as a result of researchers—typically university professors or others trained as researchers—who conduct and report their research on educational topics and the needs of practicing classroom teachers. In an effort to reduce this gap between theory and research and actual practice, it is imperative for teacher-researchers to share the results of their action research projects. A wide variety of options exist for teacher-researchers to share their research, ranging from local presentations to professional conferences and academic journals. In addition, there are numerous electronic means for communicating the results of action research. Although both Chapters 8 and 9 address issues related to publishing or otherwise disseminating the results of your action research studies, it is important to note that the focus of the present chapter is on the big picture—namely, presenting and discussing alternatives for sharing

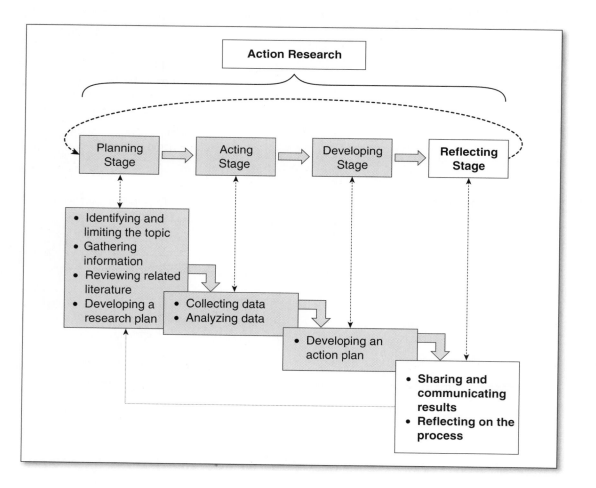

your action research. In contrast, Chapter 9 is more technical, focusing on the how-to of writing up your action research studies. After presenting information on these various alternatives for disseminating research results in this chapter, I will once again reiterate the importance of professional reflection as part of this process.

Communicating the Results of Action Research

gap   *out of touch*

For quite some time, a gap has existed between research conducted in the broad field of education and the ultimate, and supposed, users of that research (i.e., teachers). In Chapter 1, this gap was described as follows: Educational research tends to occur in the ivory towers of higher education, whereas the practical application (i.e., the education of children) takes place in schools and classrooms. What goes on in public school classrooms often does not reflect research findings related to instructional practices and student learning (Johnson, 2008).

Research is routinely written and published in such a way that does not consider a teacher's typical day-to-day schedule. The resulting research articles are often overly descriptive and highly technical and utilize research methods that do not fit with the *daily* needs of and resources available to teachers (e.g., they use true experimental designs, complete with random selection and assignment, or highly labor-intensive and longitudinal data collection methods). The research findings do not appreciate or often take into account teachers' points of view or factor in the practical challenges teachers must address in their classrooms on a daily basis. This has been alluded to numerous times throughout the book: In a manner of speaking, the teacher-researcher—through the act of designing and conducting action research studies— becomes the missing link between the theoretical researchers and the practicing educators.

Video Clip 8.1
View a clip of Dr. Mertler discussing the importance of sharing and reflecting on your research.

However, simply conducting an action research project will not automatically facilitate the reduction of this gap. Sharing the results—either formally or informally—is the real activity that helps bridge the divide between research and application. Communicating your results lends credibility to the process of conducting action research because teachers and others in the education profession tend to see this process as one that gives teachers a voice. Suddenly, research is not far removed from the classroom; they have, in a way, become one. Research is no longer an isolated activity, separate from the instructional process. It has become an integrated process such that the *advantages* of research (e.g., research designs, data collection methods, validity, and reliability) and the *advantages* of teachers' "voices" (e.g., knowing about the instructional process, having familiarity with teachers' day-to-day schedules, resource availability, and time constraints) can be realized in concert with one another. Perhaps more important, the act of sharing, communicating, or otherwise disseminating the results of your action research allow other educators to see this as well.

Not only does sharing the results of teacher-led action research projects with members of the teaching profession help narrow the gap between theory/research and practice, but it also provides the teacher-researcher with the opportunity to gain additional insight into the topic under investigation, as well as into the research process itself (Mills, 2011). If at the outset of your study you believed that the topic you had decided to investigate was an *important* one and in fact *worthy* of studying, in all likelihood there are other teachers, administrators, counselors, and so on who would feel the same way and would also be interested in your findings. This act of sharing—and, in fact, *celebrating*—the findings of your action research can actually be a very satisfying and rewarding *professional* experience (Mills, 2011). There is a tendency for teacher-researchers to feel intimidated at the thought of presenting or publishing their research, almost to the point of outwardly resisting the notion. As human beings, none of us likes to feel the wrath of our critics. However, I would strongly encourage you to take this next step in the action research process. Regardless of the types of reactions garnered by communicating your results, whether they be unfavorable or overwhelmingly positive, you will almost certainly experience professional growth.

Locally

There are several possible audiences for local presentations of your research, but probably none will be more interested than your colleagues (Johnson, 2008). More than anything, these presentations tend to promote professional discussion among teachers, counselors, and principals. These types of discussions are essential for facilitating professional reflection and growth in the teaching profession (Johnson, 2008). Do not become concerned about the notion of a full-blown presentation; it may not be necessary. These "presentations" may run the gamut from formal to informal. They may take the form of a formal teacher in-service session, a brief talk at a regularly scheduled faculty meeting, or perhaps an ongoing discussion among teachers within a school. Regardless of the level at which the presentation occurs, Johnson (2008) recommends that your audience of colleagues will tend to find your presentation more interesting if you keep it brief and focused and include only the details that other teachers might find helpful in their classrooms.

I would also strongly urge you to use some sort of visual aids to assist you in your presentation. Most of our *students*—regardless of the age or grade level at which we teach—do not like to simply be talked to or at; your colleagues will probably also appreciate visuals that increase the quality of your presentation and keep their attention. These visual aids might include overhead transparencies with a bulleted outline of your discussion, a handout of your major points and results, or perhaps even a technology-enhanced presentation using such software as PowerPoint or Keynote. The main aspects of a presentation should include the following:

1. *Background information.* Briefly summarize the literature review you conducted, trying not to mention everything you read. Simply mention three or four key aspects of your review, focusing on anything that provided you guidance in your study.

2. *Purpose of your study.* Share with your audience why you chose to study what you did. What personal experience led you to this topic? What were you trying to find out as a result of your study? Try to make a compelling argument for why your topic was worth investigating.

3. *Methodology employed.* Briefly describe the methodology used, focusing on the data you collected and how you collected them.

4. *Results.* This portion of your research presentation along with Numbers 5 and 6 below should comprise the majority of the time you have for your presentation. The results, along with your conclusions and action plan, are the aspects that your colleagues will be most interested in learning about. Tell your audience what you discovered by succinctly describing your findings. This may be an excellent time to use visuals, such as tables, graphs, or charts, if appropriate.

5. *Conclusions.* Share with your colleagues what you think your results *mean.* How do your results relate back to the original purpose of your study? What kinds of implications (i.e., for practice) can you draw from your conclusions?

6. *Action plan.* Based on your results and conclusions, describe what you plan to do from this point forward, in terms of both practice and future cycles of your action research. You may want to seek additional input from your colleagues regarding your action plan.

7. *Questions and answers.* Finally, always be sure to leave at least a few minutes for questions and answers. This is yet another opportunity for professional discussion and reflection.

Video Clips 8.2 & 8.3 View clips of educator-researchers discussing the importance of sharing and reflecting on their action research.

Another possible audience for your presentations is an audience consisting of your district's administration. This includes members of the school board, the superintendent, the assistant superintendent, directors of curriculum and instruction, directors of special education services, and so on, as well as building-level administrators (i.e., principals, assistant principals, deans of students, etc.). Often, district-level decisions regarding teaching and learning are made apart from considering any research related to them. Johnson (2008) believes that this can result in bad educational practice or perhaps even educational *mal-practice.* The results of action research can be used as an effective means of enabling your school or district to make educational decisions that are better informed. These decisions then are based on actual data collected, as opposed to being based on hunches or simply on what "looks good" to those making the decisions.

Action Research Communities

Along similar lines of sharing action research with audiences local in nature is the concept of creating action research communities. An **action research community** can be defined as a professional learning community made up of educational professionals driven by a common goal of practicing reflective teaching as a means of improving classroom instructional practice or other aspects of the educational process. Generally speaking, *professional learning communities (PLCs)* are comprised of educators committed to working collaboratively in ongoing processes of collective inquiry and action research to achieve better results for students they serve (DuFour, DuFour, & Eaker, 2008). They are based in the notion that the key to improved student learning is continuous, job-embedded learning for educators. This notion is similar to what James, Milenkiewicz, and Bucknam (2008) refer to as "communities of practice," or CoPs (p. 202).

The term "professional learning community" has been used to denote so many different types of activities that there continues to be a lack of clarity among the educational community. It has been used to describe grade-level teams, school committees, a content area department, an entire school building, or an entire school district (Baccellieri, 2010). In my opinion, the "level" of the learning community is not important, provided several important criteria are met. DuFour, DuFour, and Eaker (2008) describe six key characteristics of PLCs. At a minimum, they should include:

- a shared mission, vision, values, and goals all focused on student learning;

- a collaborative culture;

- a collective inquiry into best practices and current reality;

- an action orientation, or learning by doing;

- a commitment to continuous improvement; and

- an orientation focused on results, and not on intentions.

Note that the fourth item on this list—i.e., "an action orientation"—essentially delineates the integration of action research into the culture of a collaborative group of professional educators. Another key characteristic of PLCs is that innovation and experimentation are not viewed by the members of the PLC as tasks or projects to be completed, but rather as the way of conducting day-to-day business forever (DuFour, DuFour, & Eaker, 2008). PLCs have become extremely valuable approaches to initiating and sustaining school improvement and reform (Baccellieri, 2010).

Action research communities can be established within an individual school building or school district but can also "branch out" to include multiple buildings or even perhaps multiple districts (typically within a relatively small geographic area). These can be very meaningful professional development organizations, not only for sharing the results of action research but also for lending encouragement and support to teachers during just about any stage of the action research process. In addition, they can play an important role in the process of experienced teachers serving as mentors to novice teachers. These types of formal "learning communities" can provide significant levels of professional support. They can offer opportunities for both formal and informal sharing and reflecting on classroom teaching practice. Communities can be set up within a formal structure—perhaps with monthly meetings—or can be less formal. In the case of the latter, meetings might occur on an "as needed" basis. This idea of "grass-roots professional development" represents a substantial shift in mindset for many educators. Historically, district-level administrators have made decisions about what *they* believe their teachers should receive in the form of professional development opportunities. Furthermore, those decisions typically operate under a "one-size-fits-all" model, meaning that all teachers in a building, for example, require the same kinds and levels of continuing training in order to effectively deliver instruction, assess student learning, etc. In my opinion, this practice has been shown to be highly ineffective. Additionally, it has only served to alienate teachers from the process of determining and providing what each feels is needed to help them grow professionally (Mertler, 2010).

In contrast, professional development that is grounded in a process of individualized reflection can only be more meaningful to individual educators. In other words, when educators—either individually or collectively—reflect on their professional practice and identify areas in which *they* believe they need additional training, they tend to feel a much more vested interest in that training. Perhaps more importantly, they develop ownership over an entire process—i.e., implementing action research by reflecting on practice, identifying an area in need of improvement, and engaging in a process designed to improve the particular area—of professional development. To me, this notion is really the epitome of customized professional development.

Developing PLCs that formally integrate action research into the process can result in numerous positive outcomes. These include the fact that a collaborative approach to systematically improving educational practice and formally connecting theory to practice can be incredibly empowering for educators, at all levels. Educators develop skills and abilities to make well-informed decisions about their own practice. Furthermore, the PLC/action research approach provides opportunities for educators to effectively increase their knowledge and positively affect their practice, and can do so by focusing on what they see as their own particular professional development needs (Mertler, 2009). A process of reflecting on one's own practice as a means of answering questions about that practice, or of investigating issues related to that practice, enables educators to customize their own professional development. The bottom line is that educators who engage in this integrated process experience professional growth that is *specifically* related to their own areas of professional interest.

All of this being said, the integrated PLC/action research approach is not without its limitations. First and foremost, it requires a shift in mindset, or perhaps even in philosophy. This certainly constitutes an approach in complete opposition to the standard top-down, administrator-driven leadership models (Mertler, 2009). In a manner of speaking, the locus of control shifts away from the principal's office, providing educators with a much-needed voice in their own practice. Many educators—from the classroom teacher to the district superintendent—may experience a great deal of difficulty making this shift. Additionally, for those who desire such a shift in mindset, time and resources must be made available to them.

However you and your fellow colleagues decide to structure your action research community, I strongly encourage its use as you will likely view it as an important part of your ongoing professional development as an educator.

Professional Conferences

Local presentations are certainly acceptable outlets for presenting research and are typically beneficial to the teacher-researcher from the local point of view. However, sharing your research among a much broader community of educators provides even greater opportunities for professional dialogue, reflection, and brainstorming. Professional conferences are wonderful environments for communicating the results of research, sharing ideas for future cycles of action research, and networking with other educators who have similar research interests. Professional conferences are typically sponsored by state, regional, or national organizations and are usually held annually. The organization releases a call for proposals anywhere from 4 to 10 months in advance of the conference. Included in the call is a description of everything you need to include in your proposal. The proposal usually consists of a three- to four-page summary of your study. Once you have submitted it to the organization, it is sent out to other professional educators for a blind review, meaning that they do not know who the authors are at the time they review it. They review your proposal based on a preestablished set of criteria and either recommend it for inclusion in the conference program or not. If it is accepted, you receive notice a couple of months in advance of the conference in order to have time to prepare your research report and presentation. The seven main aspects to include in a presentation that were provided in the previous section also apply to presentations made at professional conferences. Depending on the nature and size of the professional conference, you will likely have anywhere from 15 to 75 minutes to present your study. If you are not familiar with professional conferences in your areas of interest, a search of the Internet will lead you to the websites of various organizations, which typically include links to information about their conferences. I am a big supporter of presenting research studies at professional conferences, as they can truly open the door to so many new opportunities and ideas!

District-Level Action Research Conferences

Similar to larger professional conferences—but perhaps a little less intimidating and a bit more meaningful—is the notion of district-level action research conferences. If your district promotes school- or district-wide action research as an integral part of the professional culture (implying that numerous educators might be simultaneously conducting action research projects), then providing a forum for those educators to share their findings and experiences serves as a potentially powerful mechanism for professional sharing, reflection, and future action planning, as well as for professional development in general. These types of conferences tend to be less intimidating because all of the presenters come from the same school or district. Furthermore, they tend to be more meaningful due to the fact that the action research topics (e.g., educational programs, interventions, curricula) being shared have taken place within the district where all conference presenters and attendees work. The presentations, therefore, tend to be more "personal," meaning that conference participants can more easily relate to and apply the action research being disseminated.

Several districts—as well as universities and colleges of education—throughout the United States routinely conduct such conferences.

Academic Journals

Since academic journals have the potential to reach larger audiences than professional conferences can, you may want to consider submitting your study to a journal in your particular field—one that focuses on the topic you studied or that focuses broadly on classroom-based action research. Similar to proposals submitted to conferences, **academic journals** are also **refereed**, meaning that any study submitted receives a blind, peer review by a minimum of two reviewers who provide comments on the quality of the study, as well as on the written manuscript detailing the study. Typically, comments provided by reviewers are both positive and constructive. Good reviewers will provide complimentary feedback about the good things done in the study. They will also provide suggestions for improving the quality of the manuscript. Their final comment is usually a recommendation to publish the paper or not. There are usually three types of recommendations:

1. *Accept as is.* If your paper receives this recommendation, no revisions are necessary. The paper is ready to be published in its current form. This type of recommendation is seldom given by any reviewer.

2. *Accept with revisions* (also referred to as *conditionally accept*). This is a much more typical recommendation for well-written papers of well-conducted studies. Almost every paper accepted for publication in an academic journal will require some revisions.

3. *Reject.* If your study had substantial methodological flaws or if the research paper was written poorly or simply not written clearly, perhaps because you did not pay attention to common stylistic conventions of academic writing (see Chapter 9), you may receive this recommendation. If this occurs, try not to become too discouraged—it happens to all of us! Consider taking the feedback provided by the reviewers, revising your paper, and submitting it to another journal. Sometimes when a manuscript is rejected, the editors may suggest that you "revise and resubmit" the paper. This may occur when the paper is poorly written and may need a complete reworking, but the topic may be of great interest to the readers of the journal.

As an example of this process, in Figure 8.1 I have included a copy of a letter that I received from a journal editor whose recommendation was to "conditionally accept" my manuscript. You will also notice that, as I made revisions to the final version of the manuscript, I marked off each suggested revision appearing in the letter. Although this process can be a bit intimidating at first—and can create anxiety throughout one's professional career!—receiving this type of feedback and specific comments on your action research studies and ability to write them up is one of the best ways to improve your writing (Johnson, 2008).

Figure 8.1	Sample Letter From a Journal Editor; Manuscript Conditionally Accepted for Publication

December 16, 2003

Craig A. Mertler
Bowling Green University
College of Education & Human Development
Division of Educational Foundations & Inquiry
School of Leadership and Policy Studies
Bowling Green, OH 43403

Re: "Secondary Teachers' Assessment Literacy: Does Classroom Experience Make a Difference?"

Dear Dr. Mertler:

On behalf of the Editorial Board, I am pleased to report that your manuscript is conditionally accepted for publication in American Secondary Education. Reviewers felt that the article dealt with a timely topic that "has not been emphasized enough in the literature" and that it was "professionally crafted." To prepare it for publication, however, please address the following issues

1. The article could be strengthened through an increased attention to audience. Although the topic of assessment is clearly one of general interest, the article should make some reference to the relevance of the topic for secondary educators since that is the focus of this journal. Similarly, the discussion should include some implications for the secondary teachers and administrators who read the journal as well as some suggestions for researchers.

2. One reviewer felt that the Conclusions should include a discussion of why preservice and in-service teachers score differently in their highest category. Another felt that some reference should be made to the testing emphasis in No Child Left Behind. Do you recommend more preservice instruction, or do you believe that the emphasis should shift to "on-the-job" learning—perhaps through ongoing professional development?

3. Reviewers raised a number of questions about the design and reporting of the study:
   • Clarify participants' characteristics
   • Add a table with frequencies by item or at least by aggregated items by standard
   • Describe what "correct" means on the scale (congruency with the standards?)
   • Address the low reliability coefficient for in-service teachers as a limitation of the study. Should it be used in future research?
   • Address psychometric properties of your modified instrument since it is different from the original
   • Cite some support for the assertion that the "trend is changing" away from an emphasis on standardized testing in teacher preparation (p. 17)
   • The section of the results on page 17 that talks about "5 of the 35 items" etc. is rather confusing. Readers cannot see what those items said, and the relevance of this finding to the research questions is unclear. Suggestion b. above might help, or you might just omit it.

4. The organization of the article could be tightened to reduce redundancy
   • Eliminate the introduction on page 2. The points made in that section are all made in the literature review. The Rogers article cited in this section may also be too old to be used as a basis for stating that there is currently a problem.
   • Begin instead with the definition of assessment literacy and explanation of the seven standards.
   • Omit Tables 1 and 2 since most of the information they contain is included in Table 3. It seems that the three could be combined into one.

5. Please note that APA format calls for consistent use of the past tense in the literature review. Also, try to reduce the use of passive voice (e.g., "Stiggins provided a similar description" rather than "A similar description was provided by Stiggins").

You may return your revised manuscript on a 3.5 disk in Microsoft Word. Also, please complete and return the enclosed Copyright Assignment Form. American Secondary Education cannot publish your article unless it holds exclusive rights to the article.

Thank you for considering the *American Secondary Education* journal.

Sincerely,

James A. Rycik

James A. Rycik,
Editor

JAR/gv

Source: Reprinted with permission of the *American Secondary Education* journal.

Mills (2011) offers some sound guidelines to keep in mind when considering submitting your study to a journal. First, it is important that you peruse the journal(s) that you are considering for your submission(s). Realize that the articles you are reading represent those that have been accepted for publication. Pay close attention to the writing style, as well as the structure and format of the articles themselves. Do not feel that you have to *copy* the particular format and style; rather, use them as guides for your paper as you prepare it for submission. Second, it is suggested that you use a clear, reader-friendly writing style. Action research should be written up using straightforward language and vocabulary. Do not try to impress your readers with flowery language or polysyllabic words, especially when their use is not necessary. Let your data and your interpretations of those data speak for themselves. You should strive to make your paper readable and understandable not only by those who are knowledgeable about your topic but also by those who are not. Third, Mills suggests that you develop a paper that guides your readers to the site at which your study occurred. Provide a description of the setting, the participants, the length of the study, and the focus of your investigation. Fourth, you should also include a brief description of what you actually did in the course of your study. Focus on explanations of your research design, data collection, data analysis, and ultimate interpretations. Also, do not forget to attend to other various data collection considerations, such as validity, reliability, and ethics regarding your participants. Finally, it is critical that you make every effort to keep your readers' attention. Granted, academic journal articles of classroom-based teacher research will probably never make a best-seller list, but that does not mean that they cannot be interesting and rewarding to read. Enjoyable and engaging reading does not have to be mutually exclusive in academic writing, but it does take some effort on the part of the author.

There are several journals—all of which are refereed—whose articles focus on classroom-based, teacher-conducted research. This list of journals includes the following:

- *Action Research*
- *Action Research International*
- *Educational Action Research*
- *Networks: An On-line Journal for Teacher Research*
- *Reflective Practice*
- *Teaching & Learning: The Journal of Natural Inquiry & Reflective Practice*
- *The Journal of Scholarship of Teaching and Learning*
- *The Ontario Action Researcher*

More information about these journals, including information available at their websites, has been included in the Related websites section appearing later in this chapter.

Sharing Results Electronically

More and more opportunities are being created for teachers to share the results of their research electronically, especially in various online environments. There are various types of electronic media in which results can be shared or ideas exchanged. Before I discuss them, however, let me offer a word of caution. The Internet can be a wonderful place to find information and materials that one might not have access to otherwise. However, it is important to be cautious about information and research results that you read online. There exists a common misconception that if something is "published" (that is to say, if it appears in print), it must be important, meaningful, and of high quality. Just because something appears in print—even if it is refereed—does not *necessarily* mean that it is of substantial quality. It is important to be a critical consumer of anything you read online.

One of the nicer aspects of sharing research and ideas online is that teachers can be provided with the sense that the world is a much smaller place and that input and feedback are readily accessible from literally all corners of the globe. Online resources typically fall into one of three categories: action research websites, electronic mailing lists, and electronic journals (Mills, 2011). We will briefly look at each of these, although additional information—including URLs for various websites—appears in the Related websites section.

Numerous action research websites are available on the Internet. These sites are sponsored and hosted primarily by institutions and individuals in Australia, Canada, the United Kingdom, and the United States. Most of them offer a variety of features, including electronic journals, electronic discussion boards, print as well as electronic action research resources, and links to other action research sites. The sites featured later in this chapter include the following:

- Action Research at Queen's University

- Action Research Resources

- Educating as Inquiry: A Teacher/Action Research Site

- EmTech's Action Research Page

- Teacher Research

In addition to worldwide websites, many school districts are also developing and hosting their own action research web pages on district websites. The specific purpose of these sites is to allow teachers in the particular district to share their results of action research, primarily districtwide, although with the World Wide Web, dissemination would not be limited only to members of that district. As a concrete example of this relatively new electronic means of sharing action research, let me highlight one district's efforts. On several occasions throughout this book (primarily in the Related websites sections at the end of various chapters), the Madison (Wisconsin) Metropolitan School District has been featured.

The district's action research website (http://oldweb.madison.k12.wi.us/sod/car/carhomepage.html) includes links to all types of helpful information related to conducting classroom-based action research. One link in particular (http://oldweb.madison.k12.wi.us/sod/car/search.cgi) takes you to a searchable index of abstracts of action research studies conducted by their teachers from 1990 through 2009. Several of the abstracts also include links to the complete research papers written by the teachers themselves. This is an absolutely wonderful outlet for teacher-conducted action research projects, as well as being a very valuable resource for teachers' professional development. If your district does not currently have such a means for locally (and more broadly) sharing the results of your action research, pursuing such an opportunity with district-level administrators may be time well spent for the benefit of all teachers in your district. Another example of a school that maintains its own action research website is Highland Park High School (http://hphs.dist113.org) in Highland Park, Illinois. The school's Action Research Laboratory page (http://hphs.dist113.org/Academics/Pages/ActionResearch.aspx) contains more than 25 complete action research reports and presentations written by Highland Park teachers and administrators.

An **electronic mailing list** is an online discussion forum conducted via e-mail, typically located on a large computer network and hosted by a university (Mills, 2011). Electronic mailing lists provide opportunities to participate in discussions on a wide variety of topics within a given field (e.g., action research) with individuals from all over the world. Information and links to several of them are included in the sites listed above. If you subscribe to an electronic mailing list, you should be aware that you will likely receive several e-mail messages per day on one or more discussion topics, known as "discussion threads." The messages can add up quickly if you do not check your e-mail on a regular basis.

Although it can be interesting and educational to simply sit back and read the various postings to an electronic mailing list, do not hesitate to post your own questions or ideas; electronic mailing lists tend to be very collaborative and collegial environments. I have been able to offer suggestions to members of an electronic mailing list, as well as to seek their advice for my own projects. In addition, I have been able to establish several professional relationships over the years with individuals who have interests similar to mine by doing just that. These are individuals with whom I likely would never have come into contact had it not been for the electronic mailing list.

Finally, the Internet has also enabled publishers to put entire journals online. Over time, more and more full-text, refereed teacher-researcher **electronic journals** are becoming available online. Several of the journals listed earlier in this chapter are entirely electronic or online journals, including *Action Research International, Educational Action Research, Networks: An On-line Journal for Teacher Research,* and *The Ontario Action Researcher.* These electronic journals make the submission process relatively painless, since the manuscripts are typically submitted electronically via e-mail as attachments. Furthermore, the turnaround time from submission to (hopefully) publication tends to be several months less, simply due to the technology involved. Another benefit of these electronic journals can be experienced by the teacher-researcher as a *consumer* of action research. Electronic journals make access to teacher research articles much easier. Since they are available in full-text format, one does not even have to travel to a local university library and make a photocopy of the article, as was necessary in the past and still is for print journals. The articles are usually available in HTML or PDF formats and can therefore easily be saved to a hard drive or computer disk or printed out. The fact that nearly all of these online action research journals are only a few years old serves as an indication of the extent to which teacher research is truly a field that is experiencing a great deal of growth and that is creating progressively more interest across the broad field of education.

Reflecting on the Action Research Process

At the risk of once again sounding repetitive, professional reflection is a key component of the action research process and should be integrated thoroughly throughout each of the steps along the way. The acts of sharing, disseminating, and communicating the results of your action research provide yet another opportunity to reflect on the process itself. Reviewing all that you have done and accomplished in conducting your study—which is necessary when preparing to put pen to paper and draft your final research report or when developing an outline for a presentation of your study—is another way that you can introspectively examine your practice of teaching. It is essential to your professional growth and development that you seize each and every opportunity—prior to, during, and following your action research study—to engage in reflective practice.

WRITING UP ACTION RESEARCH:
REFLECTING ON RESEARCH

Recognizing that there is an incongruency between my teaching beliefs and my teaching practice is the first step. I now wish to explore several options which should help me facilitate better teacher-student communication in my classroom. Some of these are: giving written directions so students can refer to them during the lesson as needed; providing students with an outline, covering important points in the lesson; asking questions that promote thinking, relating questions to students' previous experiences; and encouraging students to talk freely amongst themselves in groups.

Conducting this study has given me insight into my classroom. I now realize that students come to class with a sense of inquiry. They are ready to explore and find answers on their own. I feel students are excited about engaging in the process of science, and they show this by their willingness to share ideas and beliefs with others. It is my job to step back and trust this sense of student inquiry. By not monopolizing the classroom I feel I can now provide rich opportunities for students to investigate the world of middle school science at a much deeper level than ever before.

Source: Graham, 1995.

One of my primary focuses for this study was to carefully choose my groups so that they were clearly heterogeneous from both an academic and cultural standpoint. Another main focus was to assign specific roles or jobs within the groups so that each member would be perceived as a valued player. The roles worked, were also designed to make the group members more dependent on each other and less dependent on the teacher. However, according to the respondents of Kathy's survey, 92% indicated that they would have changed their jobs if they could. When the jobs were assigned, the intent was to "bring out" the very behaviors that were not being observed. For example, when one student was observed as being passive and unsmiling, we assigned her the job of Principal Investigator to bring out more assertive behavior in her. All of the roles were assigned to all of the students with similar objectives in mind. Perhaps allowing the students a part in the decision making for jobs would be a good idea next time.

Cooperative group learning is much more than just putting students in groups and giving them assignments to complete. In doing this study, I set higher expectations of my students than I ever had before. The conceptual learning and creative problem solving that took place was clearly indicated from the data sources. The rocket science unit of instruction challenged all of the students, especially in terms of the difficult mathematics concepts. However, all of the other aspects of the unit were equally challenging, and the sharing of ideas and group problem-solving strategies were prevalent throughout the unit. Student motivation was higher than I had ever seen when we were in the midst of rocket science. In fact, one student became so motivated about rocket science that he won third place in the 1995 State Science Fair and an overall "Best of Show." If anyone else can benefit from the model of middle school teaching that I developed, I would be ecstatic, but the model was truly for myself and the students that I teach. I certainly intend to keep improving the model in the years to come.

Source: DuBois, 1995.

⫷ ACTION RESEARCH PORTRAIT 1 ⫸

Enhancing Academic Performance
Through Improved Classroom Assessment

Recall that the purpose of this action research study is to improve teachers' classroom-based assessments in an effort to improve student achievement.

Following the development of their action plan, Susan, Larry, Cathy, and John approached their building principal about sharing the results of their action research study with the rest of the teachers at Jones Middle School. She had always been quite supportive of the teachers engaging in growth activities, and she agreed to let them give a brief presentation at the last faculty meeting of the year in June. The team believed that this would also be a great opportunity to share with their colleagues the action plan for next year's cycle of implementation of Improving Student Achievement by Improving Teachers' Assessments.

In preparation for their presentation at the end-of-the-year faculty meeting, the team of teachers met to develop an outline for their 20-minute presentation. They developed an outline and divided up the presentation as follows:

Improving Student Achievement by Improving Teachers' Assessments
Jones Middle School Faculty Meeting
June 15, 2:45 p.m.

1. *Background to the study* (Why did we decide to do this?)—Susan

2. *Related research and purpose of the study* (What were we trying to investigate? Had anyone done anything like this before?)—Cathy

3. *Methodology* (So, how did we do it?)—Larry

4. *Results* (And what did we discover?)—John

5. *Conclusions* (What does this all mean for our teaching? Our students? Our school?)—Susan

6 *Action plan* (Where do we go from here . . . ?)—Larry

7. *Questions and answers*—you!

The team printed out the outline and provided it as a handout for the other teachers in the meeting. In addition, because they knew that they had limited time for their presentation, they highlighted their main statements in a brief PowerPoint presentation. They felt that bulleted points under each of the first six items on their outline would help them stay on task. An example of one of their PowerPoint slides appears below:

Improving Student Achievement by Improving Teachers' Assessments

- Results
  1. Team North scored higher than Team East on all 4 subsets.
  2. Two scores (LA & MATH) were significant.

Independent Samples *t* Test Results

SUBTEST	Mean Difference (Gp. 1–Gp. 2)	*t* test value	*Df*	*p*-value
LA_2	34.0833	3.532	60	−.001
MATH_2	40.9167	2.046	60	−.045
SCI_2	13.8542	1.684	60	−.097
SS_S	19.0833	1.302	60	−.198

Following the presentation, their principal suggested that the group make the same presentation of the study to the board of education and other district administrators. The teachers agreed, and their principal set up the presentation for the July board meeting.

❧ ACTION RESEARCH PORTRAIT 2 ❧

Improving Reading Comprehension in a Title I Program

Recall that the purpose of this action research study is to improve students' reading comprehension skills within a Title I context.

Kathleen was very happy with the results of her action research study and was excited about her plans to continue it into the next school year. She felt fairly sure that her fellow Title I teachers from within the district would also find the results interesting and very meaningful. She approached the director of the district's Title I program and requested some time at their monthly meeting at the district's offices. The director willingly agreed to provide Kathleen with some time to share her study and results with the other Title I teachers.

(Continued)

(Continued)

Following the meeting where Kathleen presented her study, several of the other teachers approached her about the possibility of publishing it. Kathleen was a little hesitant at first, but the teachers offered to support her and even help her with editing and putting the finishing touches on a draft of a research report that she had been working on. They brainstormed ideas for possible publications, and all agreed that a popular reading journal, The Reading Teacher—a publication of the International Reading Association—might be a very appropriate outlet for her study. Included in each edition of The Reading Teacher is a section where teachers and other researchers can publish the results of research studies in the form of brief articles. The teachers went online, first to the main page for the International Reading Association (http://www.reading.org) and then to a page titled "Writing for The Reading Teacher" (http://www.reading.org/publications/for_authors/rt.html) or "Writing for the Journal of Adolescent & Adult Literacy" (http://www.reading.org/publications/for_authors/jaal.html) where they found information specifically directed toward individuals wishing to submit articles for possible publication. There they found information about the nature of articles published in The Reading Teacher, the desired length of published manuscripts, and the length of time that authors could expect the review process to take. Specifically, they found the following passage:

Authors are generally notified of a decision within three months of receipt of submission. Articles are judged primarily for their contribution to the field, usefulness to teachers or researchers, timeliness, freshness of approach, and clarity and cohesiveness of presentation.

Kathleen was very excited about the prospect of having her action research published, although she was aware that there was no guarantee. She would do her best to put together a sound manuscript, focusing specifically on her study and the process of reflection she used in order to make meaning of her results.

Related Websites: Communication and Discussion About Action Research

This annotated list of related websites provides information about several online action research organizations, electronic journals, and electronic mailing lists. You will notice that several of the electronic mailing lists and electronic journals are sponsored by organizations also appearing below.

Action Research Websites

- Action Research at Queen's University **http://resources.educ.queensu.ca/ar**

  This action research site is maintained by Queen's University, located in Kingston, Ontario, Canada. Included on the university's site are links to action research reports, several articles on reflective practice, and numerous action research reports from both undergraduate and graduate students at the university.

- Action Research Resources **http://www.scu.edu.au/schools/gcm/ar/arhome.html**

  This site is a wealth of resources! Sponsored by Southern Cross University in Lismore, New South Wales, Australia, it includes links to Action Research International (an online journal), a 2-week online course in action research and evaluation, various resource papers, five different electronic mailing lists (see below under Action Research Electronic Mailing Lists), and abstracts from several action research theses and dissertations.

- Educating as Inquiry: A Teacher/Action Research Site **http://www.lupinworks.com/ar/ index.html**

  Developed by Dr. Judith M. Newman of Mount Saint Vincent University, this site features articles by teachers who have conducted action research on a number of topics and an online conference on the Reflective Practitioner. There are also links to a number of related sites.

- EmTech's Action Research Page **http://www.emtech.net/actionresearch.htm**

  EmTech, or Emerging Technology Consulting, provides a lengthy web page of links to useful sites related to action research.

- Teacher Research **http://gse.gmu.edu/research/tr**

  Run jointly by Dr. Diane Painter from the Fairfax County (Virginia) Public Schools and Dr. Leo Rigsby from the Graduate School of Education, George Mason University, this site discusses a variety of issues in action research and also provides numerous links.

Action Research Electronic Journals

- *Action Research International* **http://www.scu.edu.au/schools/gcm/ar/ari/arihome.html**

  This journal consists of an electronic discussion list to which papers can be submitted for comment and another list that provides papers that have been accepted. Extensive author guidelines are also included for potential authors at http://www.scu.edu.au/schools/ gcm/ar/ari/ari-auth.html.

- *Educational Action Research* **http://www.tandf.co.uk/journals/titles/09650792.asp**

  EAR is published by Routledge, a member of the Taylor and Francis Group. Similar to other journals, guidelines for prospective authors are provided. By clicking on the eJournal: Online Contents button, you can review sample issues of EAR, going back to its first edition in 1993 (http://www.informaworld.com/smpp/title ~content = t716100708 ~ db = all).

- *Networks: An On-line Journal for Teacher Research* **http://journals.library.wisc.edu/ index.php/networks**

  Networks is arguably the premier online journal for teacher action research, mainly because it is the first journal dedicated solely to teacher research. Sponsored by the University of Wisconsin–Madison, the journal provides a "place for sharing reports of action research, in which teachers at all levels, kindergarten to postgraduate, are reflecting on classroom practice through research ventures. It also provides space for discussion of other ways in which educational practitioners, alone or in collaboration, use inquiry as a tool to learn more about their work with the hope of eventually improving its effectiveness." The editors of the journal strongly encourage teachers to share their classroom research with colleagues from around the world! By clicking on Current or Archives, readers can view and print the full text of all articles published in Networks since its inception in 1998.

- *Reflective Practice* **http://www.tandf.co.uk/journals/titles/14623943.asp**

  This journal is published by the Taylor and Francis Group. *Reflective Practice* includes "papers that address the connections between reflection, knowledge generation, practice and policy." Its focus is entirely on the nature and meaning given to the process of professional reflection.

- *Teaching & Learning: The Journal of Natural Inquiry & Reflective Practice* **http://www .und.nodak.edu/dept/ehd/journal**

  This journal is sponsored by the College of Education and Human Development at the University of North Dakota. Its focus is on the "values of thoughtful observation as an educational method." The articles, all of which are available on the site in full-text (HTML or PDF) format, center on naturalistic inquiry in educational settings.

- *The Journal of Scholarship of Teaching and Learning* **http://www.iupui.edu/~josotl**

  JoSoTL, sponsored by Indiana University, encourages educators to share their knowledge and experiences about the teaching-learning process. The editors specifically state that "submissions that include reflective commentary about the result of the investigation will be considered of greater value to our readership and more appealing for publication." All articles are available both for preview (in your web browser) and for download (in PDF format).

- *The Ontario Action Researcher* **http://www.nipissingu.ca/oar/**

  OAR is sponsored by Nipissing University in North Bay, Ontario, Canada. It is made possible through a partnership of the Grand Erie District School Board, the Elementary Teachers' Federation of Ontario, and Nipissing University. As a goal, OAR tries to mend "the rift between the researcher and the practitioner. Within this context, the journal strives to:

  o Publish accounts of a range of action research projects in education and across the professions with the aim of making their outcomes widely available, providing models of effective action research and enabling educators to share their experiences

  o Demonstrate connections between practice and theory through articles of a general nature on methodological and epistemological issues related to action research

  o Disseminate reviews of books, websites and products related to action research o And finally, to provide a forum for dialogue on the various action research projects that are taking place around the province."

Similar to many of the other journals in this list, all articles in The Ontario Action Researcher are available online in full-text format, free of charge.

- *Voices From the Field* **http://www.alliance.brown.edu/pubs/voices**

This online periodical was produced from the fall of 1999 through the spring of 2002 by the Northeast and Islands Regional Educational Laboratory, a program of the Education Alliance at Brown University. The purpose of this free publication was to present issues from the perspectives of teachers experiencing change, challenges, and growth as education reform took shape. Although no longer in production, there are some wonderful articles of action research written by teachers.

Action Research Electronic Mailing Lists

Most electronic mailing lists operate in a similar fashion. You simply send an e-mail message to the specified e-mail address for the given electronic mailing list, with nothing in the subject line and no signature included. The contents of the e-mail message—in a generic format—usually read as follows:

---

subscribe < name of electronic mailing list >   < your first name >   < your last name >

Another added advantage of electronic mailing lists is that there is no cost to subscribe or participate in the electronic discussions.

- **arlist-L**—Action Research Mailing List
  Details about this electronic mailing list, including subscription instructions, can be found at: **http://www.scu.edu.au/schools/gcm/ar/arr/arlist.html**

- **armnet-L**—Action Research Methodology Mailing List

  Information about this electronic mailing list can be found at: **http://www.scu.edu.au/schools/gcm/ar/arr/armnet.html**

- **qual-L**—Qualitative Research Mailing List
  Information about this electronic mailing list is available online at: **http://www.scu.edu.au/schools/gcm/ar/arr/qual.html**

- **partalk-L**—Participatory Action Research Network Mailing List
  Information about this electronic mailing list is available online at: **http://www.accessexcellence.org/LC/TL/AR/ardiscuss.html**

- **xtar**—Teacher-Researchers Mailing List
  Information about this electronic mailing list is also available at: **http://www.accessexcellence.org/LC/TL/AR/ardiscuss.html**

SUMMARY

★ Sharing the results of action research studies conducted by teacher-researchers can help reduce the gap that exists between research/theory and practical application in educational settings.

- Sharing the results of research studies also provides an opportunity for teacher researchers to gain additional insight into their study and ultimate findings.

- The act of sharing and celebrating the findings of action research can be a very rewarding professional experience.

- Results can be shared locally, with fellow teachers, students, and your district's administration.

- Keep any local presentation brief and focused, highlighting the following: background information, purpose of the study, methodology, results, conclusions, and action plan. Remember to always leave time at the end for questions and answers.

- Action research communities can serve as outlets for sharing the results of action research, for lending encouragement and support to teachers, and for mentoring other teachers.

★ Results can also be shared at professional conferences and in academic journals.

- Most professional conferences and journals are refereed, meaning that they use a blind peer-review process to determine the merits of a proposal submitted for presentation or publication.

- When writing for a journal, it is important to keep your audience in mind, use a clear and reader-friendly writing style, and strive to keep your readers' attention.

★ In increasing fashion, results of action research studies can be shared electronically via action research websites, electronic mailing lists, and electronic journals.

★ The act of communicating the results of your action research provides yet another opportunity to reflect not only on the topic of your investigation but also on the action research process itself.

QUESTIONS AND ACTIVITIES

1. Describe ways in which presenting or publishing your action research is beneficial in terms of professional reflective practice.

2. Develop a list of alternative techniques, not discussed in the chapter, for sharing the findings of your action research. These techniques may simply be adaptations of other forms of professional communications.

3. Conduct a web search for other types of outlets for sharing findings from action research studies, perhaps in a specific area of education (e.g., mathematics education, special education, early childhood education, gifted and talented education) that is important to you. Describe your search and what you found online.

4. Subscribe to one of the electronic mailing lists identified in this chapter. Monitor and/or contribute to the online discussions over the course of several days or weeks. What did you learn? Did you contribute to any of the discussions? If so, what was your reaction to that experience?

5. Visit one of the electronic journals listed in the chapter. Review and make a list of the steps involved in the process of getting an article published in that particular journal.

STUDENT STUDY SITE

Visit the Student Study Site at **www.sagepub.com/mertler3study** for these additional learning tools:

- Video clips
- Web resources
- Self quizzes
- E-flashcards

- PowerPoint slides
- Sample action research reports
- Full-text SAGE journal articles
- Chapter summaries

CHAPTER 9

Writing Up Action Research

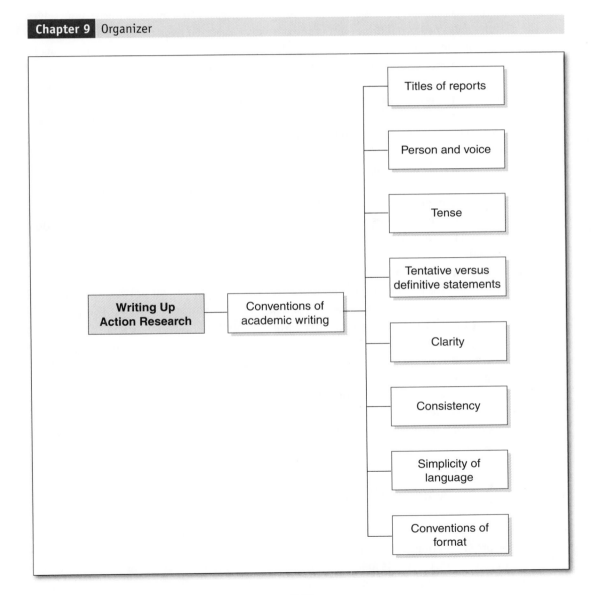

In Chapter 8, our discussion focused on the big picture of sharing your action research and, specifically, communicating the results of that research. I outlined various mechanisms through which you could share and disseminate the results of your action research studies, including presentations, academic journals, and electronic formats. In this chapter, the discussion will center on more technical aspects of formal written reports of action research—the kinds of reports that you would typically find in academic journals, for example.

At this point, and after having read Chapter 8, some of you may be saying to yourselves, "Getting *published* is not important to me or to my career. There is no real reason for me to write about my action research." Mills (2011) would argue—and I would most emphatically agree—that there is real value in writing up your research. As a community of professional educators, it is critical that we move beyond the expectation that writing up research is something that is done only by academics at colleges and universities. Mills goes on to suggest that the actual process of writing up action research requires the teacher-researcher to clarify various *meanings* throughout your report. You must choose your words carefully, thoroughly describe the events that you experienced during your study, and reflect on those experiences. Through engaging in this process, you will likely continue to learn more about your topic of study, your students, their learning, your teaching, and so on—things that perhaps you had not considered or thought through. In addition, the act of formally writing up your research study forces you to be honest, accurate, and thorough, thus promoting a better final product (Mills, 2011).

In addition to the clarification of various meanings associated with your action research, Mills (2011) also lists several other reasons for formally writing up action research. The feedback you receive from reviewers and readers of your research will provide you with *validation* for who you are and what you do as a professional educator. The act of continuously reflecting on your instructional practices will *empower* you to continue to strive for better ways to educate your students. Finally, writing up your research will quite honestly provide you with a terrific sense of accomplishment. It can be both gratifying and humbling when colleagues read your work and recognize your accomplishments (Mills, 2011).

All of this being said, academic writing is not necessarily an easy task for everyone. It represents a different type of writing—one that is more technical and "scientific." The aim of this chapter is to help you better understand this type of writing, as a process, and to share with you some of its primary conventions.

Conventions of Academic Writing

When writing up a formal report of your action research, you will need to follow a style guide. If you are submitting the report to a journal for possible publication, it is even more important that you use *the* style guide followed by the particular journal. A **style guide** is an instruction manual of sorts, providing authors with various requirements for stylistic matter, including, but not limited to, punctuation, grammar, abbreviations, reference styles, headings, quotations, statistical notation, and captions for figures and tables. The most commonly used style guide for academic-style writing in the United States is the *Publication Manual of the American Psychological Association* (6th edition). If you have ever had to write a paper for a graduate course, you are likely familiar with APA style. If not, you likely will want to invest in the manual as a reference, as it is not very expensive, retailing for about $30.

Most journals will specify the style guide they follow in their guidelines for authors; however, some journals, especially electronic journals, do not specify any sort of stylistic requirements. For example, the passage below appears on the website for *Teaching & Learning: The Journal of Natural Inquiry & Reflective Practice,* specifically on its "Guidelines for Contributors" page (http://www.und.nodak.edu/dept/ehd/journal/submissions.html):

> *Teaching and Learning* is a refereed journal devoted to the values of thoughtful observation as an educational method, of description as a technique for understanding, and of lived experience as a source of knowledge construction. The journal is in the process of being converted to the online environment.
>
> We encourage the submission of articles, essays, and critical commentary grounded in observed experience in natural settings; of parts of reflective journals; of situated descriptions on teaching/learning practice; of action-oriented research; of ethnographic studies; of semiotic analyses; and of evaluation studies. We will also consider creative works focused on issues related to teaching and learning.
>
> We define teaching and learning broadly and invite contributors to stretch or dissolve traditional categories of education. We invite contributions from educators, critical theorists, researchers, social scientists, human-service professionals, historians, philosophers, administrators, students, parents, and artists.
>
> Due to the interdisciplinary character of this journal, articles should be written in a manner that facilitates communication across domains; a style of intelligent informality is preferred. Use American Psychological Association (APA) style, double spaced, with wide margins. All manuscripts should be accompanied by a brief biography of the author or authors. Due to the online format, please submit the manuscript as an e-mail attachment, preferably in Microsoft Word (4.0 or higher), and save the manuscript as a rich text format (rtf) document.

Notice that the announcement does not specify much about writing style but does state (in the last paragraph) that potential authors should follow APA style. It is then the author's responsibility to consult the *Publication Manual of the American Psychological Association* for guidance and to prepare the manuscript accordingly.

   Conventions of academic-style writing are simply agreed-upon procedures that help ensure the readability and credibility of research reports (Mertler & Charles, 2011). Readers of journals and other outlets for research reports have certain expectations regarding format and style. When writing up the results of action research, it is important for teacher-researchers to follow these conventions. Failure to do so does not invalidate the research, but a researcher's credibility can be damaged by using unconventional report styles and formats (Mertler & Charles, 2011). Consider how a classroom teacher's credibility can be tarnished by handing out to students a test that is replete with spelling and grammatical errors. The failure of teacher-researchers to follow standard conventions of writing style can result in a fate similar to that of the careless classroom teacher. The conventions of style we will examine include the following:

1. Titles of reports

2. Person and voice

3. Tense

4. Tentative versus definitive statements

5. Clarity

6. Consistency

7. Simplicity of language

We will also take a look at two essential conventions of format, namely a generic format for the major sections of a research report and guidelines regarding the length of a research report.

Titles of Reports

The title of any written work is, at least at the outset, one of the most important aspects of the work from the readers' perspective. The title is the initial screening mechanism for anyone considering reading the work. Unless you are familiar with an author's works, the title of a novel is typically the first thing that grabs your attention or that turns you off. In a manner of speaking, the title of a research report operates in a similar fashion. The title should indicate clearly what the study and the report are about. Researchers and teacher-researchers are sometimes inclined to develop cute, clever titles that pose riddles or that are extremely vague. If my time as an educator is limited, I am less likely to pick up and read an article with such a title as this. There is nothing inherently wrong with a clever title, provided it accurately describes the topic and study at hand (Mertler & Charles, 2011).

The titles of my research papers tend to be fairly straightforward and very descriptive. For example, I recently published a journal article titled "The Role of Classroom Experience in Preservice and Inservice Teachers' Assessment Literacy." Notice the descriptive nature of this title. It includes the independent variable *(classroom experience),* the dependent variable *(assessment literacy),* and the populations studied *(preservice and in-service teachers).*

I tend not to get too clever in the development of my titles. However, sometimes I do try to create some that are a bit more entertaining. Consider the following two titles from recent studies that I conducted, one presented at a professional conference and the other published in a journal:

> "What . . . Another Survey??? Patterns of Response and Nonresponse From Teachers to Traditional and Web Surveys"

> "The Mouse or the Pencil? A Psychometric Comparison of Web-Based and Traditional Survey Methodologies"

Even though I tried to get a bit clever in the interrogative portion of these titles, the part that follows is still fairly descriptive of the topic and actual study conducted. My basic advice to you when writing up your action research is to keep the cutesy aspect out of your titles and simply create a thorough, but brief, descriptive title—grab your readers' attention!

Person and Voice

Video Clip 9.1
View a clip of Dr. Mertler discussing academic writing.

One of the features of academic writing—and, specifically, of more traditional forms of research, such as experimental research—that distinguishes it from other forms of writing is that it is typically written as objectively as possible (Johnson, 2008). You will seldom see any use of *first-person pronouns*. Usually, the authors do not refer to themselves as "I," "we," or "me." Authors will make reference to themselves using *third-person* terms, such as "the authors" or "the researchers." Personal observations, conclusions, and recommendations are reserved for a special section, usually at the very end of the report, and even those are written in third person (Johnson, 2008). Remember that the goal of experimental research is to remove any and all bias and subjectivity from the perspective of the researcher and let only the data communicate to the reader.

Consider the following passage from a paper of mine published a few years ago in an academic journal:

> An original survey instrument, the *Ohio Teacher Assessment Practices Survey,* was developed by the researcher for purposes of collecting the data. The literature was relied upon heavily in order to guide the development of the specific items appearing in the survey instrument. The instrument consisted of 47 items and included both scaled (forced-choice) and open-ended items. For purposes of the study at hand, teachers were asked by the researcher to respond to items concerning the validity and reliability of their classroom assessments, specifically requesting information on the steps that they follow and the extent to which they do so.

Notice that I have described the fact that I developed the survey instrument myself, specifically for use in this research study. However, in two places in this paragraph, I purposely refer to myself as "the researcher."

In contrast, and similar to more qualitative forms of research, action research is written in a much more subjective style. A teacher-researcher is a central part of the action research study; therefore, it is not possible—nor is it desirable—to remove the thoughts and perceptions of the teacher-researcher. However, it is important to bear in mind that this is not a license to voice explicit biases or hidden agendas in your research report (Johnson, 2008). In your action research report, it is crucial that your descriptions, interpretations, and conclusions are fair, accurate, honest, and trustworthy if your research is to be considered professionally credible. Consider the following passage from the report that I wrote on the preschool study to which I have made reference on several occasions throughout the book:

> One boy had been carelessly mixing his paints together and accidentally got some on his shirt. Marilyn noticed it quickly and said, "That's okay. We'll clean it up." She reacted calmly and not at all in a negative manner. This type of reaction typified this activity. There were not a lot of obvious examples of positive reinforcement. However, the comments provided by Marilyn were all of a positive nature and tone. I consistently witnessed Marilyn talking *with* the children, instead of *at* them. In observing the effects that these comments had on the children, I could easily classify these interactions as forms of positive reinforcement.

Here, notice that not only did I refer to myself in the first person, but I also integrated my observations and perceptions of those observations directly into the discussion of a particular event that I observed.

As with the use of personal pronouns, there is a bit of a discrepancy between the type of voice used in traditional types of research reports and the type used in action research reports. In traditional research, the *passive voice* is used fairly extensively (Mertler & Charles, 2011). The passive voice is characterized by the use of phrases such as the following:

> "The following conclusions were reached . . ."

> "It was concluded by the researchers that . . ."

Note that in the first example, the primary noun is "conclusions," and something is being done to them. In contrast, the *active voice* is more appropriate for action research reports. Here the primary noun is the person or the teacher-researcher—it is this person who is performing the action (hence, the *active* voice). The active voice is characterized by sentences such as these:

> "The researcher developed the following . . ."

> "I discovered very quickly that . . ."

Observe how the active voice tends to be a more reader-friendly form of writing. The primary difference between the two voices can be seen in the following two versions of the same statement:

It was expected by the researcher that some positive behaviors would be heard being praised in addition to the negatives being addressed. (*passive* voice)

I just expected to hear some positive behaviors being praised in addition to the negatives being addressed. (*active* voice)

Tense

Research reports are generally written in the *past tense* (Mertler & Charles, 2011). The main reason for this is that the research has already been conducted and, in some cases, completed. The review of related literature is almost exclusively written in the past tense, since you are summarizing research that has already occurred and been published or otherwise disseminated. Your methodology, results, and conclusions sections, as well as any reflective accounts, are also written in the past tense for the same reason in that they have already occurred. However, some sections may be written in the *present tense*. Introductory sections of reports—where the topic is introduced and the research questions and hypotheses are stated—are typically written in the present tense. This is because the teacher-researcher is describing a *current* situation, problem, or concern. Since the situation or concern is ongoing—and likely was not resolved as a result of the study—it remains a current issue and should be described in that manner. Also, any recommendations for the future, including your action plan, are probably most appropriately written in present or future tense.

Tentative Versus Definitive Statements

When writing up your action research, you must be careful to avoid statements made with too much confidence or certainty. In some sections of your report, you can be definitive, while in others it is critical to remain at least somewhat tentative (Mertler & Charles, 2011). When describing your methodology (i.e., your research design, data collection), you should be quite definitive and precise. You are trying to create for your readers a very clear picture of your study. In addition, when reporting the results of descriptive statistical analyses, you can also be quite definite. If you report the number of students involved in your study, the mean and standard deviation for a set of test scores, or the percentage of students who indicated that they like the current class schedule in your building, you can report very specific numbers, even to decimal places if you desire. Since there are customary and *objective* methods of calculating the mean, standard deviation, and percentages, there will be no question (i.e., nothing left to individual interpretation) regarding the values you obtain and report. In other words, two individuals cannot take the same set of data, independently calculate the mean, and obtain different values. Thus it is acceptable to write such statements as the following:

"The mean was equal to 29.11 and the standard deviation equal to 2.45."

"Sixty-eight percent of students indicated that they liked the current class schedule."

"The coefficient of correlation was equal to +0.54."

In contrast, when reporting your conclusions and any subsequent implications of your research, you must be more tentative. It is not ethical to present any conclusions with absolute certainty. In contrast to descriptive statistical analyses, your inferential analyses (in the case of quantitative data) or inductive analyses (in the case of qualitative data) inherently contain subjective interpretations. These results, conclusions, interpretations, or implications may, in fact, differ from individual to individual. When stating conclusions or implications, your statements might read similarly to the following:

> "There seem to be different contexts, or situations, within the preschool setting where positive reinforcement is more appropriately utilized."

> "As these results suggest, it may be critical that instruction on this topic be presented by experts in the field who are also knowledgeable about the reality of K–12 classrooms."

In the case of these two sample statements, notice the tentative nature of each as typified by "There seem to be . . ." and "it may be critical that. . . ." Here nothing has been presented as an absolute.

Clarity

The clarity of your written research report is also crucial to your potential readership. Your final written report should be clear enough for another person to read and duplicate the methodological steps you employed with relative ease (Johnson, 2008). One of the contributing factors to enhanced clarity is the use of as few words as possible. The simple result of doing so is that your report becomes more readable. Johnson (2008) also suggests that you can enhance the clarity of your report by "entering a teaching mode" (p. 178). Assume that your readers know nothing about your topic and your procedures and you must explain everything to them—in the simplest terms possible. Finally, organizing your report in a logical format can improve its clarity and readability (Johnson, 2008). The use of headings and subheadings allows the reader to follow the same sort of outline you used to write the report. This also creates a nice flow to your report. Additional information about formatting research reports will be presented shortly.

Consistency

Striving for consistency in your writing style will also enhance the clarity of your report. Your stylistic decisions, word usage, meanings, special symbols, abbreviations, and acronyms should remain as consistent as possible (Mertler & Charles, 2011). For example, if you symbolize the mean with an italicized uppercase *M* early in your report, do so throughout the remainder of your report. The same can be said for formatting, such as indentations, quotes, spacing, and headings—however you format them the first time (perhaps in APA style), do so the same way *each and every time.* You should also format sections, tables, charts, figures, and references in a consistent manner throughout your research report. All of these efforts enable you to create a report that is easier and less cumbersome for your readers to comprehend.

Simplicity of Language

I always remind students in my graduate research methods courses that when writing up their research, they are not trying to create a novel for the best-seller list! Research reports should be written in straightforward and simple (rather than fancy and flowery) language (Mertler & Charles, 2011). Remember that you are trying to get straight to the point, without adopting a literary style. A key is to try to avoid the *overuse* of adjectives and adverbs. Excessive use of these descriptive terms simply makes reading your report more difficult. People, and in particular other teachers, choose to read your report not for entertainment (as they would a novel) but rather to become better informed about the topic you investigated. Do not try to impress your readers with your mastery of a dictionary or the thesaurus button in your word processing program. You need to explain your research procedures, your results, and your conclusions clearly enough for readers to understand them, but you also need to do so by keeping your message short and simple. After all, their time is limited—you do not want them to give up or completely avoid reading your report simply because they find it to be a difficult read.

Conventions of Format

Research reports, regardless of the type of research they stem from, tend to follow a general structure. This structure is based on several *conventions of format,* which essentially provide a generic outline, or at least suggested components, to be included in a typical research report. Most traditional reports contain four to six sections, depending on the type of research conducted (Mertler & Charles, 2011). Standard components of reports include an introduction, a description of the methodological procedures followed, a presentation of the findings, and a summary of the conclusions. The organizational outline, as indicated by various headings and subheadings, typically used in traditional quantitative research reports follows this format (Mertler & Charles, 2011):

Introduction
    Statement of the Problem
    Purpose of the Study
    Research Questions or Hypotheses
    Limitations and Delimitations
Review of Related Literature
Methodology
    Participants
    Data Collection Procedures
    Data Analysis Procedures
Results
Conclusions and Recommendations
References

Notice that there are six main sections, which appear in bold type. These six sections are fairly standard. In fact, if you decide at some point to conduct a quantitative thesis or dissertation study, the first five sections—excluding the references—usually correspond to the five chapters that make up the final product. Subheadings can be added wherever they may be appropriate. For example, subheadings are normally added into the literature review section—which can be anywhere from 30 to 100 pages in a thesis or dissertation—in order to make it more readable. Imagine how difficult it would be to read a 100-page review of literature that does not appear to have a structural organization—each paragraph simply leads to the next.

The format of action research studies is not quite as standard as the one listed above. However, the organizational format characteristically follows the main steps of the action research process, as I outlined them in Chapter 2 and specifically in Figure 2.1. Each and every action research study will be unique in terms of its format and outline; however, action research reports will generally adhere to the following format (adapted from Mills, 2011):

Introduction
    Area of Focus
    Defining the Variables
    Research Questions
Review of Related Literature
Description of the Intervention or Innovation Data Collection and Considerations
Data Analysis and Interpretation
Conclusions
Reflection and Action Plan

Video Clips 9.2 & 9.3 View clips of educator-researchers discussing writing up action research.

In some action research reports, all of these sections may not be labeled as such (i.e., through the use of formal headings), but the material included in them will appear somewhere in the report. It is important that all of this information appears in the report, because its inclusion is necessary in order for the reader to fully understand all aspects of the study. You do not want to force your readers to have to figure some things out for themselves—they may do so inaccurately. Provide them with all the information they will need for understanding your topic, procedures, results, conclusions, and action plan.

Numerous times in this book, I have made reference to the research study I conducted on the topic of positive reinforcement in a preschool setting. The final research report that I wrote for that study was about 30 pages in length. Below I have listed all the headings and subheadings that I used in that report:

Introduction
    The Central Issue—Background Literature Description of the Study
    Description of the Site
    Description of the School Staff
Methodology
    Discussion

Gail's Story

What Positive Reinforcement Means to Me

What Positive Reinforcement Means to Children

Use of Positive Reinforcement

Carol's Story

What Positive Reinforcement Means to Me

What Positive Reinforcement Means to Children

Use of Positive Reinforcement

Marilyn's Story

What Positive Reinforcement Means to Me

What Positive Reinforcement Means to Children

Use of Positive Reinforcement

Eric's Story

Summary and Conclusions

References

You will quickly notice that I did not follow exactly the format I listed previously. However, all important components were included: an introduction (including descriptions of the topic and the study, as well as a literature review), a description of my methodological procedures (which included data collection and analysis), my discussion of results, and my summary and conclusions. If you glance at the appendix found on the student study website (http://www.sagepub.com/mertler3study), you will notice that the two final research reports presented include the essential components, but the authors have customized the format to fit their needs.

A final formatting issue that needs to be addressed is the length of the final research report. This is another one of those questions commonly asked of me by my graduate students: How long does our report have to be? The easy answer to that question is: As long as it needs to be in order to thoroughly and accurately tell your story. They typically do not like that answer, but it is often the most appropriate one I can provide. There are, of course, more formal guidelines for the length of research reports that depend largely on their purpose. If you are presenting your study to fellow teachers and administrators in your district, I would suggest keeping your write-up very brief, perhaps two to three pages. You might consider simply starting with your main headings—they really provide a strong structure, in outline form, to anything you write up—and then providing a brief paragraph summary for each one. An alternative would be to again start with your main headings but only list bulleted highlights for each section. Remember that in your oral presentation you will likely be filling in all the gaps in your bulleted outline.

If you are submitting your paper for presentation at a professional conference, you will need to have something that provides a much greater level of detail about all aspects of your action research study. Most papers that I present at my professional conferences range from 20 to 30 double-spaced pages, although there is typically no limit specified for this type of report. Ultimately, you are the best judge of the length of your research reports because you must decide if you have included enough context and detail so that your audience will have a clear understanding of your study (Mills, 2011). In addition, if you are submitting your paper for possible publication in an academic journal, the particular journal typically provides prospective authors with guidelines for the length of your report. Journals will vary, but if I had to guess, I would estimate that the average length of a journal article is approximately 20 to 25 double-spaced pages. In their sections for guidelines for contributors, the editors of journals typically provide the desired length of reports in terms of total words. This can seem a bit overwhelming when you see that you have to write several thousand words! In order to facilitate this process, I have a general conversion rate that I use to determine the approximate—and I emphasize *approximate*—number of typed pages and the corresponding number of formatted pages: *Roughly two and one-half pages of double-spaced type will equal one page of final, laid-out print.* Of course, electronic journals are not limited by the same space issues that paper journals are. For example, the editors of *Networks* state that they prefer articles that are "normally 2,000–3,500 words." The guidelines for contributors to *Reflective Practice* provide only an upper limit—6,000 words.

You also need to realize that if and when your article is accepted for publication, the journal will reformat it in order to meet its publication style. At a minimum, this usually means that your double-spaced report will be reformatted in a different font style and font size and will probably be single-spaced. For example, an article that I recently had published in a journal was 28 double-spaced pages when I sent the final version to the editor. When it appeared in the journal, it spanned only 16 of the journal's pages.

Practical Guidelines for Writing

Writing—some people love it; others detest it. Regardless of which side of that fence you fall on, it is important to recognize that writing of an academic nature is arguably the one aspect of every profession that keeps that profession changing, growing, and expanding. Communication—especially of research and research findings—among the members of any given profession allows those members to stay abreast of new ideas, innovations, and opportunities. Writing is the primary mechanism through which we can learn more about a given topic, share with others what we know about a topic, and gather ideas for new things to try in our profession. In addition, professional communication about a specific topic can provide exceptional opportunities to network. I have communicated, and in some cases actually met, with people from all over the country and throughout the world with whom I share common professional interests. Only through my writing and the act of reading the written works of others have I been afforded these wonderful opportunities to broaden my network of professional contacts.

If you had told me several years ago that by this time in my career I would have written numerous research articles and several textbooks, I probably would have laughed. I never thought I was capable of producing such written works related to my profession. However, now that I have been engaged in the writing process for a number of years and several projects, I can honestly say that I thoroughly enjoy it! For me, the key has always been to follow several tips that I have developed for myself. Keep in mind that when developing your "rituals for writing," you have to find out what works best for *you* in order to be successful. With that in mind, I offer the following suggestions:

1. *Establish a writing routine.* Writing takes time; there is no sense thinking that it is something that can be done quickly. One of the best things you can do to facilitate your writing is to make it part of your professional life. Find time where it falls or make time if necessary. It is really no different than any other aspect of teaching—we all make time for lesson planning, grading, and developing a unit test, and so on. Writing simply becomes another one of our important professional activities. In addition, find a comfortable place to write—perhaps at your home computer or with a legal pad and a pencil at your kitchen table. Find a place that works for you and make it part of your routine.

2. *Try to write at the same time every day.* Along with establishing a writing routine, try to build into your daily schedule some time for writing. Perhaps that time will consist of 30 minutes or an hour. Regardless of the amount of time, make it a regular part of your daily routine. For example, you might decide that before school for 30 minutes is the best time for you to write, or maybe a period of time after school or even after dinner will be the best time for you to write.

3. *Write as if you are talking to a friend.* Remember that you are trying to communicate your study and the results as clearly as possible. When you write, imagine that you are telling a friend about your study. This friend knows nothing about the topic, so you must communicate all aspects of the study in understandable, simple terms.

4. *Begin with an outline and organize your thoughts accordingly.* When I write, I begin by developing a thorough outline. Then all I have to do is to fill in the blanks of the outline. The outline helps keep me on track and focused; plus, it creates somewhat of a series of checkpoints for my finished product.

5. *Do not worry initially about spelling, grammar, and how your report reads.* When developing the first draft of your action research report, do not become too concerned about how your report reads. I believe that many people who are new to academic writing fall victim to this—they try to make their reports read "perfectly" the first time out. Do not concern yourself with finding the ideal phrase or with the correct spelling of a given word. At this point in the writing process, you should only be concerned with getting your thoughts, ideas, and information on paper. At this stage, Mills (2011) advises teacher-researchers to

"look for progress, not perfection" (p. 181). You will have ample opportunities to refine your writing at a later stage.

6. *Realize that writing a first draft is only the first step in the writing process.* When you begin to write, it is important to realize that you are writing a first draft. You will have opportunities to edit and revise and then edit and revise again. This part of the process enables you to further refine and clarify your thoughts and ideas; each time, they become a little more coherent, with an improved sense of flow to the report.

7. *Last, but in my mind most important, develop a realistic writing schedule.* If you begin writing with no clear sense of schedule, you essentially lack the incentive to continue making progress on your report. Developing a realistic—and I stress the word *realistic*—schedule for your writing is the first thing you should do before ever putting your first word on paper.

A writing schedule, along with the detailed outline you developed in Number 4 above, really provides the skeletal framework for your finished action research report. As an example, I have provided a schedule that I used to write a research report for a recent conference presentation (see Figure 9.1). Notice that the schedule somewhat parallels a detailed outline and that I included check boxes so I could monitor my progress.

These suggestions—especially Number 7—have helped me throughout my various writing projects. The closer I can stick to my writing schedule, the more successful my writing project will be. In addition, there is something to be said for being able to check off sections of your report as you complete them—it creates a sense of accomplishment, provides you with repeated opportunities to pat yourself on the back, and provides the necessary encouragement to keep going, because there is a light at the end of the proverbial tunnel! Just remember to find what works for you and stick with it.

Related Websites: Writing Up the Results of Action Research

This annotated list of related websites provides suggestions for writing up the results of your action research studies, as well as several additional examples of reports of classroom-based teacher research.

- Classroom Action Research: Ideas for Your Final Write-Up **http://oldweb.madison.k12.wi .us/sod/car/carwriteupideas.html**

  Throughout these sections in previous chapters, I have highlighted several pages developed by the Madison (Wisconsin) Metropolitan School District on its action research website. This page provides a bulleted list of suggestions for things you may want to include in your action research report. The final two thoughts are worth noting here:

Figure 9.1	A Sample Writing Schedule for a Research Paper

<table>
<tr><td colspan="3">Writing Schedule (beginning July 5, 2008)
for
**The Role of Classroom Experience in Preservice and
In-Service Teachers' Assessment Literacy**</td></tr>
<tr><td>**Writing Activity**</td><td>**Due Date**</td><td>**Completed?**</td></tr>
<tr><td>**Background**
What is "Assessment Literacy"?
"The Standards . . ."
Research on Assessment Literacy and
"The Standards"</td><td>August 2, 2008</td><td>☑</td></tr>
<tr><td>*Purpose of the Study and Research Questions*</td><td>August 4, 2008</td><td>☑</td></tr>
<tr><td>**Methods**
Participants
Instrumentation
Procedures
Analyses</td><td>August 13, 2008</td><td>☑</td></tr>
<tr><td>**Results**
Descriptive results—preservice teachers
Descriptive results—in-service teachers
Comparative results—two groups of teachers</td><td>August 25, 2008</td><td>☑</td></tr>
<tr><td>**Discussion**</td><td>September 3, 2008</td><td>☑</td></tr>
<tr><td>**Recommendations**</td><td>September 10, 2008</td><td>☑</td></tr>
<tr><td>**References**</td><td>Ongoing</td><td>☑</td></tr>
</table>

"All write-ups should not/will not look alike" and "Remember you are telling a story. You can organize this chronologically, by themes, by data source (i.e., students, parents, staff), or some other way. It's up to you!" Both are excellent suggestions to bear in mind.

- Purdue University's Online Writing Lab (OWL) **http://owl.english.purdue.edu**

  The **O**nline **W**riting **L**ab (OWL) at Purdue University is a fabulous writing website, providing more than 200 free writing-related resources. Included on the site are the following:

  o *OWL Exercises* **http://owl.english.purdue.edu/exercises**—various interactive exercises providing the user with practice related to grammar, punctuation, spelling, sentence structure and style, paraphrasing, and writing numbers.

  o *APA Style and Formatting Guide* **http://owl.english.purdue.edu/owl/resource/ 560/01**—a thorough summary of APA style (updated to the 6th edition), including in-text citations, reference formatting, levels of report headings, and formatting tables and figures; there is even a downloadable PowerPoint presentation (http://owl.english.purdue.edu/media/ppt/20081208070939_560.ppt).

o *Avoiding Plagiarism* **http://owl.english.purdue.edu/owl/resource/589/01**— includes a section clearly describing what constitutes "plagiarism," practices to help you avoid plagiarizing, and an interactive exercise.

Still More Examples of Action Research Reports

The three URLs listed below all contain examples of final reports of action research written by individuals or groups of teachers. I suggest that you take a look at them in order to see additional variations of formal written products of teacher-led research projects.

- The Nature and Impact of an Action Research Professional Development Program in One Urban School District **http://oldweb.madison.k12.wi.us/sod/car/carspencer report.html**

  This final report to the agency that funded the project was written by Cathy Caro-Bruce of the Madison Metropolitan School District and Ken Zeichner of the University of Wisconsin–Madison.

- Action Research Questions *(and Reports)* **http://www.alliance.brown.edu/dnd/ar_ quests.shtml**

  This site, the Development & Dissemination Schools Initiative at Brown University, provides a list of action research questions and, in most cases, copies of the final reports written by the teacher-researchers. Some of the reports are complete written reports, while others take the form of outlines, perhaps used for presentations.

- Action Research Reports **http://www.alliance.brown.edu/dnd/ar_cover.shtml**
  This second page from the Development & Dissemination Schools Initiative provides more action research reports. Again, these final reports are presented in a variety of formats.

SUMMARY

★ Formally writing up the results of action research projects is important because it promotes further clarification of various aspects of the study, can provide you with valuable feedback, tends to further empower teachers to improve their practice, and can provide a great sense of accomplishment.

★ Academic writing follows certain agreed-upon conventions of style, most of which are found in various style guides, such as the *Publication Manual of the American Psychological Association*.

- Some of the most common conventions of academic writing include person and voice, tense, clarity, tentative and definitive statements, consistency, and simplicity of language.

- It is important to remember that the title of your report is the initial screening mechanism for potential readers—it should be brief but also accurately describe the topic and study.

- Most reports of traditional research studies tend to be written using third-person pronouns; however, it is quite appropriate to use first-person references when writing up the results of action research studies.

- Use of the active voice, as opposed to the passive voice, is more appropriate for action research reports.

- Generally speaking, the introductory section of a research report is written in present tense; the review of related literature, methodology, and results are written in past tense; and any recommendations and an action plan are typically written in future tense.

- It is always best to err on the side of caution and use tentative statements when discussing your conclusions and implications.

- Any written report of research should be as clear and consistent as possible.

- Do not try to impress your readers with flowery language; use simple, straightforward language in your write-up.

★ Although there is no universally agreed-upon organizational structure for formatting a research report, most action research reports contain the following sections:
  o Introduction
  o Review of Related Literature
  o Description of the Intervention or Innovation
  o Data Collection and Considerations
  o Data Analysis and Interpretation
  o Conclusions
  o Reflection and Action Plan

- The length of a final research report often depends on the purpose the report will serve.

- When reporting the results of qualitative data analysis, it is important to be as objective as possible, to include references to yourself where they may be warranted, to thoroughly describe all aspects of your study, to include representative samples of your data only when they will enhance your presentation of the results, and to include interesting but nonessential information in appendices at the end of your report.

- When reporting the results of quantitative data analysis, it is important to follow various conventions for reporting numerical data as either numbers or words, to report arithmetic data in descending order, to report the total number of participants involved in the study before reporting numbers in categories, and to use tables and figures where appropriate in order to enhance your presentation of numerical results.

★ When preparing to write up a final research report, teacher-researchers should establish a writing routine, try to write at the same time each day, write as if conversing with a friend, begin with an outline and organize thoughts accordingly, not worry about spelling and grammar in an initial draft of the report, and develop a realistic writing schedule.

QUESTIONS AND ACTIVITIES

1. Select a published research article, or another research report, on a topic of interest to you. Based on the various guidelines and suggestions presented in this chapter (i.e., conventions of style, conventions of format, and guidelines for presenting the results of analyses), write a brief critique of the report highlighting those aspects of the written report that the author(s) did well and those aspects that could be improved.

2. Locate a report of qualitative research related to an area of interest to you. What types of things do you notice about the writing style? Which of the suggestions presented in the chapter did the author(s) follow? Which suggestions were not followed?

3. Locate a report of quantitative research related to an area of interest to you. What types of things do you notice about the writing style? Which of the suggestions presented in the chapter did the author(s) follow? Which suggestions were not followed?

4. Conduct a quick survey of at least 20 people, asking them to indicate their favorite color. Once you have collected your data, analyze them using both qualitative and quantitative techniques. First, use inductive analysis to develop groups and numbers of people within each group. Report your results in narrative fashion. Second, analyze your data quantitatively by counting the number of responses for each color identified. Report your results three ways: narratively, using a table, and using an appropriate type of graph or figure.

STUDENT STUDY SITE

Visit the Student Study Site at **www.sagepub.com/mertler3study** for these additional learning tools:

- Video clips
- Web resources
- Self quizzes
- E-flashcards

- PowerPoint slides
- Sample action research reports
- Full-text SAGE journal articles
- Chapter summaries

Appendix A

Sample Action Research Report

The Achievement Gap at Highland Park High School

Judi Elman, Facilitator

Holly Skiba

Beth Peterson

Kate Piorkowski

For many years, teachers and administrators at Highland Park High School have been concerned about differing patterns of achievement for different populations of students at our school. To help teachers address these gaps in student achievement, we have created new courses to meet the needs of struggling students, and we have offered a variety of professional development opportunities for teachers to help them to improve their understandings of the various, and varying, needs of students with whom they work each day.

At its inception, our action research team wondered about whether our school structures were in any way responsible for the gaps in achievement that our faculty and administration is trying so hard to correct. We observed that our higher-level classes and the majority of student activities did not have students of color in them. As we pursued our inquiry together, we realized that we had three specific questions that we wanted to answer.

1. How does the culture of our school impact student learning?

2. How do we empower students to improve academic achievement? What strategies can teachers/faculty/administration employ to empower the marginalized students in our classroom/our school?

3. How can we, as a school, create a welcoming climate for marginalized students, who feel otherwise disempowered?

These daunting questions required us to seek information from a variety of sources. First, we accessed several articles from *Educational Leadership,* a professional journal published by the Association for Supervision and Curriculum Development. One article that guided our thinking and our continued work was "Confronting the Racism of Low Expectations" by Julie Landsman. In this article, Landsman argues that:

> In U.S. schools "the system that sets up the hierarchy of intelligence and excellence is racist." Racist attitudes—some subtle, some blatant—and the way criteria are set up for admission into gifted programs, advanced placement classes, and similar "tracks" ensure that minority and low-income youth are less represented. Landsman cites examples she has seen of how teachers' assumptions—such as that minority students can't answer complex questions, or that their families will be unsupportive—have hurt minority students' achievement. She describes how the definitions of "giftedness" many schools use are based on "acquaintance with certain authors, certain ways of reasoning, or certain ways of behaving." Drawing on the work of [African-American psychologist and educator] Joseph White, she recommends five steps educators should take to eliminate racism from their teaching and administrative practice—and from the entire U.S. public education system.

Landsman suggests that one of the first things educators and administrators must do is educate themselves about the cultures of students who are not particularly successful in their school environments. To advance our understanding, we read Ruby Payne's Framework for Understanding Poverty. This text helped us to understand why some of our students are not invested in school and why they cannot hold a vision of the future in their heads. We also watched a film entitled, *A Day Without a Mexican,* which painted a picture of the ways in which Mexican immigrants earn a living in the United States and the extent to which our economy relies on their existence in the workforce.

Another article from *Educational Leadership* that proved to be useful to our inquiry was "Increasing Diversity in Challenging Classes" by Eileen Gale Kugler and Erin McVadon Albright. In this article, Kugler and McVadon discuss how

> In the late 1990s, the recently diversified Annandale High School in Virginia pulled together administrators, teachers, parents, and other elements in its community to build an accepting climate and draw students from all cultural groups into advanced classes. Rapid changes in the student body led to a school that now serves students from 92 different countries, speaking more than 45 native languages. The school chose an intentionally broadened International Baccalaureate program as a vehicle for extended entrée into advanced classes to students from many races and cultures. They capitalized on the international nature of IB's curriculum, assessments and approach, even offering advanced classes in cultures other than English, to widen the circle of students enrolled in

challenging classes. African American students' participation in 11th and 12th grade IB classes has doubled in the past three years, and participation by Latino students has tripled. Individual portraits of several IB diploma candidates from non-majority cultures reflect the success of Annandale's crusade.

From this article, we gleaned a number of ideas that have the potential to influence our contributions to curriculum proposals in our disciplines.

Finally, we devised, and administered, a survey about Highland Park High School to over 100 students in order to get a sample of students' attitudes about our school. We gave this survey to students in all grade levels and all levels of courses (remedial, college prep, and honors.) The questions, and students' responses that we found particularly instructive to our inquiry, follow:

Question #1

You wake up in the morning, and you are not feeling that great. You think for a moment about not going to school. What makes you go to school? What makes you stay at home? Explain.

- Seeing my friends makes me go to school when I don't feel well. Also interesting classes influences me.

- It depends on what day or how much work we have done. Bad week would make me stay home. Monday will make me stay home. Friday I will go so that I can go out.

- I'm tired. Getting an hour more of sleep helps! On late starts I am much more on task and energized, and I am happier.

- What makes me go to school is to not miss my homework because you won't know how to do it.

- Getting to see my friends would make me want to go to school.

- The reason I would go to school would be because I wasn't feeling like I would go crazy if I went and I would be all right. I wouldn't want to make up all that work for my classes so I would just go. If I felt like if I went to school I would probably have to home for being too sick, then I wouldn't go.

- I would go to school so I don't get behind in class.

- I stay home because if I wake up feeling like I do not want to go to school. If I come to school I will be in a very bad mood all day.

- Waking up knowing I can see my child in Child Development. Staying at home because I think of all the snob North Shore teens and sometimes it makes me sick.

- Baseball would be the overwhelming decision maker. I can't miss school.

- I go to school because I know if I miss a day, I will have way too much homework. I stay at home only if I am really sick. But unfortunately this year has been so filled with homework, I don't think I would want to miss school. If I had a 102.0 temperature.

- What makes me go to school is that my friends are there and it is fun to be at school at least for me. What makes me stay at home when I'm totally [stressed?] out.

- Obligations to groups in classes for projects. Obligations to be in school. Mother would make me go to school.

- I might be sick, school gives me something to do. I would get really bored during the day if I didn't have school.

Question #2

What would teachers say or do to make you feel as though you belonged at school?

- Asking how I am doing, and asking about the weekend and non-academic topics.

- You are a great contribution to class. You're a great student. You make my class flow.

- I'm not sure. It all starts with one's mind and feeling towards education/school. I guess it also starts within the home of the student. If he/she has great problems within their home, they will most likely have troubles outside of home like in the street or school.

- They would say that you are smart, and you would do better if only you came to school every day.

- Encourage us and ask how we are doing, asking if we need help on something.

- You are a good student, you need to apply yourself and I think you will go far in life.

- That we only have a certain amount of time to finish something at school.

- Nothing—they just have to be understanding and supportive.

- Make comments to me as if I was nine years old again . . . fake comments.

- Encourage you to participate, and ensure that you felt comfortable with kids in the class.

- If they take time to help me and make sure I get everything. It is easy to tell what teachers care and what teachers just teach the lesson every day and act like they care by calling our parents if we do bad. It is the student's responsibility to get the help and materials but also the teachers.

- Hey, my teachers love me. Well, maybe not all of them but they like me.

- I don't recall them saying anything that makes me feel like I should be here.

- I have no idea. I don't think I belong here.

Question #3

Do you have a classroom that you feel comfortable in because of the way it looks? If so describe it. If not, what would that classroom look like?

- No I do not have a classroom that I feel comfortable in because of the way it looks. If I did, I am not sure what it would look like, but possibly it would have more comfortable looking chairs that aren't as structured as desks.

- All that I would like for a comfortable classroom would temperature that is comfortable to my outside surroundings. Windows and desks that do not connect to the chair.

- Yes, Mrs. Elman's, Mr. Sutherland's, and Mrs. Levin. It's all about the teacher. A teacher is like a mother in the room of the home they make the place comfortable and good. More like "love."

- To me all the classes are the same, but if I had more friends in one then I would feel more comfortable with that class.

- Yes, my English class has a variety of people. Some I already knew and others I got to know as the school year progressed. Everyone is nice and respectful and listen to you without judging you.

- If I did it would be just a comfortable room with couches and chairs to make you feel more comfortable.

- The smaller the class is, the better.

- No, I don't know.

- No, the classrooms all look the same. The classroom would be bright and welcoming.

- One where all the students are visible from every seat, no rows! Circles or "V" shapes work best.

- It matters who is in it and who isn't.

- The classroom that I like the most is Graphic Design because it's dark and gloomy. Love that place.

- English classroom. Posters around, books, chairs in order.

- Open classrooms with fresh air.

Question #4

Is there diversity in your group of friends? If so, describe.

- No.
- There is a lot of diversity. 2 of my friends are black, one is Hispanic, 3 are Jewish and 3 are Italian.
- Yeah, somewhat. Now that I'm more mature, I try to keep a peaceful environment. I like to be cool with everybody. Life is better without problems.
- Yes there is, there are Latinos, white, African American, and Asians. We all get along very well.
- Yes, I have Hispanic, African American, and Caucasian friends.
- Yeah, there is. I have all different types of races. I am friends with black, white, Hispanic, Asian, and mixed kids who are half something, half something else.
- No.
- Yes, there are people from every race.
- Yes.
- Absolutely, race, age, sex. I hang out with people who are of many races, different ages, and boys and girls . . . most girls.
- In my close group, no there isn't, but I have many diverse friends.
- No, only [paisas?].
- Yes, I have Latino friends, African American friends, I don't see the difference.
- I don't have any here.

Question #5

Your classroom teacher asks you to take a note to another teacher down the hall. When you enter the room, you make a judgment about what level class is being taught. How would you know what level class it is? Provide specific examples.

- There are a few things that would give me a clue as to what level class is being taught. Some of these things include the particular teacher (knowing what kind of levels they teach), the students in the classroom and the behaviors of the students (if following directions, paying attention, particularly, and level of material).
- More people, street looking class. I really wouldn't be able to tell.
- I'm not sure. I don't like to put people in "smart" or "dumbass" levels! This crap *bothers me!*

- Well, if the students were all Hispanics then I would think that they are in a lower class. If the students are all white and some others different and they are doing something hard then I would think it's a hard class.

- Maybe the classroom has a lot of non-English speaking students like the TPI classrooms.

- The teacher and how she is exampling certain things would tell me what level and sometimes who is in the class.

- The amount of notes on the board and the amount of people in the class.

- How many students are in there, what the students are doing.

- Mostly Caucasians are in level 2 classes. Level 3 is diverse.

- You can tell by the kids in the class. When you are in a school you know how smart different kids are, just from being around them, hearing their conversations . . .

- Because it is obvious all these years to know who is in the higher level classes and who isn't.

- I don't know. Me, Mexican. I learned to take classes and not to judge them.

- The way the teacher talks to the students, the way the students respond to the teacher.

- If it's the same subject and they are behind, it's a lower level.

Question #6

Do your teachers care about your success? How do you know?

- Yes, they ask how my work is going. They give me extended time if I need it to complete major projects.

- They do a lot. They are always making sure I am on track. They nag me to get late assignments in.

- Some. Like I said, it's all about the teachers HPHS hires.

- You know if they are always on your case.

- Yes, because they push you to do your best and help you whenever you need it.

- I think so. Teachers are about students' success because they will push you into trying to do good and that shows they care.

- Some do, and some don't. The teachers that do care would tell you if you're missing something.

- Some of them do, others just do it for the money.

- Some do, not really.

- Some do. They will make an effort to improve your performance. Some teachers will give work back that might not be what they had expected, but there are no suggestions on how to improve the work quality.

- Only a few do. When I can see that teachers don't care about me and just getting through class, I lose all my ability to work in the class, because it is hard for me to come to work (school) every day, just to have my boss (certain teachers) not care about me and/or my future.

- Hell yeah, they do. They are always bugging me with going to college or stuff like that. I hate it.

- I feel one or two care about it because they take me aside and tell me they are genuinely concerned if I miss a few things. Like Mrs. Elman took the time to call my mother, regardless if it started a fight. It still helped.

- Yes, they encourage me all the time.

Question #7

As a student at HPHS, how much pressure do you feel? Circle the number that matches your level of stress. (1 is the lowest, 10 is the highest)

- 5

- 7

- 10—Because stress is always felt; we all can control how much we get. I believe that the harder you work on something, the more stress you get.

- 8

- 6

- 5

- 5

- 3—I really do not feel a lot of pressure. I'm just trying to graduate.

- 9

- 10—More like Highland Park University than High School. Most classes leave me with more stress than knowledge.

- 10—I think that about 75% of classes I have taken here are just here to stress me out, but I don't learn from them. Senior year has been my most stressful year. I also feel that some teachers don't realize we have other things going on outside of school, which makes everything more stressful.

- 6
- 7—I feel like we have to get things done quicker than a normal school.
- 5

Question #8

What do you think are the unwritten or hidden rules of our school?

- Pushing students to do their best academically. Students should participate in activities outside of the classroom. Encouraging diversity.

- Stay within your group at school. There are people you talk to and there are some you just don't. Some people don't belong in the commons—really they feel unwanted. Gossip—you heart it, you spread it.

- Not sure. Sometimes I think that if you're white, you have better chances.

- Watch your language. No making out in hallways and no throwing up gang signs.

- There are none.

- Accuse students or interrogate them for their "wrong doings" such as overdosing, alcoholism, etc. I think it is a bunch of BS.

- Senior year for many people is harder than any other time. Workloads in most classes are increased. Teachers say that they are "preparing us for next year." Teachers should explain what next year will be like, not make this year next year.

- I think there are way too many rules. I feel that at least seniors should be treated different. I feel that a lot of the teachers here treat us like we are in 5th grade even though they think they are preparing us for the future. I feel that the rules here are so strict, all the seniors are going to be in shock once they see the freedoms of college.

- Down with the Mexicans. Not. Just kidding, I don't know.

- No clue.

Question #9

The school is cleaned every night, which shows that cleanliness is valued here. What else do you think the school cares about? Give specific examples.

- Grades and student success. Students going to college. Its image as a perfect school. Its students.

- The way we dress. Sex is so hushed up here, anything provocative is quickly taken care of. Drugs are, but they are handled in the wrong way.

- Not sure.

- That they get a good education.

- Keeping students safe by having cameras around the school and having someone at every exit to make sure whoever is entering the school has signed in and has a specific reason for being in the school building.

- The way students dress. If someone is in a gang or not.

- The image of the school. We are #1 or at least that is the goal of HPHS.

- How we look as a school. HPHS tries to be perfect.

- I believe the school cares about its reputation as a very successful, learning environment, which is why classes are so difficult.

- Excluding all the sports, because I can see that the school has a lot of pride. I have been very disappointed with my high school experience and I believe if some of the teachers actually did care, my future could be different.

- The health of the students, the welfare of the students, the opportunities presented to the students, and the resources that the students need.

- Representation of gangs, drugs, clothing.

- Freedom of choice. Caring about student opinions

The task for our action-research team, as we enter our second year, is to observe, analyze, and interpret the data that students provided in this survey. Clearly, some students do not find HPHS to be the "home" that we desire it to be for *all* students. As we gain more understanding of our students, our school structures, and strategies that we can employ to improve learning and a sense of belonging for all, we anticipate that our gaps in student achievement will begin to shrink.

References

Kugler, G. & Albright, E. (February 2005). Increasing diversity in challenging classes. *Educational Leadership, 62,* 5.

Landsman, J. (November 2004). Confronting the racism of low expectations. *Educational Leadership, 62,* 3.

Payne, R. (2005). *A framework for understanding poverty.* Highlands, TX: aha! Process, Inc.

Appendix B

Sample Action Research Report

Motivation in Social Studies

Collaborative Teacher Action Research 2000–01

Tom Koulentes

Social Studies Department

Highland Park High School

Highland Park, Illinois

During the 2000–01 school year, three teachers examined methods of increasing their students' motivation to learn. The process started with these teachers looking at motivation and exploring the various factors that affect student motivation. After identifying the attributes of a motivated student, each teacher designed methods which they hoped would increase student motivation and therefore student learning in their classrooms. This web-site briefly examines each teacher's project, and then offers discussion as to why the data offered here may be meaningful to other teachers as well.

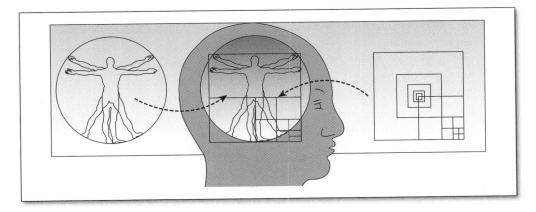

Question

The question that I researched this year was, "How can I motivate seniors?" This question is probably universal to every high school in the United States, but it is especially relevant to me as I teach all senior courses and I notice a significant drop in my students' level of motivation as spring draws closer and college acceptance letters start being received in the mail. I believe that senior year is the time when my students are best prepared to do their finest academic work, and I am not content to simply let them slide off into summer and graduation. Thus, understanding that seniors are unique creatures in the high school environment, I was determined to find unique ways of motivating them to stay focused and productive right up to graduation day.

The Classroom

My research was conducted throughout two semesters using two different courses that I teach. First semester I taught a Political Science class. This class is an introduction to American government course that focuses on teaching the Constitution, the structures of the federal government and current issues in American politics. The class is composed solely of seniors and is a semester elective course. The students enrolled in political science bring a wide variety of academic skills with them to the class. The majority of the students are college bound and have a genuine interest in law and politics; most of these students are on high academic tracks. A significant portion of the students however, are low achieving students who need one more social studies credit to graduate high school. Demographically, most of the students (approximately 85%) are white and are middle/upper class children. The remaining 15% of my students are Hispanic and African-American, some of whom come from families living at or near the poverty line. This mixture of student demographics and academic abilities possess some unique instructional challenges and opportunities.

Second semester I taught a psychology course. This class is essentially an introduction to the field of psychology as most students have never taken a psychology course before. Among the topics the class examines are: the history of psychology, research methods, the brain, sensation and perception, learning and memory, personality and identity, and abnormal psychology. The class is composed primarily of seniors, though sophomores are eligible to enroll in the course and many do. Out of a class of 25 students, I will usually have 3 to 5 sophomores enrolled. The majority of students who take this class are college bound, high achieving students. Recently, however, more academically challenged students have begun to take the course.

Demographically, the course is nearly identical to the political science course described above.

The Idea: Real World Projects

After reading several articles about student motivation, and after reflecting on methods of teaching that I believe are engaging and effective, I decided that the focus of my study this year would be to try to motivate my students by challenging them to participate in "real world" projects. "Real world projects" is a term I use to describe the learning activities that I created for my students to work on during the semester. It was my hypothesis that if I reduced the amount of traditional classroom instruction and evaluations (i.e. lecture and exams) and increased the number of alternative assessments (student centered projects), that I ultimately would find my students more motivated to complete my coursework. Thus, my work this year centered around me designing and implementing real world projects into my curriculum to attempt to increase the motivation my students had for learning my course content.

The Process and the Research Process

Step 1: Designing the Projects

This year I decided to use real world projects to try to motivate my seniors to produce high quality work. The real world projects that I created are amalgamations of several pedagogically sound methods of instruction. For example, all real world projects that I developed were experiential, collaborative, interdisciplinary, and authentic in their design (for a more thorough explanation of the projects and the philosophy behind them, please visit my "Real World Projects" link).

For every class of seniors that I taught, I carefully examined my curriculum and searched for areas where a project might be incorporated into the curriculum. Once I identified areas where projects would fit, I began designing the projects. In designing projects I took several factors into consideration:

- **Theme**—All my projects revolve around a theme. The reason a theme is important is because many of the projects require a great deal of time to complete and as a teacher you will be covering many topics in your course. You don't want to be stuck talking about one topic for four weeks so a good theme enables you to discuss many different topics in your curriculum, but all of them relate to your central theme in some way. For example, in political science a theme I use is "representation." With this theme I can discuss topics of: direct vs. representative democracy, the presidency, the congress, the judiciary, and even local politics. Students also enjoy a curriculum designed on themes because it affords them a great deal of freedom. Each of my projects allow my students to explore an aspect of the theme that is particularly interesting to them.

- **Skills**—All my projects are designed to teach my students academic skills as well as course content. I feel this is vital to any good project because I am hoping to teach my students to become "life long learners." If I just teach my students content, they will only be able to use this knowledge in few, specific situations. If I, however, teach my students skills (such as research, computer, and writing skills) they will be able to apply these skills to any new situation they may encounter in their futures.

- **Relevance**—All of my projects must be relevant to my students lives. The key here is that the project (or content of the course) must be relevant to their lives NOW, not five years from now. My students must believe that the work they are completing will have an immediate and obvious impact upon their present lives. Very few students (and for that matter, very few adults) are motivated to work on projects that they think will only benefit them four years from now.

- **Audience**—All of my projects are designed so that the students must present their work to an audience. If you want to really hold students accountable for their work, they must believe that other people (aside from their teacher) are going to see and evaluate their work. When I design a project I think about "what audience could my students present this information to?" I have used audiences of kindergartners, parents, community members, senior citizens and other high school students with equal success.

- **Final Product**—All of my projects are designed with the end in mind. What will be the final product the students are responsible for creating? How can I make this a "fun" product to create? The key here is making the final product something relevant to the students and something requiring creativity to create. In my opinion, one problem affecting student motivation in a negative way is that students are not asked to be creative. Thus, all of my projects offer and encourage my students to use creative thinking skills. It is amazing how designing a children's book on the Constitution, rather than simply writing an analytical essay about it, will stimulate my students' interest and effort on this topic.

Step 2: Gathering Data (Measuring Motivation)

After designing these projects, I began implementing them into my curriculum. As I did this, I was faced with the challenge of monitoring and measuring my students' motivation levels. This, I learned, was a very difficult task to complete. How could I determine if a student was motivated or not? How could I measure if a student's level of motivation had increased or decreased as the semester progressed? With students' lives being incredibly complex, and with my students attending six other classes throughout the day aside from mine, how could I know if my projects were making a difference to my students or not? These questions challenged me to think critically about my research and they led me to the development of the following research methods.

- **Method One: Student Surveys**

    The easiest method for gathering information on student levels of motivation was through the use of surveys that were designed solely for measuring motivation levels. I administered these surveys to my students several times throughout the semester, each time looking to see how their motivation had increased or decreased from the time before. I also used this survey to determine what aspects of my course were affecting my students' motivation. For example, was the difficulty of my class affecting motivation? Did the projects affect motivation? Did the classroom environment affect motivation? The surveys yielded invaluable data and allowed me to sharpen my understanding of how to motivate my students. For a more thorough explanation of the survey and a complete discussion of the data it produced, click here or see my "data" page.

- **Method Two: Natural Observation**

    As a teacher, I am acutely aware of my students' moods, attitudes, feelings, and actions. I observe my students daily and I come to know their behaviors quite well throughout the year. Thus, to measure student motivation I simply observed my students' class performance and participation and made judgements as to what this revealed about their motivation levels. Though I watched all aspects of my students' behavior, I was particularly interested in the following actions:

- **Preparedness**—Did students come to class ready to learn and participate? Was homework complete, assigned readings read, and all necessary course materials brought in? A motivated student would generally be well prepared for class.

- **Engagement**—Were students actively engaged in class discussion and activities? Did the students spend a great deal of time on task when given class time to work? Were class debates lively and intelligent? Were class discussions used for teacher-student interaction? Motivated students would be engaged and interested in what was occurring during class time.

- **Enthusiasm/Enjoyment**—Did students appear to be excited about what they were doing? Did the class enjoy working on the projects that were assigned to them? I believe that motivated students would generally enjoy working on class assignments more than non-motivated students.

- **Attendance**—Did my students attend class or were there large amounts of absences? Motivated students would attend class more, thus I monitored my attendance closely.

- **Making Connections**—Did my students make connections of my course content to other aspects of their lives? Did students stay after class to talk to me about a movie they had seen that related to our course? Did students tell me that they know understood something in their lives that they hadn't before? Did students bring me clippings from the newspaper related to our class? Motivated students tend to reflect on their learning outside of the classroom, thus, I was looking to see if my classes were recognizing the concepts we had discussed in class in their daily lives.

Throughout the semester I kept a journal and recorded thoughts and observations about these qualities in my classes. For a complete discussion of this journal see my "data" page.

- **Method Three: Student Reflections**

    A third and final method of collecting data was for me to ask my students to reflect upon their learning and their levels of motivation throughout the year. To do this, I would ask my students to write reflections at the conclusion of our units, and whenever they had completed a project. Educational research supports student reflective thinking, claiming that in order for students to internalize their learning, they need to actively reflect upon what they have learned. I utilized the reflection process not only to increase student learning, but to gather data about how their levels of motivation shifted throughout the year.

For a more thorough discussion of this data please see my "data" page. Results of this work are detailed on the following pages.

Data Collection

As the year progressed, I gathered a great deal of data about my research question. Much of that data is summarized here.

Course Survey

A survey was issued to the students in the class on five separate occasions throughout the year. On each occasion, student motivation was measured along with the degree of difficulty for the course, the students' level of enjoyment for the course, and the value of the content to the students' lives. An example of an acutal survey's results is shown as follows:

Student Survey Results (March 2001):

Topic of Survey Question	Student Response (scale of 1-5 / 1 = low 5 = high)
Overall Motivation	4.5
Value of Content	4.1
Overall Enjoyment	4.6
Degree of Challenge	3.2

From this data I have concluded that at that time, students were very motivated to participate in my course and that they valued and enjoyed the content they were studying. At different times throughout the year, I found that motivation would frequently decline as the value of content and enjoyment also declined. In turn, as value and enjoyment increase, so too does motivation. I believe that is a positive correlation between motivation, value of content, and student enjoyment, though it is important for me to state that no scientific analysis of this correlation has yet been conducted. As a teacher, this validates my belief that my students will be more motivated to perform in my class if I can design curriculum that is both relevant and enjoyable for them to study. I think that in order to do this effectively, I must seek my students' input into what it is they feel they should learn about my course content and how they would enjoy doing this.

Anecdotal Evidence and Student Reflections

In keeping a journal this year, there were several occasions on which student behaviors yielded insight into levels of their motivation. What follows are examples of student behaviors that I observed this year or comments students made to me in their reflective activities. Students continually stayed after class to discuss ideas for their final projects with me. The students frequently commented about how they were nervous about presenting to audiences and wanted to make sure they did a good job.

Students frequently brought in articles from magazines or newspapers that dealt with our course content. Three students even taped television programs that dealt with topics I had taught them and gave me these tapes to use with my classes next year.

In choosing topics for their final projects, many students told me that they chose their topic because "it was very relevant to my life." In psychology, many students chose to complete projects about Alzheimer's disease to better understand the illness their grandparents had, and one girl chose to complete a project about grieving to better understand how to deal with her own mother's death.

During the political science "voter education symposium" many students told me that they had "never worked so hard on a project." The reason for their efforts was due to the fact that they knew they would have to present their information to a live audience and that they did not want to be embarrassed.

On student evaluations of my course, the vast majority of students commented that the projects made them more interested in what we were studying.

Political Science Projects

For political science I chose to create three projects for my students to work on. Two of the projects were short (3–4 weeks) unit projects that were used as alternative to unit exams.

The third project was an entire semester long project that I developed in an attempt to give my students a more intensive project to focus upon.

Project One: Tinkering Toward Utopia (3–4 weeks)

This project was assigned for students to work on during our "Utopia" unit. The utopia unit is the first unit of the semester and it introduces students to the idea of a utopian society. This concept is appropriate for political science because the students are asked to think critically about the nature and purpose of government and society. Among the questions posed during the unit are: Can a perfect government or society ever be created? If so, how? What type of government will lead to a utopia? What are the responsibilities of the citizens living in a utopian society? Will human nature ever allow a utopian society to be created? To answer these questions the students read several pieces of political philosophy and literature which are provided to them by the teacher. Among the works read are excerpts from: Thomas More's *Utopia*, George Orwell's *1984*, Thomas Hobbes' *Leviathan*, Machiavelli's *The Prince*, [and] William Golding's *Lord of the Flies*. We read short stories such as: Kurt Vonnegut's "Harrison Bergeron," Ray Bradbury's "The Veldt," [and] Stanislaw Lem's "Trurl's Machine." Finally we used treatises written by John Locke, Jacques Rousseau, and Thomas Jefferson.

After reading and discussing these works, the students are prepared to work on the unit project. The project asks them to create an argumentative essay that argues whether or not they believe a utopian society can ever exist. To support their thesis the students must use evidence from the pieces of literature that they have read. In addition to the literature that I have provided for them, the students are required to find *three* other sources of information to help support their thesis. The students are told to use film, literature, art and music to find works that explore the concept of utopias. Many students use obvious examples such as Aldous Huxley's *Brave New World* or Alex Zamyatin's *We*, but others find examples of utopias from less obvious choices like Bob Dylan's "Hurricane" and Stanley Kubrick's film *2001: A Space Odyssey*. The cumulating activity is for the students to bring their sources to class and to use them as they engage in a debate with their classmates about the possibility of a utopia's existence. The students enjoy this piece of the project because they like seeing the resources their classmates have discovered.

Project Two: Time to Make a Change (3–4 weeks)

This project has been created as a final project for our unit on "Social Policy." The students read the Alex Kotlowitz book *There Are No Children Here* to introduce them to the nature of urban poverty in the United States. After reading this book the students are given a project that challenges them to develop a solution to one of the problems that the characters in the book face. The students spend a great deal of time researching current government programs to combat such social problems as: gangs, drugs, school violence, homelessness, welfare, and poverty. Next, they propose ways in which to improve the current government initiatives and ultimately help more people overcome their problems. After conducting research, and developing their program ideas, the students must present their ideas to their peers. The students enjoy this project because they believe that the work they are engaged in can truly make a difference in the lives of many of our nation's poor.

Project Three: Presidential Election Symposium (Semester Project)

This project was a natural fit for a political science course in the year 2000. As the nation prepared to elect a president, I developed a project that would challenge my students to learn about the presidential candidates and then teach their community about where each candidate stood on the important issues of the election. To complete this project the class was divided into democrats and republicans (sorry third parties!) The students in the democrat group researched Al Gore's position on the environment, abortion, gun laws, capital punishment, health care, education, and civil rights. The students in the republican group did the same for G. W. Bush. After spending 8–9 weeks researching their candidates, watching the televised debates, and evaluating their candidates' websites, the students were prepared for the final phase of the project. The cumulating activity was for the class to design a "voter education symposium." The class chose an evening 1 week prior to the election. They invited members of their families, members of the community, and members of the student body to attend an informational meeting about the candidates and the election. At the symposium, different groups of students presented the information they had gathered on each candidate; each group made a concerted effort to explain how the policies of Gore or Bush would affect the community of Highland Park. From the advertisements, to the organization, to the refreshments, the students were responsible for planning the entire event. The symposium was attended by approximately 250 people and for many students, it was there first opportunity to speak in front of a large audience. The class received rave reviews for their thorough and accurate analysis of the candidates and the issues.

Psychology Projects

In psychology I teach my students many theories about human behavior. One thing that my reflective research helped me understand was that while my students were learning and remembering the theories, they were often unable to understand how those theories related to their daily lives. Thus, in order to help my students connect my course content in a relevant way to their lives, I devised the following project.

Psychology Semester Research Project

With the majority of my students being seniors, I wanted to allow them as much freedom as possible in creating their psychology project. I believed that a true "self-directed" learning project would motivate my students at this point in their academic careers. Thus, the students were able to choose any topic they wished to study (as long as it related to psychology). In addition, the students were able to choose to work independently or with a partner, and they were able to decide exactly how they would present their information at the conclusion of the project.

The project the students were given to complete was to formulate a question about human behavior, research the answer (or possible answers), and then present and educate their peers and community about what they had learned. The focus of the presentations was not to be solely on regurgitating the information the student had learned about his or her topic, but to also recommend how this information may be useful for someone to use.

As the students worked on developing and answering a question, they were instructed in a number of skills that would help them successfully complete this project. First, the students were instructed in various methods of research. In addition to traditional research, each student had to find an expert to interview about his or her topic. This component was built into the project so that students would develop confidence in their interview skills and so that the students would be exposed to a number of careers that involve psychology. A third skill built into the project was for the students to complete a book review. Each student was allowed to pick his or her own book, and then methods of critique and analysis were discussed in class. Many students enjoyed reading an in-depth account of the concept they were studying. Finally, all students were instructed in computer skills such as PowerPoint, FrontPage, and HyperStudio so that this software might become a method for each student to present his or her data to an audience.

At the end of the semester, all of the students completed their final project and then presented their question and findings to the class.

Final Reflection

The action research lab was an excellent experience for me. Through my participation I learned better how to motivate my senior students and I believe I have become a better, more reflective educator. I look forward to refining my study in the future. I think that next year I will search for more ways of motivating my students by trying to incorporate actual internships and volunteer experiences into my class projects. I remain thoroughly committed to real world projects and hopefully I will be able to place some more authentic experiences into my curriculum.

Glossary

Abstract   Brief summary of the contents of a research article, typically including the results and conclusions of the study.

Academic journal   A periodical that publishes manuscripts detailing empirical research studies.

Acting stage   The second stage of the action research process, consisting of collecting and analyzing data.

Action plans   Formal or informal plans that follow from the results of action research, designed to guide either future cycles of action research or strategies for implementation or both.

Action research   Any systematic inquiry conducted by teachers, administrators, counselors, or others with a vested interest in the teaching and learning process or environment for the purpose of gathering information about how their particular schools operate, how they teach, and how their students learn.

Action research community   A learning community made up of educational professionals driven by a common goal of practicing reflective teaching as a means of improving classroom instructional practice.

Alpha level   Value that indicates the percentage of the time (usually 5%) that we can be reasonably certain that the differences we obtain actually are due to chance.

Analysis of variance (ANOVA)   Variation of the independent-measures t test; used when there are more than two groups being compared.

Assent   A child's agreement to participate in a research study.

Assent form   An agreement (either written or verbal, and in age-appropriate language) that describes the nature of the research study, as well as the level of involvement of minors to be involved in a research study; necessary for permission to use data collected from children in a research study.

Authority   Source of answers to questions; based on opinions of experts.

Bar chart   Graph similar to a histogram, but where adjacent bars do not touch due to the categorical nature of the variable.

Boolean operators   Keywords (e.g., *and, or*) that enable the retrieval of terms in specific combinations within searchable databases.

Case study   In-depth qualitative research study of an individual program, activity, person, or group.

Causal-comparative research   Quantitative research design used to explore reasons behind existing differences between two or more groups.

Checklist A list of behaviors, characteristics, skills, or other entities that a researcher is interested in investigating; presents only a dichotomous set of response options.

Chi-square test Inferential statistical test used to compare frequency counts by groups.

Class journal A less formal version of a student journal.

Classroom artifacts Written or visual sources of data, contained within the classroom, that contribute to our understanding of what is occurring in classrooms and schools.

Coding scheme System of categorization used to group qualitative data so that they provide similar types of information.

Collaborative action research Action research that is designed and implemented by collaborative teams.

Constant comparative method A research design for studies involving multiple data sources, where data analysis begins early in the study and is nearly completed by the end of data collection.

Construct A human characteristic, unable to be directly observed.

Control group The group of participants in an experimental study that receives the "standard" treatment.

Conventions of academic-style writing Agreed-upon procedures that help ensure the readability and credibility of research reports.

Correlation coefficient The quantitative measure resulting from a correlational study, which reports the direction of the relationship and the strength of the relationship.

Correlational study Type of nonexperimental study; determines the degree of relationship that exists between two or more variables.

Credibility The trustworthiness of qualitative data; the results of qualitative research are credible or believable from the perspective of the participant in the research.

Criterion-referenced Standardized test scores, which provide data such as how many questions students attempted and how many correct answers they gave for each category of question.

Data journals Narrative accounts or records kept by a variety of sources within a classroom setting.

Deductive reasoning A top-down approach to reasoning, working from the general to the more specific.

Dependability Emphasizes the need for the researcher to account for the ever-changing context within which research occurs; contributes to the trustworthiness of qualitative data.

Dependent variable The ultimate, or outcome, variable of interest.

Descriptive statistics Statistical techniques that allow researchers to summarize, organize, and simplify data.

Developing stage The third stage of the action research process, consisting of the development of an action plan.

Directional research hypothesis Hypothesis that not only states that an effect (or a difference or relationship) will be found but also specifies the direction or nature of that effect.

Districtwide action plan Broad-based action plan resulting from a districtwide action research project.

Educational research Application of the scientific method to educational topics, phenomena, or questions in search of answers.

Educational Resources Information Center (ERIC) The largest existing database for locating research in education.

Electronic journal An academic journal appearing entirely in electronic format (as opposed to print format), usually accessible online.

Electronic mailing list An online discussion forum conducted via e-mail, typically located on a large computer network and hosted by a university.

Empirical research Research studies that are based on the firsthand collection of data, as opposed to those that simply provide an author's individual opinions and perceptions.

Ethnographic study Type of qualitative study that attempts to describe social interactions between people in group settings.

Existing documents or records Data that already exist, typically collected for another reason but that can also be used for research purposes.

Experimental group The group of participants in an experimental study that is exposed to a new or an innovative treatment or another type of condition.

Experimental research Type of research design where the researcher has control over one or more of the variables included in a study that may somehow influence the participants' behaviors.

Field notes Written observations of what you see taking place in your classroom.

Focus group A simultaneous interview of people making up a relatively small group, usually no more than 10 to 12 people.

Formative classroom assessment Assessments that are administered *during* instruction for purposes of revising or adjusting instruction while it is ongoing.

Formative evaluation Evaluative decision making that occurs during the implementation of a project.

Frequency distribution table A table showing the distribution of scores, where individual score values are arranged from highest to lowest, moving down the table.

Full participant At one end of the participant-observer continuum, the researcher is simultaneously a fully functioning member of the "community" as well as a researcher.

Google Scholar A large database for locating research in education.

Grounded theory Type of qualitative study, attempting to discover a theory that relates to a particular environment.

Group comparison design A quantitative research design that attempts to investigate cause-and-effect relationships by comparing groups that differ in treatment conditions.

Histogram A graphical representation of the distribution of a set of scores.

Human Subjects Review Board A board that reviews proposed research studies in order to ensure the protection of participants in a research study; see also *institutional review board*.

Hypothesis Tentative, but intelligent and informed, guess about the findings of a study, made before the study begins.

Independent-measures *t* test An inferential statistical technique appropriate for research designs where two groups are compared on a common dependent variable.

Independent variable The variable in an experimental study over which the researcher has control; assumed to be the cause of something else.

Individual action plan Action plan resulting from action research carried out by one person.

Inductive analysis Process of logically analyzing qualitative data in order to reduce the volume of collected information, thereby identifying and organizing the data into important patterns and themes in order to construct some sort of framework for presenting the key findings of the action research study.

Inductive reasoning A bottom-up approach to reasoning, working from the specific to the more general.

Inferential statistics Statistical techniques that allow researchers to test the statistical significance of the difference between two or more groups or to test the degree of relationship between two variables.

Informal interviews Spontaneous interviews that take place throughout the data collection process, typically part of the daily interactions with students in a classroom setting.

Informed consent form A form that describes the nature of the research study, as well as the level of involvement of the participants; necessary for permission to use collected data in a research study.

Institutional Review Board (IRB) A board that reviews proposed research studies in order to ensure the protection of participants in a research study; see also *human subjects review board.*

Internal consistency A statistical estimate of the reliability of a test that is administered only once.

Interview Conversation between a teacher-researcher and a participant, or group of participants, in the study, in which the teacher poses questions directly to the participant(s).

Interview guide List of either general or specific questions to be asked during an interview.

Kuder-Richardson formula 21 Statistical formula used to calculate internal consistency.

Likert scale Statements provided on surveys or questionnaires to respondents where individuals are asked to respond on an agree-disagree continuum.

Likert-type scale Scale similar to Likert scale, but where something other than extent of agreement is being measured.

Literature review An examination of journal articles, books, research papers, and so on; related to an action research project; helps guide the development of future research projects by examining previous research on the topic.

Logico-inductive analysis A thought process used to analyze qualitative data that uses logic to make sense of patterns and trends in data.

Mean The arithmetic average of a set of scores.

Measures of central tendancy Statistical procedures that indicate, with a single score, what is typical or standard about a group of individuals.

Measures of dispersion Statistical procedures that indicate what is different within a group of scores.

Median The specific score in the set of data that separates the entire distribution in equal halves.

Member checking Procedure involving the sharing of interview transcripts, analytical thoughts (such as observation notes with observer's comments), and drafts with the participants of the study in order to help ensure the quality of data.

Mixed-methods research design A research design that combines both quantitative and qualitative research designs and data.

Mode The most frequently occurring score in the overall set of scores.

Negative correlation A correlation coefficient whose value is less than zero, indicating that as the scores or values on one variable increase, the values on the other variable decrease.

Nondirectional research hypothesis Hypothesis that states that there will be some sort of effect (or difference or relationship) discovered in the results of the research study, without stating the nature of the difference or relationship.

Nonexperimental research A type of research design where the researcher has no control over any variable in the study, either because it has already occurred or because it is not possible for it to be influenced.

Norm-referenced Standardized test results that allow performance comparisons with other groups of students taking the test.

Null hypothesis Hypothesis that states that no effect will occur in the study or that no differences between groups or no relationship between variables will be found.

Observation Act of carefully watching and systematically recording what you see and hear going on in a particular setting.

Observational case study Case study involving the examination of a particular organization or some aspect of the organization.

Observational research (quantitative) A quantitative research design, focusing on a description of a specific aspect of behavior, perhaps a single particular variable.

Observational study (qualitative) Qualitative study similar to case study but not necessarily focused on organizational aspects.

Observer as participant Researcher is primarily an observer but has some level of interaction with the participants.

Observer's comments Preliminary interpretations of what has been observed; usually interpretations of field notes.

One-group pretest-posttest design A pre-experimental design involving two groups of participants who are pretested, exposed to different treatment conditions, and then posttested.

One-shot case study Very primitive type of experimental design; involves one group that is exposed to some sort of experimental treatment and then posttested after the passage of time.

Open-ended interviews Interviews that provide the respondent with only a few questions, very broad in their nature.

Open-ended questions Questions used in surveys or questionnaires where individuals provide their own responses.

Parental consent form A form that describes the nature of the research study, as well as the level of   involvement of minors to be involved in a research study; necessary for permission to use data collected from children in a research study.

Participant as observer Researcher continues to observe but also has the opportunity to interact with the participants in the study.

Participant observation The act of observing as a researcher but also participating in the group or setting as an equal, active member of that group or setting.

Pearson correlation coefficient The most common measure of the relationship between two variables; symbolized by r.

Phenomenological study Type of qualitative study that engages the researcher in a long process of data collection in order to fully understand a phenomenon.

Pie chart A circular type of graph, showing the distribution of categorical scores in a data set.

Planning stage The first stage of the action research process, consisting of identifying the topic, reviewing related literature, and developing a research plan.

Polyangulation The process of relating or integrating two or more sources of data in order to establish their quality and accuracy.

Population The group of people of primary interest in a research study, although not necessarily studied in its entirety; the group about which conclusions are drawn.

Positive correlation A correlation coefficient whose value is greater than zero, indicating that as the scores or values on one variable increase, the values on the other variable also increase.

Practical significance Determination of the significance of group differences based on a subjective decision.

Preexperimental designs
Quantitative research designs seen as precursors to true experimental designs in that they are lacking several key elements.

Pretest-posttest control group design
Quasiexperimental design similar to the one-group pretest-posttest design but including the addition of a control group for comparison purposes.

Primary sources Firsthand accounts of original research.

Principle of accurate disclosure Rule of research that states that participants should be informed accurately about the purpose and specifically what they will be asked to do as participants.

Principle of beneficence Rule of research that states that research should be done in order to acquire knowledge about human beings and the educational process in order to benefit someone or a group.

Principle of honesty   Rule of research stating that honesty should be exhibited throughout the entire research process.

Principle of importance   Rule of research indicating that the findings of research should somehow be likely to contribute to human knowledge or be useful elsewhere in the field of education.

Prolonged engagement and persistent observation   Idea that the more time you spend in the field, the more you are able to develop trust with and get to know your participants, learn the culture of their setting, and observe patterns of behavior to the point of being routine.

ProQuest   A large database for locating research in education, including dissertations and theses.

*p***-value**   Statistical measure indicating the probability of chance occurrences in the actual study.

Qualitative research methodologies
Those research methodologies that require the collection and analysis of narrative data; utilize an inductive approach to reasoning.

Quantitative research methodologies
Those methodologies that require the collection of and analysis of numerical data; utilize a deductive approach to reasoning.

Quasiexperimental design   Closest relative to true experimental designs, the only difference being that there is no random assignment of participants to groups.

Questionnaire   Survey that is administered in written form, where the researcher asks participants to answer a series of questions or respond to a series of statements and then return it to the researcher.

Range   Measure of dispersion calculated by subtracting the lowest score in a set of data from the highest score.

Rating scales   Questions or statements used in surveys or questionnaires where individuals simply select their response from a set of options provided to them; also known as "closed response items."

Reconnaissance   During preliminary stages of action research, taking time to reflect on your own beliefs and to gain a better understanding of the nature and context of your research problem.

Refereed   Characteristic of an academic journal, meaning that any study submitted receives a blind, peer review by a minimum of two reviewers, who provide comments on the quality of the study, as well as on the written manuscript detailing the study.

Reflecting stage   The fourth and final stage of the action research process, consisting of communicating the results of action research and reflecting on the process.

Reflection   The act of critically exploring what you are doing, why you decided to do it, and what its effects have been.

Reflective teaching   A process of developing lessons with thoughtful consideration of educational theory, existing research, and practical experience, along with the analysis of the lesson's effect on student learning.

Reliability   Concept related to the consistency of quantitative data.

Repeated-measures *t* test   Inferential statistical test that compares two measures taken on the same individuals.

Research design A specific type of plan that will be used to carry out a research study.

Research ethics Moral aspects of research, including such values as caring, honesty, fairness, and openness.

Research methodology The specific plan for collecting data in a research study.

Research question The fundamental question inherent in the research topic under investigation.

Rigor Refers to the quality, validity, accuracy, and credibility of action research and its findings.

Sample A representative subset of a population.

School-level action plan Broad-based action plan resulting from a schoolwide action research project.

Scientific method Systematic, step-by-step method for investigating questions and resolving problems.

Search engine Web site that searches other Internet Web sites by keyword.

Secondary sources Summaries, compilations, or interpretations of primary research information.

Semistructured interview Interview where the researcher asks several "base" questions but also has the option of following up a given response with alternative, optional questions that may or may not be used by the researcher, depending on the situation.

Semistructured observation Observation that allows the teacher-researcher the flexibility to attend to other events or activities occurring simultaneously in the classroom or to engage in brief, but intense, periods of observation and note taking; also known as "unstructured observation."

Standard deviation The average distance of scores away from the mean.

Statistical significance A decision made from the results of inferential statistical procedures that enable researchers to conclude that the findings of a given study are large enough in the sample studied in order to represent a meaningful difference or relationship in the population from which the sample was drawn.

Structured interview Interview where the researcher asks only predetermined questions listed on an interview guide.

Structured observation Observation that requires the observer to do nothing else but observe, looking usually for specific behaviors, reactions, or interactions.

Student journals Journals kept by students that provide information similar to homework to the teacher and through which teachers can gain a sense of students' daily thoughts, perceptions, and experiences in the classroom.

Style guide An "instruction manual" for academic writing.

Summative classroom assessment Assessments that are administered *after* a substantial unit of instruction for purposes of assigning grades or some other sort of formal decision.

Summative evaluation Evaluative decision making that occurs following the completion of a project.

Survey Collective group of quantitative data-collection techniques that involve the administration of a set of questions or statements to a sample of people.

Survey research   Quantitative, descriptive design involving the acquisition of information from individuals representing one or more groups—perhaps about their opinions, attitudes, or characteristics—by specifically asking them questions and then tabulating their responses.

Teacher empowerment Process highlighted by teachers collecting their own data in order to assist in making decisions about their own students and classrooms; concept also known as "teacher as decision maker."

Teacher journals   Journals kept by teacher-researchers that provide them with the opportunity to maintain narrative accounts of their professional reflections on practice.

Team action plan   Action plan resulting from action research carried out by a network of teacher-researchers.

Test   Standardized or teacher-developed formal assessments, where the scores may also be used as research data.

Tradition   Source of answers to questions; based on past behaviors.

Treatment group   See "experimental group."

Triangulation   Process of relating multiple sources of data in order to establish their trustworthiness; used with qualitative research methods.

Trustworthiness   Verification of the consistency of various sources of qualitative data while accounting for their inherent biases; focuses on the accuracy and believability of the data.

Unstructured observation   Observation that allows the teacher-researcher the flexibility to attend to other events or activities occurring simultaneously in the classroom or to engage in brief, but intense, periods of observation and note taking; also known as "semi-structured observation."

Validity of research data   Characteristic of data that deals with the extent to which the data that have been collected accurately measure what they purport to measure.

Variables   Factors that may affect the outcome of a study or characteristics that are central to the topic about which a researcher wishes to draw conclusions.

Videotapes   Alternatives to recording observations using field notes.

References

Alsup, J. K., & Sprigler, M. J. (2003). A comparison of traditional and reform mathematics curricula in an eighth-grade classroom. *Education, 123,* 689–695.

American Educational Research Association (AERA), American Psychological Association (APA), & National Council on Measurement in Education (NCME). (1999). *Standards for educational and psychological testing.* Washington, DC: American Educational Research Association.

American Psychological Association. (2010). *Publication manual of the American Psychological Association* (6th ed.). Washington, DC: Author.

Anderson, G. L. (2002). Reflecting on research for doctoral students in education. *Educational Researcher, 31*(7), 22–25.

Baccellieri, P. (2010). *Professional learning communities: Using data in decision making to improve student learning.* Huntington Beach, CA: Shell Education.

Bachman, L. (2001). *Review of the agricultural knowledge system in Fiji: Opportunities and limitations of participatory methods and platforms to promote innovation development.* Unpublished dissertation, Humboldt University to Berlin, Germany. Retrieved January 17, 2008, fromhttp://dochost.rz.huberlin.de/dissertationen/bachmann-lorenz-b-r-2000-12-21/HTML/bachmann-ch3.html

Bogdan, R. C., & Biklen, S. K. (2007). *Qualitative research for education: An introduction to theory and methods* (5th ed.). Boston: Allyn & Bacon.

Brotherson, M. J., Sheriff, G., Milburn, P., & Schertz, M. (2001). Elementary school principals and their needs and issues for inclusive early childhood programs. *Topics in Early Childhood Special Education, 21,* 31–45.

Calhoun, E. F. (1994). *How to use action research in the self-renewing school.* Alexandria, VA: Association for Supervision and Curriculum Development.

Clauset, K. H., Lick, D. W., & Murphy, C. U. (2008). *Schoolwide action research for professional learning communities: Improving student learning through the whole-faculty study groups approach.* Thousand Oaks, CA: Corwin Press.

Creswell, J. W. (2005). *Educational research: Planning, conducting, and evaluating quantitative and qualitative research* (2nd ed.). Upper Saddle River, NJ: Merrill/Prentice Hall.

DuBois, M. H. (1995). Conceptual learning and creative problem solving using cooperative learning groups in middle school science classes. In S. Spiegel, A. Collins, & J. Lappert (Eds.), *Action research: Perspectives from teachers' classrooms. Science FEAT (Science for Early Adolescence Teachers).* Tallahassee, FL: SouthEastern Regional Vision for Education.

DuFour, R., DuFour, R., & Eaker, R. (2008). *Revisiting professional learning communities at work: New insights for improving schools.* Bloomington, IN: Solution Tree.

Fraenkel, J. R., & Wallen, N. E. (2003). Action research. In *How to design and evaluate research in education* (5th ed., pp. 571–597). Boston: McGraw-Hill.

Gay, L. R., & Airasian, P. (2000). *Educational research: Competencies for analysis and application* (6th ed.). Upper Saddle River, NJ: Merrill/Prentice Hall.

Glesne, C. (2006). *Becoming qualitative researchers: An introduction* (3rd ed.). New York: Longman.

Graham, E. (1995). What patterns of teacher-student communication exist in my classroom? In S. Spiegel, A. Collins, & J. Lappert (Eds.), *Action research: Perspectives from teachers' classrooms. Science FEAT (Science for Early Adolescence Teachers).* Tallahassee, FL: SouthEastern Regional Vision for Education.

Hendricks, C. (2009). *Improving schools through action research: A comprehensive guide for educators* (2nd ed.). Boston: Allyn & Bacon.

Hollis, J. (1995). Effect of technology on enthusiasm for learning science. In S. Spiegel, A. Collins, & J. Lappert (Eds.), *Action research: Perspectives from teachers' classrooms. Science FEAT (Science for Early Adolescence Teachers).* Tallahassee, FL: SouthEastern Regional Vision for Education.

Hubbard, R. S., & Power, B. M. (2003). *The art of classroom inquiry: A handbook for teacher-researchers* (2nd ed.). Portsmouth, NH: Heinemann.

Institute of Education Sciences. (n.d.a). *ERIC-Educational Resources Information Center.* Retrieved September 24, 2004, from http://www.eric.ed.gov

Institute of Education Sciences. (n.d.b). About ERIC. In *ERIC-Educational Resources Information Center.*

Retrieved September 24, 2004, from http://www.eric.ed.gov/ERICWebPortal/resources/html/yabout/about_eric.html

James, E. A., Milenkiewicz, M. T., & Bucknam, A. (2008). *Participatory action research for educational leadership: Using data-driven decision making to improve schools.* Thousand Oaks, CA: Sage.

Johnson, A. P. (2008). *A short guide to action research* (3rd ed.). Boston: Allyn & Bacon.

Leedy, P. D., & Ormrod, J. E. (2005). *Practical research: Planning and design* (8th ed.). Upper Saddle River, NJ: Merrill/Prentice Hall.

McLean, J. E. (1995). Improving education through action research: A guide for administrators and teachers. In J. J. Herman & J. L. Herman (Eds.), *The practicing administrator's leadership series.* Thousand Oaks, CA: Corwin Press.

McMillan, J. H. (2004). *Educational research: Fundamentals for the consumer* (4th ed.). Boston: Allyn & Bacon.

Melrose, M. J. (2001). Maximizing the rigor of action research: Why would you want to? How could you? *Field Methods, 13*(2), 160–180.

Mertler, C. A. (2002). *Using standardized test data to guide instruction and intervention.* College Park, MD: ERIC Clearinghouse on Assessment and Evaluation Digest Series, EDO-TM-07.

Mertler, C. A. (2003). *Classroom assessment: A practical guide for educators.* Los Angeles: Pyrczak.

Mertler, C. A. (2007). *Interpreting standardized test scores: Strategies for data-driven instructional decision making.* Thousand Oaks, CA: Sage.

Mertler, C. A. (2009). A systematic approach to transforming the *art* of teaching into the *science* of teaching: Developing a D-DIDM mindset (MWERA 2008 Presidential Address). *Mid-Western Educational Researcher, 22*(1), 12–23.

Mertler, C. A. (2010, February). PLCs, collaborative action research, and reflective professional development: The triumvirate for school improvement. In C. A. Mertler (Chair), *Integrating action research and professional learning communities: A powerful approach to school improvement and educator empowerment.* Symposium conducted at the annual meeting of the Eastern Educational Research Association, Savannah, Georgia.

Mertler, C. A., & Charles, C. M. (2011). *Introduction to educational research* (7th ed.). Boston: Allyn & Bacon.

Metz, M. H., & Page, R. N. (2002). The uses of practitioner research and status issues in educational research: Reply to Gary Anderson. *Educational Researcher, 31*(7), 26–27.

Mills, G. E. (2011). *Action research: A guide for the teacher researcher* (4th ed.). Boston: Pearson.

Parsons, R. D., & Brown, K. S. (2002). *Teacher as reflective practitioner and action researcher.* Belmont, CA: Wadsworth/Thomson Learning.

Piggot-Irvine, E. (2006). Sustaining excellence in experienced principals? Critique of a professional learning community approach. *International Electronic Journal for Leadership in Learning, 10*(16). Available at http://www.ucalgary.ca/iejll/vol10/irvine

Pyrczak, F., & Bruce, R. R. (2003). *Writing empirical research reports: A basic guide for students of the social and behavioral sciences* (4th ed.). Los Angeles: Pyrczak.

Riel, M. (2007). *Understanding action research.* Center for Collaborative Action Research. Available at http://cadres.pepperdine.edu/ccar/define.html

Rousseau, M. K., & Tam, B. K. Y. (1996). Practical issues for teachers conducting classroom research. *Teaching Exceptional Children, 28*(3), 52–56.

Schmuck, R. A. (1997). *Practical action research for change.* Arlington Heights, IL: SkyLight Professional Development.

Schwalbach, E. M. (2003). *Value and validity in action research: A guidebook for reflective practitioners.* Lanham, MD: Scarecrow Press.

Smith, M. K. (2007). *Kurt Lewin: Groups, experiential learning, and action research.* Retrieved January 23, 2008, from http://www.infed.org/thinkers/etlewin.htm

Stringer, E. T. (2007). *Action research* (3rd ed.). Thousand Oaks, CA: Sage.

Trochim, W. M. K. (2002a). *Deduction & induction.* Retrieved August 26, 2004, from the Research Methods Knowledge Base website: http://www.socialresearchmethods.net/kb/dedind.htm

Trochim, W. M. K. (2002b). *Positivism and post-positivism.* Retrieved August 26, 2004, from the Research Methods Knowledge Base website: http://www.socialresearchmethods.net/kb/positvsm.htm

Trochim, W. M. K. (2002c). *Qualitative validity.* Retrieved October 26, 2004, from the Research Methods Knowledge Base website: http://www.socialresearchmethods.net/kb/qualval.htm

Weldon, W. H. (1995). The use of cloze procedure as an instructional tool in a middle school classroom. In S. Spiegel, A. Collins, & J. Lappert (Eds.), *Action research: Perspectives from teachers' classrooms. Science FEAT (Science for Early Adolescence Teachers).* Tallahassee, FL: SouthEastern Regional Vision for Education.

Credits

Chapter 3, page 60, top: From "A Comparison of Traditional and Reform Mathematics Curricula in an Eighth-Grade Classroom," by J. K. Alsup and M. J. Sprigler (2003), *Education, 123,* pp. 689–695. Reprinted with permission.

Chapter 3, page 61, bottom: From "The Use of Cloze Procedure as an Instructional Tool in a Middle School Classroom," by W. H. Weldon (1995), in S. Spiegel, A. Collins, & J. Lappert (Eds.), *Action Research: Perspectives From Teachers' Classrooms. Science FEAT (Science For Early Adolescence Teachers).* Tallahassee, FL: South-Eastern Regional Vision for Education. Reprinted with permission.

Chapter 4, page 94, top: From "The Use of Cloze Procedure as an Instructional Tool in a Middle School Classroom," by W. H. Weldon (1995), in S. Spiegel, A. Collins, & J. Lappert (Eds.), *Action Research: Perspectives From Teachers' Classrooms. Science FEAT (Science For Early Adolescence Teachers).* Tallahassee, FL: South-Eastern Regional Vision for Education. Reprinted with permission.

Chapter 4, page 94, bottom: From "Conceptual Learning and Creative Problem Solving Using Cooperative Learning Groups in Middle School Science Classes," by M. H. DuBois (1995), in S. Spiegel, A. Collins, & J. Lappert (Eds.), *Action Research: Perspectives From Teachers' Classrooms. Science FEAT (Science For Early Adolescence Teachers).* Tallahassee, FL: SouthEastern Regional Vision for Education. Reprinted with permission.

Chapter 5, page 127, bottom: From "Effect of Technology on Enthusiasm for Learning Science," by J. Hollis (1995), in S. Spiegel, A. Collins, & J. Lappert (Eds.), *Action Research: Perspectives From Teachers' Classrooms. Science FEAT (Science For Early Adolescence Teachers).* Tallahassee, FL: SouthEastern Regional Vision for Education. Reprinted with permission.

Chapter 5, page 129, bottom: From "What Patterns of Teacher-Student Communication Exist in My Classroom?" by E. Graham (1995), in S. Spiegel, A. Collins, & J. Lappert (Eds.), *Action Research: Perspectives From Teachers' Classrooms. Science FEAT*

(Science For Early Adolescence Teachers). Tallahassee, FL: SouthEastern Regional Vision for Education. Reprinted with permission.

Chapter 6, page 165, top: From "Elementary School Principals and Their Needs and Issues for Inclusive Early Childhood Programs," by M. J. Brotherson, G. Sheriff, P. Milburn, and M. Shertz (2001), *Topics in Early Childhood Special Education, 21,* pp. 31–45. Reprinted with permission.

Chapter 6, page 166, bottom: From "A Comparison of Traditional and Reform Mathematics Curricula in an Eighth-Grade Classroom," by J. K. Alsup and M. J. Sprigler (2003), *Education, 123,* pp. 689–695. Reprinted with permission.

Chapter 7, page 185, top: From "Effect of Technology on Enthusiasm for Learning Science," by J. Hollis (1995), in S. Spiegel, A. Collins, & J. Lappert (Eds.), *Action Research: Perspectives From Teachers' Classrooms. Science FEAT (Science For Early Adolescence Teachers),* Tallahassee, FL: SouthEastern Regional Vision for Education. Reprinted with permission.

Chapter 7, page 185, bottom: From "A Comparison of Traditional and Reform Mathematics Curricula in an Eighth-grade Classroom," by J. K. Alsup and M. J. Sprigler (2003), *Education, 123,* pp. 689–695. Reprinted with permission.

Chapter 8, page 201, top: From "What Patterns of Teacher-Student Communication Exist in My Classroom?" by E. Graham (1995), in S. Spiegel, A. Collins, & J. Lappert (Eds.), *Action Research: Perspectives From Teachers' Classrooms. Science FEAT (Science For Early Adolescence Teachers).* Tallahassee, FL: SouthEastern Regional Vision for Education. Reprinted with permission.

Chapter 8, page 201, bottom: From "Conceptual Learning and Creative Problem Solving Using Cooperative Learning Groups in Middle School Science Classes," by M. H. DuBois (1995), in S. Spiegel, A. Collins, & J. Lappert (Eds.), *Action Research: Perspectives From Teachers' Classrooms. Science FEAT (Science For Early Adolescence Teachers).* Tallahassee, FL: SouthEastern Regional Vision for Education. Reprinted with permission.

Index

About the Author

Craig A. Mertler is currently a professor and director of the Doctoral Program in School Improvement in the College of Education at the University of West Georgia. He teaches doctoral courses focused on the application of action research to promote school improvement and reform, and also teaches quantitative research methods, introductory statistical analysis, multivariate statistical analysis, and educational assessment methods. He is the author of five books, four invited book chapters, 16 refereed journal articles, two instructors' manuals, and numerous nonrefereed articles and manuscripts. He has also presented numerous research papers at professional meetings around the country, as well as internationally. He conducts workshops for in-service educational professionals on classroom-based action research and on the broad topic of classroom assessment. His primary research interests include classroom-based action research, professional learning communities, and assessment practices of classroom teachers. Before teaching and researching at the university level, he taught high school biology and earth science, and also coached track and volleyball. In his leisure time, he enjoys travelling with his family and playing golf. Dr. Mertler can be reached at the following:

Doctoral Program in School Improvement

College of Education

Carrollton, Georgia 30118

cmertler@westga.edu

http://www.westga.edu/eddsi